Themes in Dicker

D1548170

Themes in Dickens

*Seven Recurring Concerns
in the Writings*

Peter J. Ponzio

McFarland & Company, Inc., Publishers
Jefferson, North Carolina

FRONTISPIECE: Photograph of Charles Dickens taken by
George Herbert Watkins in 1858 after the publication
of *Little Dorrit*. The portrait is one of a group of five by
Watkins and first appeared in John Forster's *Life of Dickens,
1872–1874* (British Library, London).

LIBRARY OF CONGRESS CATALOGUING-IN-PUBLICATION DATA

Names: Ponzio, Peter J., author.
Title: Themes in Dickens : seven recurring concerns in the
    writings / Peter J. Ponzio.
Description: Jefferson, North Carolina : McFarland & Company,
    Inc., Publishers, 2018. | Includes bibliographical references
    and index.
Identifiers: LCCN 2017055848 | ISBN 9781476672571
    (softcover : acid free paper) ∞
Subjects: LCSH: Dickens, Charles, 1812–1870—Criticism and
    interpretation. | Dickens, Charles, 1812–1870—Themes,
    motives.
Classification: LCC PR4588 .P66 2018 | DDC 823/.8—dc23
LC record available at https://lccn.loc.gov/2017055848

BRITISH LIBRARY CATALOGUING DATA ARE AVAILABLE

ISBN 978-1-4766-7257-1 (print)
ISBN 978-1-4766-3135-6 (ebook)

Front cover image of London © 2018 iStock

Printed in the United States of America

*McFarland & Company, Inc., Publishers
    Box 611, Jefferson, North Carolina 28640
    www.mcfarlandpub.com*

To the memory of two of my instructors who guided me and introduced me to Charles Dickens:

the late DR. CHARLES HART,
and the late MR. JAMES KUCIENSKI

Acknowledgments

I wish to thank the following people for their assistance with this book. For their efforts in proofing, editing and suggestions for this book, I thank Dr. Deborah Deacon and Dr. Marcus Conley at Harrison Middleton University. In addition, Dr. Deacon also acted as my mentor throughout the doctoral process. I also wish to thank the following instructors at Harrison Middleton University for guiding me through the various classes that led to my Doctor of Arts degree: Dr. Marcus Conley, Michael Curd, Dr. Deborah Deacon, Rebecca Fisher, Dr. Margaret Metcalf, Gary Schoepfel, Dr. Philip Stewart, Andy Tafoya, Dominique Wagner, and Dr. Robert Woods.

I also wish to thank several instructors who helped me in my research on Dickens, and who encouraged me to continue my studies. Dr. Charles Hart, Mr. James Kucienski, Dr. Daniel Born, and Dr. Nancy Carr.

Contents

Abbreviations

AN	*American Notes*
BH	*Bleak House*
BR	*Barnaby Rudge*
CC	*A Christmas Carol*
D&S	*Dombey and Son*
DC	*David Copperfield*
GE	*Great Expectations*
HT	*Hard Times*
HW	*Household Words*
LD	*Little Dorrit*
MC	*Martin Chuzzlewitt*
NN	*Nicholas Nickleby*
OCS	*The Old Curiosity Shop*
OMF	*Our Mutual Friend*
OT	*Oliver Twist*
PP	*Pickwick Papers*
SB	*Sketches by Boz*
SL	*Selected Letters of Charles Dickens*
SP	*Speeches Literary and Social*
TTC	*A Tale of Two Cities*

Dates of Publication

Preface

Like many readers in the United States, I first became acquainted with Charles Dickens in high school. In one of the years at school (I can't recall whether it was freshman or sophomore year), we were required to read *Hard Times*, and I must admit that I neglected to do so, and instead made use of *Cliff's Notes* to fake my way through the novel.

In my senior year, we were assigned *David Copperfield*, and this time, rather than consult *Cliff's Notes*, I read the novel. It was a revelation, and in the summer between graduation and the start of college, I read *Oliver Twist, Martin Chuzzlewitt, Dombey and Son*, and *Our Mutual Friend*. My apprenticeship as a Dickens scholar had begun.

It is now more than forty years since I read *David Copperfield*, and my appreciation for Dickens has only increased since then, not only as a novelist, but as a man interested in effecting changes in his society. It is hoped that this book will provide an understanding of Dickens through an examination of a number of themes to which he returned in his writings. This book examines the themes of class and class distinctions; naming, identity and self; dreams and dreaming; society and social pretension; ineffective institutions; and prison at a macro level, and then performs a detailed analysis of several of his works under each broad theme, illustrating how Dickens returned to these themes in an attempt to understand and reconcile himself to his world.

I hope that this book will help others become more familiar with his life and work.

Introduction

More books have been written about Charles Dickens than any other English author, with the exception of William Shakespeare. It would seem, therefore, that another book about Charles Dickens would add little to the understanding of the literary merits of the author's works, or of his philanthropic and societal contributions. Yet, it is hoped that this book about Dickens's writing and social thinking will help expand the reader's knowledge of the man and his work.

It is my belief that to arrive at an understanding of an author's works, it is imperative to attempt to understand his beliefs and to examine them over a long enough period of time so that his thoughts and life-work illumine his literary accomplishments. This sort of belief is seen to be somewhat old-fashioned in the era of literary "isms" that have been promulgated in the twentieth and twenty-first centuries. Dickens was not allied to one of these "isms," nor was he one of the "ists." He was not a Marxist, socialist, nationalist, structuralist, deconstructionist, historicist, behaviorist, economist, or one of the many other "ists" that have sprung up like so many Hydra heads in the past century. He was, however, a *novelist* and was actively involved in writing about the social problems of his era.

This book provides an understanding of Dickens through an examination of a number of themes to which he returned in his writings. Other books have explored Dickens's use of themes but have done so by examining a single theme in a selected novel(s) or non-fictional writing, in isolation as it were, and without tracing the influence of these themes throughout the author's career and his various works. It is my belief that Dickens, who was a critic of many aspects of Victorian society, attempted to portray the many ills he witnessed in that society through his fictional and non-fictional writings. Because he was not a social scientist or politician, he did not propound a series of reforms which would solve the problems that he described. Rather, he approached these problems from a viewpoint that was symbolic, emotional and empathetic and provided tentative solutions in his early writing that were based on individual good deeds and hard work. As he matured, his belief that social problems could be ameliorated through individual effort faded; at the same time, he did not believe that serious reform could be accomplished by Parliament, the court system, philanthropy or organized religions. Ultimately, Dickens's writings are those of a man who is attempting to understand his world, to cry out "like a voice in the wilderness" about the injustice and social ills he witnesses in his society and who attempts to construct a fictional world where these ills are recognized but where solutions to the problems he writes about are not easily found. His writing may be viewed as an antidote to the sickness he saw in Victorian society, but unlike a good physician, he could not prescribe an effective cure.

The book is intended for use by readers who have a working knowledge of Dickens's writing as well as a familiarity with his life and times. A listing of books for further reading is provided in the Appendix to this work. For consistency, chapters in Dickens's novels will be referred to by chapter number expressed in Arabic numerals and will eliminate the use of Roman numerals which are used in some versions of the novels. The book will also appeal to scholars who may be interested in the themes to which Dickens returns in various novels and in his journalism. Initially, the book examines the themes of class and class distinctions; naming, identity and self; dreams and dreaming; society and social pretension; ineffective institutions; and prison. Each chapter is arranged so that it presents an overview of the theme covered in the chapter. It then presents a view of the theme that spans several of Dickens's works. Finally, a detailed analysis is performed under each broad theme illustrating how Dickens returned to these themes in an attempt to understand and reconcile himself to his world. That he was somewhat ineffective in constructing an alternate world and reconciling himself to the Victorian era is beside the point. An artist is not a sociologist or political reformer; it is enough that he recognized society's ills and tried to make his reading public aware of them. He also encouraged his readers through his fiction and essays to consider the plight of those less fortunate than they were.

Chapter One begins with a discussion of class and class distinctions that focuses on the gulf between the upper and lower classes in terms of wealth and the provision of social services in Victorian England. The chapter proceeds to an overview of the spread of capitalism which led to an emphasis on material possessions at the expense of the moral and spiritual values which Dickens endorsed. Finally, the chapter covers the migration from rural to urban areas which resulted in a sense of isolation that is evident in Dickens's writing. The chapter makes use of contemporary reports by Edwin Chadwick regarding the living conditions of workers in London, as well as commentary by Edward Said to provide background on this topic. *Sketches by Boz* is used to discuss these concepts in greater detail.

The second chapter explores Dickens's interest in names and personal identity in his works. This chapter examines how Dickens viewed the relationship of names and character development in his writing, and focuses on the novel *David Copperfield* to explore the concepts of naming and identity in greater detail. This chapter draws upon recent research in psychology and the social sciences to inform the reader of the importance of naming and family relationships in the formation of personal identity.

Chapter Three examines Dickens's understanding of psychology with particular emphasis being paid to his speculation on dreams and dreaming as well as his practice of mesmerism as a way to understand the human psyche. Several novels are explored to understand Dickens's use of dreams and reveries including *The Old Curiosity Shop, A Tale of Two Cities, Great Expectations, Little Dorrit, Martin Chuzzlewitt, The Pickwick Papers* and *A Christmas Carol*. The works of Oliver Sacks, Sigmund Freud and Mary Ainsworth are used to provide background information relating to Dickens's conception of psychology.

The concept of society and social pretention is the subject of Chapter Four and includes the topics of misguided philanthropy, hypocritical religious practices and the reliance on money as a panacea to solving the problems Dickens associated with Victorian society. Dickens's non-fictional essays, as well as speeches, are used to explain his disdain for governmental and philanthropic institutions which profess to help the poor and indigent but, in reality, do little to ameliorate their suffering. The novel *Dombey and Son* is examined to explore these concepts in an expanded fashion.

Toward the later stages of his career Dickens believed that Parliament was ineffective and that unbridled capitalism and the lack of standardized education in Great Britain would result in a society that lacked "fancy" or imagination, leading to a joyless form of existence. The subject of ineffective institutions comprises the fifth chapter and the novel *Hard Times* is used to illustrate Dickens's concerns about agencies which no longer function properly.

Prisons and workhouses are present in every Dickens novel. Chapter Six examines the workings of the penal system in Great Britain and Dickens's perspective, based on first-hand experience, of the effects prison has on those who have been incarcerated. *Little Dorrit* is used to understand the extended metaphor that Dickens uses to illustrate that the entire world is a prison. Foucault's conception of the nature of prisons and confinement provides background material and context for Dickens's writings about prisons and prison life.

Charles Dickens, aside from writing some fifteen novels, several travel journals, hundreds of journal articles, editing two magazines and a number of newspapers, was a Parliamentary reporter, a philanthropist, an outspoken proponent of universal copyright laws, and social reformer. The common thread that unified his disparate interests was a belief in the common man who was poorly served by an inefficient government and ineffective social institutions. As a result of the lack of adequate social services, people were often reduced to poverty, homelessness, illiteracy, prison or transportation, conditions which Dickens abhorred and to which he would return, time and again in his writing and speeches.

As might be expected in a writer with the literary output like Dickens, there are a number of original manuscripts to work with, including the novels themselves, his speeches, as well as correspondence to and from many of his friends, literary acquaintances, and the reading public. Many of Dickens's speeches, delivered to philanthropic organizations, social clubs, dinners organized on the behalf of charitable institutions or in his honor, are vehicles which he used to present his views on leading social institutions, governmental effectiveness, and the state of the law in Victorian England, are used in the work. In addition, the number of biographers and critics who have written about Dickens is quite extensive, and the list of such critics includes John Forster, Edgar Johnson, Michael Slater, Jane Smiley, Philip Hobsbaum, J. Hillis Miller, and Peter Ackroyd, to name a few.

John Forster was a literary critic for the *Examiner* and had reviewed Dickens's early works for that paper. In 1837, he was introduced to Dickens by Harrison Ainsworth, a mutual friend and popular author at the time. Forster was Dickens's closest personal friend and was named Dickens's executor and was personally selected by Dickens to write his biography. The biography is an exhaustive exploration of Dickens's life and works and was originally published in three volumes. Forster had the advantage of knowing Dickens for a period of some thirty-odd years and his biography is filled with details known only to a few people during Dickens's lifetime. Forster's biography provides the basis for much of what we know of the author's early childhood. Dickens relied on Forster to remain discreet and Forster avoided expressing his personal opinion about Dickens's breakup with his wife, Catherine, and did not provide details about his subsequent relations with Ellen Ternan. It is difficult to imagine writing about Dickens's life without a knowledge of Forster's work.

Edgar Johnson was chairman of the Department of English at City College, New York. His biography, *Charles Dickens: His Tragedy and Triumph*, was published in 1953 and like Forster's book, provides details of Dickens's early childhood. Johnson's primary contribution to Dickens scholarship, aside from the sheer abundance of detail and insight provided in the book, is his linking of the events of Dickens's early life to his later published works. Johnson provides an empathetic reading of Dickens's life and makes a case that despite his impoverished childhood, Dickens was able to overcome his early misfortunes and develop into one of the greatest English authors. Johnson's insights into Dickens's character and psychological make-up have helped in understanding Dickens's approach to writing, as well as his views on politics, social reform, Parliament and philanthropy.

Michael Slater, emeritus professor of Victorian literature at Birkbeck College, University of London, is considered by many to be the foremost Dickens scholar of this generation. His biography, *Charles Dickens*, published in 2009 is both scholarly and highly readable. Like the biographies of Forster and Johnson, Slater's book abounds with details of Dickens's life as well as providing insights into Dickens's publishing and writing habits and provides details concerning the planning that went into Dickens's works. Slater is one of the founding members of the Dickens Society and contributes articles, insight and advice to its members.

Jane Smiley is a prolific author writing novels as well as non-fictional works including her book *Charles Dickens: A Life*. Although her biography of Dickens is short, it is an insightful portrait of Dickens as a writer, journalist and social reformer. She provides an understanding of Dickens's use of psychology in forming his characters that was particularly helpful in the writing of the chapter on dreams and dreaming.

As reader and then professor of literature at the University of Glasgow from 1966 until 1997, Phillip Hobsbaum wrote a number of books of criticism including works on William Wordsworth, D.H. Lawrence, Robert Lowell and Charles Dickens. His book, *A Reader's Guide to Charles Dickens*, contains a short biographical introduction followed by a critical analysis of each of Dickens's major works. He intersperses elements of Dickens's life and work habits into each chapter and his commentary on the major works is scholarly and trenchant and was helpful in the choice of themes to organize this book.

J. Hillis Miller taught at Johns Hopkins University, Yale University and the University of California at Irvine and was the president of the Modern Language Association (MLA) in 1986. His book, *Charles Dickens: The World of His Novels*, is composed of a series of essays on nine of Dickens's novels. Miller's stated goal was to demonstrate that Dickens's novels were a means for Dickens to come to grips with himself and in some ways, to create himself. Miller's argument that Dickens's novels were not a result of his psychological condition but help to develop that condition is similar to the arguments developed in this book. He also believed that culture does not so much dictate the material that an author uses but that the author engages this material in an attempt to define the existing culture.

Like Jane Smiley, Peter Ackroyd has written both fiction and non-fictional works. His non-fictional writing includes biographies of Ezra Pound, T.S. Elliot, William Blake, William Shakespeare, Geoffrey Chaucer and Charles Dickens. His biographies on Dickens include his monumental and thoroughly researched 1990 work, *Dickens*, and a shorter work entitled *Dickens: Public Life and Private Passion* which was released in conjunction with a BBC television series on Dickens. Ackroyd's books and television series helped make Dickens more accessible to readers and viewers in the twentieth century.

A brief summary of Dickens's childhood and adolescence, as well as a survey of Victorian England, will help to frame a number of issues that will be discussed later in the book. The age of Queen Victoria officially began in 1837, the year that the Queen ascended to the throne. Historical eras are delineated by the occurrence of an important event, such as ascension or death of a monarch, wars, or the violent overthrow of a government. For the vast majority of the population one era blends into another so that a line of demarcation cannot usually be drawn between the two. At the time of Victoria's ascension to the throne profound changes were beginning to be felt in the country: the French and American Revolutions had come and gone; Napoleon had been defeated and as a result, the English Navy was the most powerful in the world; the British efforts at colonization of foreign lands resumed after a brief hiatus experienced after the loss of the American colonies; industry began to expand with the invention of the steam engine; the migration of the population from the country to the city accelerated as industry expanded. The political power of the landed gentry was being challenged by the new-found wealth of the mercantile and industrial classes, while the movement of people from the rural areas of England to the cities created a new class of workers. In many cases, the skills required for farming and herding did not translate into the skills needed for industry; dislocations of people and skills produced a new form of urban poor and the social, judicial, political and sanitation systems could not keep up with the massive influx of people to the cities.

As these changes swept through English society the attitudes that were prevalent in the eighteenth century began to change and to become more conservative. The society of the eighteenth century was more open, boisterous, less prudish, and less concerned with the appearance of propriety than that of the nineteenth century. It was, according to Ben Wilson, an age where "People were encouraged to talk the talk of virtue and to judge each other by outward appearances of respectability and public rectitude, which had nothing to do with inner morality" (6).

Charles Dickens was born on February 7, 1812, into a society that was experiencing profound changes. He was the eldest son of John and Elizabeth Dickens, the family then living at 387 Mile End Terrace, Portsea. By June of the same year, the family moved to smaller accommodations at 18 Hawke Street due to John Dickens's straitened financial conditions. In December 1814, John Dickens, a payroll clerk in the Royal Navy, was transferred to London, occupying a house at 10 Norfolk Street. In early 1817, John Dickens was transferred to Chatham, where he moved the family to Two Ordinance Terrace. In the space of five years, the Dickens family moved four times, which likely placed a great deal of stress on the family; so too, did John Dickens's poor money management. While at Ordnance Terrace, the family employed two servants, Jane Bonney and Mary Weller. In later life, Dickens related how Mary told frightening tales which inspired him to continue the tradition of telling tales in later life.

In the time period from 1812 to 1817, John Dickens' s annual salary as payroll clerk went from a modest £176 per annum to a more respectable £300 per annum, yet he remained financially encumbered during this entire time. In the autumn of 1822, John Dickens was transferred back to London, but before leaving Chatham, the family was forced to sell some of its possessions to pay off creditors and rent new living quarters. One of the people who purchased some of the family's possessions was Mary Weller, Charles' old nanny. It is believed that Charles was allowed to remain at grammar school in Chatham until the end of the term at Christmas time and that he joined the family sometime after the Christmas session finished. It was Dickens's first experience of being left alone; he would later experience the same sort of isolation and loneliness when his family was sent to the Marshalsea Prison as a result of John Dickens's poor money management.

The new family household was established at 16 Bayham Street in Camden Town, a decidedly less appealing location than their previous residence in London. It was at this residence that the Dickens family engaged the services of an orphan who was a ward of the parish, and was immortalized as the "Orfling" in Dickens's most autobiographical novel, *David Copperfield*.

Despite the frequent relocations and upheaval, by all accounts Dickens was a precocious lad who at an early age performed pantomimes, songs, and dances at the behest of his father. John Dickens was known for his ability to tell engaging stories, and was prone to bits of flowery oratory, which would later find expression in the characters of Wilkins Micawber in *David Copperfield*, and William Dorrit in *Little Dorrit*. In later life, Dickens claimed that he spent his happiest years in Chatham, despite his frail health which caused him to be confined to his room. His constant companions during these times were his books which he devoured with great relish. Dickens provided Forster with a fragment of an autobiography that was never published. In this fragment, Dickens describes his early childhood and reading:

> My father had left a small collection of books in a little room upstairs to which I had access (for it adjoined my own), and which nobody else in our house ever troubled. From that blessed little room, *Roderick Random, Peregrine Pickle, Humphrey Clinker, Tom Jones*, the *Vicar of Wakefield, Don Quixote, Gil Blas*, and *Robinson Crusoe* came out, a glorious host, to keep me company. They kept alive my fancy, and my hope of something beyond that place and time,—they, and the *Arabian Nights*, and the *Tales of the Genii*,—and did me no harm; for whatever harm was in some of them, was not there for me; I knew nothing of it [I: 9–10].

It is worth noting that this same passage is repeated, almost verbatim, in his semi-autobiographical novel, *David Copperfield*. In the following quotation, Foster provides a glimpse of young Charles Dickens growing up in Chatham:

> The queer small boy was indeed himself. He was a very little and very sickly boy. He was subject to attacks of violent spasm which disabled him for any active exertion. He was never a good little cricket-player; he was never a first-rate hand at marbles, or peg-top, or prisoner's base; but he had great pleasure in watching the other boys, officers' sons for the most part, at these games, reading while they played; and he had always the belief that this early sickness had brought to himself one inestimable advantage, in the circumstances of his weak health having strongly inclined him to reading [I: 7].

When Dickens was just a boy he took a walk with his father near Rochester. It was during this walk that he first encountered Gadshill Place, and his father told him he might someday own the mansion if he worked hard enough.

Engraving on paper of Gad's Hill, Kent, Dickens's last residence. The engraving was made by J. Donkin, in 1879. As a boy, Dickens's father told him he might own the mansion someday if he worked hard enough (London Metropolitan Archives).

By 1823, Mrs. Dickens, in an attempt to earn extra income for the family, opened a school for young girls and rented an apartment at a rate of £50 per annum; not one girl attended the school and the family's fortunes declined further. Dickens made use of his mother's attempt to open a school for young girls in his novel *David Copperfield*. In the novel, Mrs. Micawber opens a girl's school with the same disastrous results; money that the family desperately needed was spent for provisioning a school that no one attended.

Continually strapped for cash, the Dickens family began pawning items to pay for their rapidly increasing debts. Among the first items to go were Charles' beloved books, a fact which he noted to Forster in his *Life of Dickens*; but perhaps more hurtful than the necessity of pawning the books was the fact that it was Charles himself who was given the task of selling them at the pawn shop: "Almost everything by degrees was sold or pawned, little Charles being the principal agent in those sorrowful transactions" (I: 21).

Shortly after the family began pawning items to pay their mounting bills, Dickens was sent to work at Warren's Blacking Factory, which was run by his maternal cousin, James Lamert. At the age of twelve, Charles worked ten hours a day, six days a week, pasting labels on bottles of shoe blacking (shoe polish) for the sum of six shillings per week. The factory was located near the Thames at Hungerford Stairs. Charles, a perceptive and sensitive little boy whose primary enjoyments were reading books, listening to his father's tales, and performing small songs and skits at the local pub for his father and friends, was aware of the great gulf separating him from the other working-class boys who labored at the factory. He was called the "young gentlemen" by the other lads who worked in the factory and his cousin arranged a separate working area for young Charles, a further indication of this divide. In the mind of young Charles, he was meant to be an educated gentleman and he feared that life as a menial factory operative would put an end to this ambition. Perhaps it was in this factory where he first became conscious of the gulf between himself and others where the notion of "otherness" first dawned in his consciousness.[1] Yet, despite the differences between himself and the other boys, he made friends with one boy, Bob Fagin, whose name later became immortalized as the leader of a gang of young pick-pockets in *Oliver Twist*, the criminal character named only Fagin.

Dickens's notion of being different from the boys in the blacking factory lingered throughout his life, as he related to Forster before the publication of his semi-autobiographical novel *David Copperfield*: "My whole nature was so penetrated with the grief and humiliation of such considerations, that even now, famous and caressed and happy, I often forget in my dreams that I have a dear wife and children; even that I am a man; and wander desolately back to that time of my life" (I: 26–27). His disgrace was so marked that he told Forster he could not bear to pass the location of the blacking factory, which had moved to Chandos Street, without the feelings of humiliation arising again like some long-repressed ghost of the past:

> For many years, when I came near to Robert Warren's in the Strand, I crossed over to the opposite side of the way, to avoid a certain smell of the cement they put upon the blacking-corks, which reminded me of what I was once. It was a very long time before I liked to go up Chandos-street. My old way home by the borough made me cry, after my eldest child could speak [I: 38–39].

As much as the disgrace of working at the blacking factory affected the sensibilities of the young boy, one more blow was to be visited upon him which would have an equally profound effect on Dickens. Shortly after Charles began his drudgery at the blacking factory, John Dickens was arrested on February 20, 1824, for non-payment of debt and was sent to a sponging house,[2] then to the Marshalsea Prison. The family, minus Charles, accompanied him to the Marshalsea. Charles, recently turned twelve, was sent to live with Mrs. Roylance, a friend of the family, at 112 College Place in Camden Town. His desolation and loneliness were now complete, as he related to Forster: "'I felt keenly, however, the being so cut off from my parents, my brothers, and sisters; and, when my day's work was done, going home to such a miserable blank; and *that*, I thought, might be corrected'" (I: 30). Charles related his loneliness to his father, and remarkably, John Dickens never considered that his son left alone on the streets of London at the age of twelve, might have felt abandoned and lonely while his family resided in the Marshalsea Prison. John Dickens subsequently arranged for his son to take up new rooms nearer to the prison at Lant Street; young Charles was now able to visit his family after work and on weekends; yet, his employment at the blacking factory continued.

John Dickens was declared an insolvent and was discharged from the Marshalsea Prison on May 28, 1824. After his discharge, he received a bequest in the amount of £450 on the death of his mother, which enabled him to achieve a somewhat stable financial footing. The family moved to 112 College Place and lived with the same Mrs. Roylance Charles had lived with some months before. Despite the family's improved financial condition, Charles continued to work in the blacking factory. It was not until Charles and Bob Fagin were seen working in the bay window at the blacking factory, now located on Chandos Street, by a friend of John Dickens that something was done about Charles's employment at Warren's. Whether John Dickens felt ashamed that his son was observed working in the factory, or whether Charles's pleas that he be allowed to return home and attend school influenced the elder Dickens can never be fully known. John Dickens, despite the protests of his wife to the contrary, decided that Charles would quit the blacking factory, and return to school. Peter Ackroyd, in his book *The Life and Times of Charles Dickens*, writes about Dickens's relationship with his mother which resulted from her wish that he continue to work at the factory: "He never forgave her [his mother] for what seemed to him to be an act of treachery, and his mother was later savagely satirized in his novels as Mrs. Nickleby and others. They were never close again" (14).

After being relieved of his duties at the blacking warehouse, young Charles returned to school at the Wellington House Academy and attended classes there for two years. The Academy, despite its somewhat pretentious name, was not a very good school and its headmaster, one William Jones, was more adept at beating his pupils than instilling a love of knowledge in them. Dickens would later portray a similar kind of teacher in the persons of Wackford Squeers, headmaster at Dotheboys Hall in *Nicholas Nickleby*, and Mr. Creakle in *David Copperfield*. Despite the less than stellar reputation of the Wellington House Academy, young Dickens was a precocious, playful student and wrote some small plays and sketches during his stay at the school.

At the age of fifteen, he was made junior clerk to Mr. Edward Blackmore, an attorney whose offices were located at Gray's Inn. During the time he spent working at Blackmore and Ellis, he attended the theater frequently and in his spare time taught himself shorthand in preparation for a career as a Parliamentary reporter. He left the firm of Blackmore and Ellis to pursue a similar position at the offices of Charles Molloy, where he labored for a few additional months as a law clerk. After leaving the employ of Mr. Molloy, Dickens was faced with a decision: should he pursue a career as a journalist and Parliamentary reporter, or should he pursue a career as an actor.

Dickens's decision on a career was guided by a series of events. He received an invitation to audition for the theatre at Covent Gardens, but was unable to accept the audition due to a bad cold; he requested a postponement of the audition until the following year but his dreams of becoming a professional actor did not produce results. In the meantime, his career as a journalist was aided by the services of his uncle, John Henry Barrow, who encouraged Dickens to become a freelance reporter in Doctor's Commons. This institution was responsible for administering civil law in England and heard cases related to wills, marital discord, and maritime law. Here, his knowledge of shorthand aided him in recording the proceedings and writing articles for his uncle's publication, *The Mirror of Parliament*. His experiences as a court reporter covering the disputes related to wills, matrimonial difficulties and the convoluted intricacies of maritime law led to Dickens's disdain for the legal profession which he expressed later in life in his writing.

At about the same time as his reporting career was developing, he fell in love with a young girl named Maria Beadnell, who was his first true love. Maria came from an upper middle class family and her father, a prosperous banker, did not approve of her courting by Dickens whose family station was beneath that of the Beadnells'. The courtship languished for a period of three years and ended when Maria chided Dickens for being "a boy" at a party he threw on his twenty-first birthday. Maria's rejection cut him deeply, and led to a reticence for expressing his love for those closest to him, a reticence which persisted throughout his life.

A combination of events which included his early life apart from his family, the destruction of his dreams of becoming a distinguished gentleman and the humiliation he suffered from working at the blacking factory contributed to his sense of being different from the other boys during this period of his life. The feeling of being different was exacerbated by the events he later experienced as a legal clerk and Parliamentary reporter, where he witnessed the great divide between the members of Parliament and the common people. His profession of love to Maria Beadnell and her subsequent rejection, due in part to their difference in social standing, also contributed to his sense of being somehow outside of polite society. In one of the most pathetic disclosures to Forster, Dickens describes his feelings of loneliness and isolation as he struggled with his life alone in London:

> I know that, but for the mercy of God, I might easily have been, for any care that was taken of me, a little robber or a little vagabond.... That I suffered in secret, and that I suffered exquisitely, no one ever knew but I. How much I suffered, it is, as I have said already, utterly beyond my power to tell. No man's imagination can overstep the reality. But I kept my own counsel, and I did my work [I: 29–30].

Somehow during the loneliness and isolation, feeling cut-off from his family and society and facing the prospect of the continuing drudgery of working as a legal reporter, Charles Dickens developed a resolution that he would not be hurt like this again. He determined that from then on, he would decide the course he would follow in life and as a result an iron will was forged from the hurt and humiliation he felt at such a young age. It was as if this young, sensitive boy developed an alternate personality, one that would not be stopped, one that would brook no fools, one that would stand on the side of the oppressed, lonely, down-trodden; one that would take on the veneer of respectability that was applied to the surface of the highest levels of Victorian society, and would win.

John Forster, commenting on this dual nature of Charles Dickens expressed what close friends would come to know about him in later life:

> All that was involved in what he had suffered and sunk into, could not have been known to him at the time; but it was plain enough later, as we see; and in conversation with me after the revelation was made, he used to find, at extreme points of his life, the explanation of himself in those early trials.... What it was that in society made him often uneasy, shrinking, and over-sensitive, he knew; but all the danger he ran in bearing down and over-mastering the feeling, he did not know.... But there they were; and when I have seen strangely present, at such chance intervals, a stern and even cold isolation of self-reliance side by side with a susceptivity almost feminine and the most eager craving for sympathy, it has seemed to me as though his habitual impulses for everything kind and gentle had sunk, for the time, under a sudden hard and inexorable

sense of what fate had dealt to him in those early years.... The never to be forgotten misery of that old time, bred a certain shrinking sensitiveness in a certain ill-clad ill-fed child, that I have found come back in the never to be forgotten misery of this later time [I: 40–41].

It was this feeling, developed at the age of twelve, and heightened by his experiences during his adolescence, that led to Dickens's sense of otherness, a sense of being different from the members of his own family and of society in general. The experiences of his early childhood caused Dickens to develop a steely will that would not be turned aside. The effects of his will were double-sided: on the one hand, he developed a sense of discipline and hard work that were to last him the rest of his life. On the other hand, it caused him to resent any interference once his mind was made up, as several of his publishers and his wife, Catherine, would learn.[3] It was this feeling of isolation that did not permit Dickens to relate his early life to his wife or children, and which led him to remark in a letter to Maria Winter (née Beadnell) that he could not show his love for his children once they were past the age of five or six years old.[4]

The man who emerged from these early childhood experiences was in many ways a series of contradictions: the greatest writer of his age who was admired and adulated but who sometimes imagined himself as a small, helpless child. A man who intensely disliked the abuses of power and wealth but who was obsessed with making money throughout his lifetime. A man whose natural exuberance and love of theatricality was the life of any party he attended but who wished to keep private his earliest childhood privations and who retreated from the throngs of people who clamored for a piece of him. A man whose friendships were deep and in some cases lifelong but who was reticent to show his affection, even towards his own children. A man who readily adopted a number of the technological advances of his era but who was also profoundly disturbed by the effects these advances might have on the quality of life for the average man. A writer who portrayed the chaotic, sprawling life of London but who insisted on an almost regimented existence in his own household, and who disliked change in his everyday habits.[5]

Dickens's early childhood experiences would shape his views of society and enable him to identify with the circumscribed social prospects of a number of characters in his novels. From his humble beginnings, he would come to understand the common man: his frustrations, anger, joys, sorrows, his feelings of bewilderment at a rapidly changing society, as well as the sense of nostalgia felt by many of his fellow Englishmen and that permeates many of Dickens's works.

CHAPTER ONE

Class and Class Distinctions

One of the primary themes of Dickens's novels is that of the tension between the individual and society. This tension is rooted in Dickens's background which can be traced, in part, to his experiences with life in London when he lived by himself at the age of twelve and his first-hand observations of the Marshalsea Prison. His stint as a Parliamentary reporter contributed to his dislike of politicians who were "full of sound and fury, signifying nothing," and did little to alleviate the poverty, overcrowding, and unsanitary conditions which plagued London during the early to mid–Victorian period.

Dickens was also aware of the profound changes sweeping through Victorian society. For perhaps the first time in history, the wholesale movement of populations which thrived in a rural/agricultural economy to an urban mercantile/industrial economy was accomplished in a period between thirty and forty years. This movement resulted in a destabilizing of society which affected job creation, education, political reform and the eventual replacement of the power of the landed gentry with that of the middle class through the expansion of the franchise to the middle class.[1]

Dickens wrote about the gulf that separated the upper classes from the lower classes in his novels and non-fictional pieces. As a result of the rigid class structure in Britain, the distribution of wealth was skewed and provided the upper classes with services and amenities that were unavailable to the poorer members of society. The gulf between the rich and the poor was exacerbated by the rise of capitalism that sprang up as a result of the Industrial Revolution and contributed to an emphasis on material possessions at the expense of the moral and spiritual values that Dickens wrote about in his novels. Finally, Dickens recognized that the migration from rural areas to the city led to a lack of identification with a larger group which contrasted with the stability provided by identifiable groups in the small towns and villages that made up rural England as recently as the 1820s and '30s.

Beginning with the novel *Oliver Twist*, Dickens started to write about the distinctions between the upper and lower classes that existed in Victorian society. The novel was written as a repudiation of the New Poor Law which was passed in 1834.[2] *Oliver Twist* is the tale of an orphan who was born in a workhouse; life in a workhouse was not easy, young children were expected to work to earn their keep. Oliver is sent to work as an apprentice to a chimney-sweep and then an undertaker; he succeeds in neither job and makes his way as a mere boy to London to find better prospects. There, he encounters a gang of pickpockets and is recruited to join in their work. The conditions of the young and those in the workhouse which are explored in the novel are harsh and might seem exaggerated to the modern reader.

An examination of the *Report on the Sanitary Condition of the Labouring Population and on the Means of Its Improvement*, written in 1842 by Edwin Chadwick, will reveal the extent of the privations suffered by young children and laborers in workhouses, factories and mines in England. Chadwick was initially employed by the Royal Commission to rewrite the Poor Laws and helped to draft the original proposal which resulted in the New Poor Law of 1834. The law, as written, provided for each parish to administer its own workhouse, a provision with which Chadwick disagreed. He then proceeded to investigate the sanitary conditions in England, Wales and Scotland in an attempt to convince the Royal Commission that a centralized administration of sanitary conditions and the workhouses was required. The *Report*, which he initiated on his own, and published at his own expense, was a scathing indictment of the sanitary conditions which existed in the United Kingdom at the time.

The *Report* was based on eye-witness accounts of the living and sanitary conditions of the poor in the United Kingdom and paints a sharp contrast between the conditions of the poor and those of the more affluent inhabitants of the kingdom. The first page of the *Report* provides a detailed breakdown of the deaths caused by disease and sanitation for the years 1838 and 1839, the same years as *Oliver Twist* appeared for publication. Chadwick provides the following categories of death relating to disease and sanitation: epidemic, endemic and contagious diseases; diseases of the respiratory organs; diseases of the brain; and diseases of the digestive organs. In total, there were 216,000 cases of death from these causes in 1838, and 215,000 in 1839 (3).

A brief listing of the causes of these unsanitary condition includes:

poor drainage of city and rural areas; overcrowding and unsanitary housing conditions; lack of potable water suitable for washing, drinking and cooking; insufficient land drainage leading to typhoid, malaria and other disease; the spreading of contagion due to filth, lack of hygiene, and overcrowding; poor working conditions in factories and mines; and inability to effectively deal with sickness by members of a household or neighborhood.[3]

By the time Dickens wrote his next novel, *The Old Curiosity Shop*, published in 1840-1841, he wished to make his readers aware of the conditions he read about in Chadwick's *Report*. The novel contains a passage that is eerily similar to several of the abuses presented in Chadwick's *Report*. In the novel, Nell and her grandfather encounter factory workers near Birmingham. Here is Dickens's description of the factory and its laborers:

> In a large and lofty building, supported by pillars of iron, with great black apertures in the upper walls, open to the external air; echoing to the roof with the beating of hammers and roar of furnaces, mingled with the hissing of red-hot metal plunged in water, and a hundred strange unearthly noises never heard elsewhere; in this gloomy place, moving like demons among the flame and smoke, dimly and fitfully seen, flushed and tormented by the burning fires, and wielding great weapons, a faulty blow from any one of which must have crushed some workmen's skull, a number of men labored like giants [*OCS* 329–330].

Not only does Dickens's description of the factory match that of Chadwick in his *Report*, it also conjures up images of hell. The workers are variously referred to as demons and giants, who are flushed and tormented; the factory is described as being lit by fire and filled with smoke. Such conditions are abysmal, hell-like, and unfortunately, too real.

Prior to his departure for Italy on holiday in 1844, Dickens confided to Forster that he was discouraged by society, and that it was in need of reform:

> I declare I never go into what is called "society" that I am not aweary of it, despise it, hate it, and reject it. The more I see of its extraordinary conceit, and its stupendous ignorance of what is passing out of doors, the more certain I am that it is approaching the period when, being incapable of reforming itself, it will have to submit to be reformed by others off the face of the earth [I: 356].

In this passage, the reader is made aware of Dickens's contempt for class distinctions and his belief that the existing institutions which were in put place to ameliorate the disparity between those classes, were ineffectual. At this period of his life, Dickens was just beginning to express his frustrations with England's stratified society. As time went on without appreciable changes occurring in society, Dickens's fictional writing about class distinction became more openly critical culminating in his attacks on social injustice in *Bleak House, Little Dorrit* and *Our Mutual Friend.*

His concern for social reform continued in a series of novels beginning with *Dombey and Son.* Dickens takes up the notion of class distinction in *Dombey and Son,* published in 1847-1848. Paul Dombey, Sr., is seen as the representative of a society which places too much value on the accumulation of wealth and as a result imbues people like Paul Dombey, Sr., with a false sense of their importance in society. Dombey Sr., believes that the world was created expressly for him, and that his employees and servants are created solely to propitiate and obey him. His two wives are not seen as real people, but as extensions of his empire; something to be trotted out on special occasions and placed back, like a trophy, after the occasion passes. He is the embodiment of that form of English snobbery which Dickens loathed, and which he believed, contributed to a society made up of two classes of people: those who have, and those who have not.

Dickens attributes the increasing disparity in wealth to laissez-faire capitalism, which is unchecked by law, and which allows merchants like Mr. Dombey to attain a power that was once reserved for the landed gentry. Thomas Carlyle, in his essay "Signs of the Times," refers to the disparity between rich and poor and attributes it to the growth of capitalism which leads to what he calls a "Mechanical Age." Dickens, an admirer of, and close friend of Carlyle, no doubt thought of Carlyle's essay when he began work on *Dombey:*

> What changes, too, this addition of power is introducing into the Social System; how wealth has more and more increased, and at the same time gathered itself more and more into masses, strangely altering the old relations, and increasing the distance between the rich and the poor, will be a question for Political Economists, and a much more complex and important one than any they have yet engaged with [Carlyle 7].[4]

As the years passed, Dickens perceived that society became more rigid, class distinctions between the rich and the poor became more prevalent, and social conventions became more fixed; as a result, social mobility became more difficult to accomplish. In *Bleak House,* Dickens emphasized the rigid class structure that would not allow Lady Dedlock to recognize her born out-of-wedlock daughter, Esther Summerson, for fear that her prominent social standing would be jeopardized. Lady Dedlock, wife to Sir Leicester Dedlock, is portrayed as an icy, haughty woman who lives in Chesney Wold, a place steeped in an aristocratic family history which seems impervious to the effects of time. Dickens's portrayal of Chesney Wold is also meant to indicate the inflexible nature of the upper classes who have held their lofty positions since time immemorial:

Illustration of Tom-All-Alone's by H.K. Browne (Phiz), in *Bleak House*. Tom-All-Alone's was a fictional slum used to depict the unsanitary conditions existing in London during Dickens's time (British Library, London).

... there is no hurry there; there, in that ancient house, rooted in that quiet park, where the ivy and the moss have had time to mature, and the gnarled and warted elms, and the umbrageous oaks, stand deep in the fern and leaves of a hundred years, and where the sun-dial on the terrace has dumbly recorded for centuries that Time, which was as much the property of every Dedlock—while he lasted—as the house and lands" [BH 388].

Lady Dedlock maintains her icy demeanor until she acknowledges her daughter in chapter 36 of the novel, but even after she takes leave of Esther she returns to her former state, for she must "be proud and disdainful everywhere else" (BH 501).

The pestilent area known as Tom-All-Alones is a product of the Chancery suit of Jarndyce v. Jarndyce and becomes a symbol for the squalor that houses all the dispossessed in the city of London. It contains:

... by night, a swarm of misery. As, on the ruined human wretch, vermin parasites appear, so, these ruined shelters have bred a crowd of foul existence that crawls in and out of gaps in the walls and boards; and coils itself to sleep, in maggot numbers, where the rain drips in; and comes and goes, fetching and carrying fever..." [BH 217].

For those unfortunate enough to live in Tom-All-Alones, their lives present a stark contrast to those privileged few who are cocooned in Chesney Wold.

In *Little Dorrit*, Dickens engages in a scathing diatribe against class consciousness, when he has Mr. Dorrit, former prisoner for debt at the Marshalsea prison, explain his position in society to his daughter, Amy:

"I was there all those years. I was—ha—universally acknowledged as the head of the place. I—hum—I caused you to be respected there, Amy. I—ha hum—I gave my family a position there. I deserve a return. I claim a return. I say, sweep it off the face of the earth and begin afresh. Is that much? I ask, is *that* much?"

He did not once look at her, as he rambled on in this way; but gesticulated at, and appealed to, the empty air.

"I have suffered. Probably I know how much I have suffered better than any one— ha—I say than any one! If *I* can put that aside, if *I* can eradicate the marks of what I have endured, and can emerge before the world—a—ha—gentleman unspoiled, unspotted—is it a great deal to expect—I say again, is it a great deal to expect—that my children should—hum—do the same and sweep that accursed experience off the face of the earth?" [LD 243]

The character of Mr. Dorrit, a former resident of the Marshalsea Prison, has adopted the affectations of the upper classes after receiving an inheritance which freed him from prison. That he adapts to his new station so readily underscores Dickens's notion that unearned money corrupts; in fact, he names this type of corruption the "Merdle contagion" in the novel.

Mr. Dorrit was not the only character in *Little Dorrit* who was too conscious of his social standing. His characterizations of the figures of Mrs. Merdle and Mrs. General are designed to be symbols of the type of person who places emphasis on an outward show of respectability while the interior of the person is described as being hollow. In chapter 20, book 1, Mrs. Merdle is introduced to Little Dorrit who has accompanied her sister, Fanny to Mrs. Merdle's house, ostensibly to return a bracelet to Mrs. Merdle. During their interview, Mrs. Merdle, aware of Fanny's true purpose which is to enforce her claim upon the affections of Edmund Sparkler, Mrs. Merdle's son by a previous marriage, engages in a homily about the nature of polite society: "We know it is hollow and conventional and worldly and very shocking, but unless we are Savages in the Tropical seas (I should have been charmed to be one myself—most delightful life and perfect climate, I am told), we must consult it'" (*LD* 122).

Mrs. Merdle eventually acknowledges Fanny's true mission, which is to marry Mrs. Merdle's son, and comments on the naiveté of her son. Mrs. Merdle then asserts that she is devoid of social pretension and wishes to remain in a state of Edenic simplicity: "'So he [Edmund Sparkler] is very impressible. Not a misfortune in our natural state, I dare say, but we are not in a natural state. Much to be lamented, no doubt, particularly by myself, who am a child of nature if I could but show it; but so it is. Society suppresses us and dominates us—Bird, be quiet!'" (*LD* 122). Dickens is, of course, satirizing the pretensions of Mrs. Merdle who professes a wish to be in a "natural" state, all the while displaying the opulence in which she lives and at the same time emphasizing to both Fanny and Little Dorrit that they do not move in the same exalted social circles. Mrs. Merdle's façade is lifted when, turning to Little Dorrit she remarks:

> I pointed out to your sister that plain state of the case; the impossibility of the Society in which we moved recognizing the Society in which she moved—though charming, I have no doubt; the immense disadvantage at which she would consequently place the family she had so high an opinion of, upon which we should find ourselves compelled to look down with contempt, and from which (socially speaking) we should feel obliged to recoil with abhorrence [*LD* 123].

Dickens's contempt for all that Mrs. Merdle stands for is manifested in his portrayal of her as a mere adornment; one of Mr. Merdle's trophies to be placed on public display at one of his many soirées where the fashionable people in London come to see and be seen. "The bosom moving in Society with the jewels displayed upon it, attracted general admiration. Society approving, Mr. Merdle was satisfied. He was the most disinterested of men,—did everything for Society, and got as little for himself out of all his gain and care, as a man might" (*LD* 125).

Not to be outdone by Mrs. Merdle in her claim to be distinguished in polite society, Mrs. General is hired as governess to Little Dorrit and

Fanny and that venerable lady inculcates the lessons of "prisms, prunes and papa" to the two young women in an attempt to make them presentable and to impart a "surface" to their characters. Dickens is juxtaposing the idea of a "surface" layer of respectability with that of the development of an inner self, and uses the person of Mrs. General to highlight the hypocrisy of people who place more emphasis on the appearance of things, rather than placing value on the reality of a person's character.

Dickens portrays Mrs. General as a sort of automaton who has no real thoughts of her own, but merely parrots the crass opinions of polite society:

> She had a little circular set of mental grooves or rails on which she started little trains of other people's opinions, which never overtook one another, and never got anywhere. Even her propriety could not dispute that there was impropriety in the world; but Mrs. General's way of getting rid of it was to put it out of sight, and make believe that there was no such thing [*LD* 229].

In keeping with the crassness of polite society, it comes as little surprise that Mrs. General's primary interest is not in her two charges, Amy and Fanny, but in William Dorrit, who, having inherited a great deal of money, is an eligible bachelor. She is ultimately frustrated in her attempts to win the hand of Mr. Dorrit, who has a stroke and becomes unaware of her presence, "They tried him with Mrs. General, but he had not the faintest knowledge of her" (*LD* 331). She is left to attempt to find another position with some other family, there to produce the "surface" that she was unable to apply to the persons of Amy and Fanny, and no doubt repeat her empty platitudes on a new set of victims.

Dickens continues his criticism of polite society in *Our Mutual Friend*. In this novel, two families are singled out for derision: the Veneerings and the Podsnaps. The Veneerings, like Mrs. General, are concerned with surface valuations of people; but more than this, they are emblematic of new money, new power, new influence and are the result of the increase in the nouveau riche in Victorian society. The very name chosen for these crass new-comers, a name which implies a false surface or veneer, is testament to Dickens's ability to match a name to a primary personal characteristic. Dickens's introduction of the Veneerings highlights their sudden rise to prominence, fueled by money:

> Mr. and Mrs. Veneering were bran-new people in a bran-new house in a bran-new quarter of London. Everything about the Veneerings was spick and span new. All their furniture was new, all their friends were new, all their servants were new, their plate was new, their carriage was new, their harness was new, their horses were new, their pictures were new, they themselves were new, they were newly married as was lawfully compatible with their having a bran-new baby, and if they had set up a great-

grandfather, he would have come home in matting from the Pantechnicon, without a scratch upon him, French-polished to the crown of his head.

For in the Veneering establishment, from the hall-chairs with the new coat of arms, to the grand pianoforte with the new action, and up-stairs again to the new fire-escape, all things were in a state of high varnish and polish. And what was observable in the furniture, was observable in the Veneerings—the surface smelt a little too much of the workshop and was a trifle sticky [*OMF* 6].

Like all of the newly minted people of money portrayed in the novel, the Veneerings are only too eager to make their mark upon society, and to be counted among those who must be seen. They throw lavish parties where the only common thread among the guests is that none of the attendees is in any way aware of the background of the Veneerings; yet each person invited to the soirée is received as one of the most cherished friends of the Veneerings. Despite having no discernable background, and no real friends to speak of, Mr. Veneering is recruited to stand for Parliamentary election:

Britannia, sitting meditating one fine day (perhaps in the attitude in which she is represented on the copper coinage), discovers all of a sudden that she wants Veneering in Parliament. It occurs to her that Veneering is a "representative man"—which cannot in these times be doubted—and that Her Majesty's faithful Commons are incomplete without him. So Britannia mentions to a legal gentleman of her acquaintance that if Veneering will "put down" five thousand pounds, he may write a couple of initial letters after his name at the extremely cheap rate of two thousand five hundred per letter. It is clearly understood between Britannia and the legal gentleman that nobody is to take up the five thousand pounds, but that being put down they will disappear by magical conjuration and enchantment [*OMF* 244].

And so, Dickens tells us, Veneering is not above bribing his way into public office as a member of Parliament (M and P being the two initials referred to in this passage). Here, Dickens conflates three of the themes of this novel: the hypocrisy of social standing, the insidious influence of money, and the lack of regard for the commonweal by the members of Parliament.

The other redoubtable family in the novel, the Podsnaps, is more firmly established in society than the Veneerings, and as a result, its members are perhaps more set in their ways. Dickens paints a portrait of Mr. Podsnap:

Mr. Podsnap's world was not a very large world, morally; no, nor even geographically: seeing that although his business was sustained upon commerce with other countries, he considered other countries, with that important reservation, a mistake, and of their manners and customs would conclusively observe, "Not English!" [*OMF* 126]

In this passage, Dickens confirms that not only are the Podsnaps set in their ways, they are representative of those members of the upper classes who are so arrogant that they look down upon other cultures simply because they are not English.

Like the Veneerings, the Podsnaps threw lavish parties, including one for the benefit of their daughter, Georgiana Podsnap, who was celebrating her eighteenth birthday. At that party, which was marked by the usual polite but meaningless banter that characterized polite society, one meek person had the temerity to intimate that several people had recently died of starvation in the city of London. This remark is considered impolite by Mr. Podsnap, who inquired of the gentleman what he meant by his intimation. The gentleman replied that something must be wrong somewhere, if people were left to die of starvation in the streets. Mr. Podsnap's reply expresses the belief system which Dickens abhorred, and which indicates the arrogance at the highest levels of Victorian society:

> "I must decline to pursue this painful discussion. It is not pleasant to my feelings. It is repugnant to my feelings. I have said that I do not admit these things. I have also said that if they do occur (not that I admit it), the fault lies with the sufferers themselves. It is not for *me*"—Mr. Podsnap pointed "me" forcibly, as adding by implication, though it may be all very well for *you*—"it is not for me to impugn the workings of Providence" [*OMF* 141].

This passage indicates that Podsnap denies responsibility for the welfare of those less fortunate than himself, and relies on the workings of Providence to justify his callous attitude. Lost in Podsnap's self-important posturing is the fact that the party was intended for the benefit of his daughter on her eighteenth birthday. But a man so shallow as Podsnap would not hesitate to put his vacuous beliefs ahead of his daughter's happiness. In fact, Podsnap

> ... stood with his back to the drawing-room fire, pulling up his shirt-collar, like a veritable cock of the walk literally pluming himself in the midst of his possessions, nothing would have astonished him more than an intimation that Miss Podsnap, or any other young person properly born and bred, could not be exactly put away like the plate, brought out like the plate, polished like the plate, counted, weighed, and valued like the plate [*OMF* 142–143].

Ultimately, Miss Georgiana Podsnap is reduced from her status as a person to a mere possession, no more valuable to her father than a piece of plate. Miss Podsnap's status is similar to that of Mrs. Merdle, who is reduced from a person to a trophy to be displayed by her husband, Mr. Merdle. The severity of Dickens's attack cannot be underestimated: he is demonizing a society that places more value on possessions than on people, especially those people who should be most loved and cherished. He is also commenting on the arrogance of the more affluent members of Victorian society who refuse to recognize the suffering of the poor, or if they acknowledge that the poor suffer, blame the poor and not an ineffective government and their own callous attitudes for the plight of the urban poor.

As societies experience rapid changes such as those experienced during the early Victorian era, a sense of dissociation occurs, a sense that somehow a connection to the past has become fractured. One method of coping with this sense of being disconnected from the past is to evoke a feeling of nostalgia. Nostalgia is an attempt to return to a simpler point in time; a time of greater stability. It is a method of conjuring up prior experiences, an attempt to relive them, to use them as a way of coping with the present.

Oliver Sacks, neurologist and author, writes about the feeling of dissociation that occurs during times of rapid social change in *An Anthropologist on Mars*. One of his patients returns to his hometown in an effort to preserve his boyhood experiences, but discovers that time has altered the village where he grew up. Sacks noted that his patient began to paint scenes of his hometown based on boyhood memories. The evocation of these memories contributed to a profound sense of "nostalgia raised to the level of art and myth" (169). In effect, the nostalgia reported on by Sacks is an attempt by his patient to isolate a relatively stable period in the patient's life as a retreat from a more hectic, disturbing, present-day existence. The same kind of retreat to an earlier, more stable time may be seen in several of Dickens's works, including *Sketches by Boz* and *The Pickwick Papers*. Like Sacks's patient, Dickens elevates this sense of nostalgia into "the level of art" in these two works. The tone of these works is openly nostalgic and indicates a backward look on the part of Dickens to an earlier time that was lost, a time that was more coherent, more stable, more understandable.

Dickens's portrayal of the emergence of cabs and omnibuses, and the slow disappearance of hackney-coaches in the sketch "Hackney-coach Stands" in *Sketches by Boz* is an example of a nostalgic tendency in Dickens's works that was exhibited early in his career. The descriptions of Seven Dials and Monmouth Street which are presented in the *Sketches*, while written as third person narrative, contain passages which are tinged with nostalgia and almost seem as if they were taken directly from Dickens's own life. As he describes the discarded clothes offered for sale in the second-hand shops on Monmouth Street and references the antiquity of the shops and the unchanging nature of the residents of the street, it is likely that he is writing from first-hand experience and that articles of his clothing were either sold or purchased from these shops.

Dickens's sense of the fragmented nature of time can be seen in his understanding of the instability of Victorian society; it seemed that time itself was unhinged, and is perhaps best reflected in his two historical novels *Barnaby Rudge* and *A Tale of Two Cities*. In both of these novels, the fabric of society is rent, and old social conventions appear to be meaningless. The dissolution of social conventions and the unfettered emotions of the crowds are shown through a series of passages where time seems to have stopped, where the unruly crowds take over the cities and social conventions no longer apply. The portrayal of the actions of the crowd seem surreal, time stops as the carnage, pillaging and lawlessness expand outward; the only thing that appears real is the collapse of the social order. The fear of social collapse was real for Dickens and a number of his contemporaries; if real change to the social order did not occur, Dickens feared that the events which led to the Gordon Riots and the French Revolution might occur again, with results that could be more devastating.[5]

As Dickens looked back to earlier, more stable times, his views of contemporary London society reflected his belief that there was a growing rift between rural and urban dwellers. This rift created a class of laborers who migrated to the city but whose skills were unsuitable for urban life. The portrayal of the brick makers and the street-sweeper, Jo, in *Bleak House* shows the plight of the uneducated and unskilled in London in the 1840s. Because they did not possess needed skills they were marginalized and in the case of Jo, discarded. Similarly, in his letter to Angela Burdett Coutts of September 16, 1843, relating his visit to one of the Ragged Schools, he almost despairs of providing adequate assistance to the young people attempting to become better educated: "My heart sinks within me when I go into these scenes, that I almost lose the hope of ever seeing them changed. Whether this effort will succeed, it is quite impossible to say" (*SL* 123). Dickens feared that without a proper education these poor students would become like Jo the street sweeper who "knows nothink."

By mid-century, London was not the only city which was experiencing profound social changes. The northern manufacturing cities of Manchester, Birmingham and Leeds were also undergoing significant changes, as were many cities on the Continent. Dickens and Thackeray wrote about the changes occurring in society in their novels set in the 1830s, '40s and '50s, and George Eliot and Thomas Hardy continued this tradition in their novels which were written later in the Victorian era. Edward Said writes about the novel as a form which deals with homelessness in his work *Reflections on Exile and Other Essays*: "The European novel is grounded in precisely the opposite experience [of stability and permanence], that of a changing society in which an itinerant and disinherited middle-class hero or heroine seeks to construct a new world that somehow resembles an old one left behind for ever" (144). Dickens, the foremost English novelist, attempts to recreate a new world in his early novels and employs the technique of writing about a changing society which causes him to act like an exile in his own city, a point noted by Said when he comments: "No matter how well they may do, exiles are always eccentrics who feel their difference (even as they frequently exploit it) as a kind of orphanhood" (144). It is significant to note that Said links the concepts of feeling like an exile, of being "other," with that of orphan-hood, themes and linkages that recur in Dickens's writing.

The large scale relocation of rural inhabitants to the city led to a fragmentation of social relationships that formed the basis of rural life. It seems almost incongruous to the modern reader that London, the largest city in Europe during the Victorian period, could be at once so populous and at the same time so conducive to a sense of loneliness, a loneliness brought about by the disruption of local communities and families. Dickens highlighted this seeming incongruity in many of his novels, an incongruity that was lost on many of the writers of this period, as Robert Douglas-Fairhurst makes clear in his work *Becoming Dickens*:

> Where Dickens differed from those other writers was in recognizing that London was not only a celebration of sociability. It was also a place that magnified loneliness. Although many people feel isolated from time to time, London seemed especially adept at transforming such moods into a way of life, like that of the pinched man Boz observes walking mechanically up and down in St. James Park, "unheeding and unheeded; his spare, pale face looking as if it were incapable of bearing the expression of curiosity or interest" ("Thoughts about People") [152].

In providing a picture of Mr. Gridley, the Shropshire Man in *Bleak House*, Dickens makes explicit the correlation between the movement from rusticity to urbanity and the disruption this causes in a person's sense of place and time. After years of watching his rural inheritance being eaten away by the interminable process of Chancery, Mr. Gridley is left to voice his anger at "The System! I am told, on all hands, it's the system. I mustn't look to individuals. It's the system. I mustn't go into Court, and say, 'My Lord, I beg to know this from you—is this right or wrong?'" (*BH* 213). Here the plight of the rural dweller is emphasized. Mr. Gridley can no longer consult real people for solutions to his problems, as he did in his town. Instead he is told that he must appeal to the nameless bureaucrats who comprise "the System"!

Mr. Gridley, for all his anger, is not yet fully diminished in capacity, for he has a sense of the injustice being done to him which preserves his sanity; yet, he is fearful of becoming something akin to Miss Flite "the poor little mad woman that haunts the Court" (*BH* 212). Miss Flite might be the ultimate expression of a person who has witnessed the effects of a social order which has lost its meaning. Because she is powerless to effect change, she has retreated from the world of the Chancery Court with its interminable, nonsensical, legal precedents to a simpler world, a world in which she lives with her birds, and watches them slowly die away, along with her chances for a verdict in the Chancery Court on the "day of judgment," which never arrives.

Dickens continued to write about the theme of class and class distinctions throughout his life, beginning with his earliest works, including his first collected writings, *Sketches by Boz*. An examination of the *Sketches* provides a detailed analysis of class and class distinctions, which served as the foundation for the theme in his later works. The *Sketches* were originally written as a series of individual pieces published in different magazines and newspapers, including *The Monthly Magazine*, *The Evening Chronicle*, *Bell's Life in London*, and *The Morning Chronicle* from 1833 through 1836. In 1836–1837, Dickens's first publisher, John Macrone, arranged these sketches into a two-volume collection, to which Dickens added some additional pieces that were not previously published. The collection was divided into four sections entitled "Seven Sketches From Our Parish," "Scenes," "Characters," and "Tales," and Boz was listed as the author of the series. The collection became an instant hit, and provided Dickens with additional writing opportunities. He began writing his first novel, *Pickwick Papers* at the same time as the *Sketches* were being published.[6]

The sketch was a popular form of writing in the 1830s, making use of observations of London life. Several collections of essays and stories were published by authors who are not well-known today, including John Poole, J. Wight, and Cornelius Webb (McEwan 34); Leigh Hunt's sketches form an exception to the relative anonymity of the authors previously listed. Virgil Grillo, in *Charles Dickens' Sketches by Boz: End in the Beginning*, outlines the function of the sketch as follows:

> As a literary form, a sub-genre of the essay, the sketch in the 1830s was primarily comic; it sought to amuse, occasionally to inform its readers. The subject matter of the sketch ranged from the depiction of a particular person or character type, to a description of a building, a neighborhood, a town, a social event, an institution, or even a peculiarly contemporary phenomenon [56].

Sales of *Sketches by Boz* were aided by the illustrations produced by George Cruikshank which complemented the writing of Dickens. Robert Patten, in his article "From *Sketches* to *Nickleby*," comments on the popularity of *Sketches by Boz*, as well as the literary form of sketches:

> The *Sketches* derive in part from a tradition of graphic representations of urban scenes. The explosive growth of London during and after the Napoleonic wars and the thousands of workers who immigrated to the metropolis in search of jobs and a new identity produced a kind of dizzying dislocation for old and new inhabitants. Streets were torn down and rebuilt, fields converted to tenements, rivers bridged over, and shops opened and closed, seemingly overnight. Finding one's way around in this city of transformations was difficult enough; understanding the babble of tongues and the semiotics of signs—printed ones, but the equally important signs of clothing and behavior—required expert guidance [22].

Dickens emphasized this sense of impermanence and rapid change by highlighting a sense of isolation in a number of the *Sketches*, as noted by Dennis Wilder:

> The image of himself arriving in London friendless and alone, at the mercy of those around him, helps us to understand the sympathetic power of his insight into the lives of the lonely and neglected; equally, however, the humorous detachment with which he views himself, and documents his direction in London, suggests his durability and appetite for experience—qualities that enabled him to observe his environment, and to survive blows such as his father's imprisonment for debt, and his spell as "a common labouring hind" of twelve [xx].

Dickens understood the feeling that accompanied a loss of identity or belonging to something larger than oneself. It is this sense of group identity which was a characteristic of rural life and was lost in an urban environment; people could no longer identify with others, they had lost their sense of belonging. As a way of illustrating this point, Dickens alludes to this sense of belonging which was becoming increasingly lost in urban London but which survived in a few of the poorer sections of the city in the novel *Bleak House*. In chapter 8, Esther, Ada and Mrs. Pardiggle journey to the home of some brick makers to engage in one of Mrs. Pardiggle's misguided attempts at philanthropy. Arriving at the brick maker's house, they found: "a woman with a black eye, nursing a poor little gasping baby by the fire; a man, all stained with clay and mud, and looking very dissipated, lying at full length on the ground, and a bold girl, doing some kind of washing in very dirty water" (*BH* 107).

As Esther and Ada watched the scene unfold before them, the small child who was gasping by the fire, died. At the same time, a friend of the baby's mother came into the house and noticing the dead baby, attempted to console the mother. Esther, observing the conduct of the two careworn women who exhibited "marks of ill-usage," reflected on their hardships and the bonds that joined them together:

I thought it very touching to see these two women, coarse and shabby and beaten, so united; to see what they could be to one another; to see how they felt for one another; how the heart of each to each was softened by the hard trials of their lives. I think the best side of such people is almost hidden from us. What the poor are to the poor is little known, excepting to themselves and GOD [*BH* 110].

Similar scenes of group identity in a rural setting can be seen in *The Old Curiosity Shop* when Nell and her grandfather meet the old schoolmaster who provided them lodging for a few days and endeavored to impart a rough-hewn education for his rustic scholars. Similarly, a sense of belonging is evident in the rural spectators who are drawn to the somewhat dilapidated figures that populate Mrs. Jarley's Wax Works and where Nell and her grandfather worked for a time.

Returning to the *Sketches*, the narrator highlights the sense of isolation which occurs in an urban setting and uses isolation as a way to observe those around him without others noticing him. Dickens employs the pronoun "we" quite extensively in the *Sketches*, and this usage is a way of distancing himself from those around him, as J. Hillis Miller and David Borowitz note:

He refers to himself here, as throughout, with the journalistic "we," which depersonalizes him, reduces him from a private man to a function, and at the same time suggests that he is divided into two consciousnesses. One is the public role of journalistic recorder who speaks not for himself but for the collective experience of all the dwellers in the city, for the universal truth which all know but do not know they know until it has been articulated for them by Boz. Such a truth is shared by all but is visible only to those who are disengaged from immediate involvement in the life of the city. Behind this collective self is Boz's other self, the private man behind the public role, who watches the journalist at work, somewhat self-consciously. This deeper self, it may be, expresses his private experience or private peculiarities covertly by way of the conventional mask [3–4].

The piece "Seven Dials," which is a reference to the junction of seven roads in the Covent Garden region of London notorious for its slums exhibits this sense of isolation using the journalistic pronoun "we" in its opening paragraph: "We have always been of the opinion that if Tom King and the Frenchman had not immortalized Seven Dials, Seven Dials would have immortalized itself" (90). The narrator describes some of the people who inhabit the Seven Dials area:

In addition to the numerous groups who are idling about the gin-shops, and squabbling in the centre of the road, every post on the open space has its occupant, who leans against it for hours, with listless perseverance. It is odd enough that one class of men in London appears to have no enjoyment beyond leaning against posts [*SB* 93].

The description of the people who inhabit Seven Dials is followed by a general description of the area:

Brokers' shops, which would seem to have been established by humane individuals, as refuges for destitute bugs, interspersed with announcements of day-schools, penny theatres, petition-writers, mangles, and music for balls or routs, complete the "still life" of the subject; and dirty men, filthy women, squalid children, fluttering shuttle-cocks, noisy battledores, reeking pipes, bad fruit, more than doubtful oysters, atten-uated cats, depressed dogs, and anatomical fowls, are its cheerful accompaniments [*SB* 94].

In both these passages, the narrator is recording his observations; he does not interact with the persons he describes. The scenes are impersonal, almost photographic, like some image in a museum or photo gallery. The effect of this photographic description is a sense of disconnection which underscores the lack of community and commonality between the narrator and the people he is describing.

The sense of isolation portrayed in the first few passages of the sketch is continued in Dickens's portrait of a man who is believed to be an author by the inhabitants in the area of Seven Dials:

The shabby-genteel man is an object of some mystery, but as he leads a life of seclusion, and never was known to buy any thing beyond an occasional pen, except half-pints of coffee, penny loaves, and ha'porths of ink, his fellow-lodgers very naturally suppose him to be an author; and rumors are current in the Dials, that he writes poems for Mr. Warren [*SB* 95].

There are a number of autobiographical elements in this portrayal of the shabby-genteel man; Dickens was himself an aspiring author at the time he wrote this sketch, lived on short rations during his family's stay at Marshalsea, and, like the shabby-genteel man, had a working knowledge of life at Warren's blacking factory, having worked there at the age of twelve.

The theme of isolation, which leads to a feeling of being different, continues in the sketch entitled "The Pawnbroker's Shop," which begins, "Of all the numerous receptacles for misery and distress with which the streets of London unhappily abound, there are, perhaps, none which present such striking scenes of vice and poverty as the pawnbroker's shops" (220). Dickens goes on to describe the nature of that shop, which provides private areas so that people pawning their possessions may be hidden from view, allowing them to escape observation or to preserve some last shred of dignity as they transact their business. In some cases, the sense of shame at having to pawn personal objects cannot be erased and has hardened into a sense of desperation, as Dickens observes in the following passage, which describes a girl and her mother who are attempting to pawn some once precious jewelry:

They are a small gold chain and a "Forget me not" ring, the girl's property, for they are both too small for the mother; given her in better times, prized perhaps once for the giver's sake, but parted with now without a struggle, for want has hardened the mother, and her example has hardened the girl, and the prospect of receiving money coupled with a recollection of the misery they have both endured from the want of it—the coldness of old friends—the stern refusal of some, and the still more galling compassion of others—appears to have obliterated the consciousness of self-humiliation, which the bare idea of their present situation would once have aroused [*SB* 228].

It is easy to think that this is a set-piece against the evils of poverty and about the necessity of pawning goods to make ends meet. It is only after recalling that Dickens himself experienced these same feelings as a child when he was recruited to sell his family's possessions at pawnshops to stave off creditors that this piece takes on a more personal note. For Dickens, the events which caused him to pawn his family's possessions also contributed to his sense of being separate and alone.

He continues the sketch in a more reflective manner, and one which is surely personal, when he writes,

There are strange chords in the human heart, which will lie dormant through years of depravity and wickedness, but which will vibrate at last to some slight circumstance apparently trivial in itself, but connected by some undefined and indistinct association, with past days that can never be recalled, and with bitter recollections from which the most degraded creature in existence cannot escape [*SB* 228].

It seems that for Dickens the experience of the pawnshop, and the degradation he experienced in being forced to pawn his family's possessions, was recalled in this sketch. Dickens later intimated to Forster in his unpublished autobiographical fragment that he was enlisted to pawn his family's possessions, including his father's books, which the young Dickens retreated to for solace. This passage is also reminiscent of the scene in *David Copperfield*, where David is asked by the Micawbers to pawn their family possessions.

Dickens continues the theme of isolation with the sketch "Shabby-genteel People." In the sketch, the narrator uses the pronoun "we" several times during the course of the sketch, causing a sense of isolation to pervade his description of another shabby-genteel man:

We were once haunted by a shabby-genteel man.... He first attracted our notice by sitting opposite to us in the reading-room at the British Museum, and what made the man more remarkable was, that he had always got before him a couple of shabby-genteel books—two old dogseared folios, in mouldy worm-eaten covers, which had once been smart. He was in his chair every morning just as the clock struck ten; he was always the last to leave the room in the afternoon; and when he did, he quitted it with an air of a man who knew not where else to go for warmth and quiet. There he used to sit all day, as close to the table as possible in order to conceal the lack of buttons on his coat, with his old hat carefully deposited at his feet, where he evidently flattered himself it escaped observation [*SB* 305].

The use of the distancing "we" imparts a notion that Dickens, or the narrator, is attempting to be non-partial or reporterly. Yet, it is difficult to dismiss the feeling that Dickens knows a little too much about how it feels to wear worn-out clothes, have second hand books that have seen better days, or to look for a place to find some warmth on cold afternoons. Perhaps the distancing effect that Dickens is looking for is an attempt to provide a way of removing the memories of his own days as one of the shabby-genteel people, and of the isolation and aloneness that he experienced in London. It is worth noting that at this period in his life Dickens frequented the reading room at the British Museum, just as the shabby genteel gentleman did, having obtained his reader's card at the age of eighteen.[7]

Part of the sense of isolation that Dickens writes about is the result of the destabilizing effect that the constant bustle of city life in London has on people. In the sketch "Meditations in Monmouth Street," Dickens writes about a second-hand shop located in the street; here, even the clothes are second hand and the vestiges of the prior owner's life seem to lend an illusory quality, a quality of incompleteness or loss to the very clothes themselves:

> This was the boy's dress. It had belonged to a town boy, we could see; there was a shortness about the legs and arms of the suit; and a bagging at the knees, peculiar to the rising youth of London streets. A small day-school he had been at, evidently. If it had been a regular boys' school they wouldn't have let him play on the floor so much, and rub his knees so white [*SB* 99].

Dickens continues the sketch with an imagined account of the boy's life, complete with a description of the boy's family and the gradual descent into poverty which necessitated the sale of the clothes:

> We saw the bare and miserable room, destitute of furniture, crowded with his wife and children, pale, hungry, and emaciated; the man cursing their lamentations, staggering to the tap-room, from whence he had just returned, followed by his wife and a sickly infant, clamouring for bread; and heard the street-wrangle and noisy recrimination that his striking her occasioned. And then imagination led us to some metropolitan workhouse, situated in the midst of crowded streets and alleys, filled with noxious vapours, and ringing with boisterous cries, where an old and feeble woman, imploring pardon for her son, lay dying in a close dark room, with no child to clasp her hand, and no pure air from heaven to fan her brow. A stranger closed the eyes that settled into a cold unmeaning glare, and strange ears received the words that murmured from the white and half-closed lips [*SB* 101].

Here is a powerful imagination at work, an imagination that would shortly produce a series of novels that would reflect a number of themes in this paragraph. These themes include the isolation of the family; the child raised by an uncaring, neglectful father; the descent into poverty; the crowded, noisy, pestilential streets of London; the workhouse; the lonely death that came to the old woman; the sense of being detached from other people dwelling in London, all painted as a result of seeing a suit of clothes in a second hand shop.

The sense of social instability can also be seen in the sketch "Gin-Shops." Here, Dickens paints a portrait of the establishments dedicated to selling cheap liquor, and the patrons of these shops:

> The filthy and miserable appearance of this part of London can hardly be imagined by those (and there are many such) who have not witnessed it. Wretched houses with broken windows patched with rags and paper: every room let out to a different family and in many instances to two or even three; fruit and "sweet stuff" manufacturers in the cellars, barbers and red-herring vendors in the front parlours, and cobblers in the back; a bird-fancier in the first floor, three families in the second, starvation in the attics, Irishmen in the passage; a "musician" in the front kitchen, and a charwoman and five hungry children in the back one—filth every where—a gutter before the houses and a drain behind them—clothes drying and slops emptying from the windows: girls of fourteen or fifteen with matted hair walking about barefooted, and in white great-coats, almost their only covering; boys of all ages, in coats of all sizes and no coats at all; men and women, in every variety of scanty and dirty apparel, lounging, scolding, drinking, smoking, squabbling, fighting, and swearing [SB 217].

This is London gone astray, a city where nothing is stable, where people are isolated while living crammed together in filthy conditions. J. Hillis Miller and David Borowitz note that, "One narrative pattern recurring in the *Sketches* is an apparently inescapable progression of the city dwellers step by step toward starvation, sickness, degradation, crime, depravity, suicide, or execution" (17–18). Such a descent is pictured in Dickens's sketch of the Gin Shop.

The social stratification so common in Victorian society led to a sharp dichotomy between those who are members of the privileged upper classes and those who have been consigned to the neglected lower classes. In the sketch "London Recreations," Dickens explores the nature of class distinctions which contributed to the gulf between the classes in Victorian society:

> The wish of persons in the humbler classes of life, to ape the manners and customs of those whom fortune has placed above them, is often the subject of remark, and not unfrequently of complaint. The inclination may, and no doubt does, exist to a great extent, among the small gentility—the would-be aristocrats—of the middle classes. Tradesmen and clerks, with fashionable novel-reading families, and circulating-library-subscribing daughters, get up small assemblies in humble imitation of Almack's, and promenade the dingy "large room" of some second-rate hotel with as much complacency as the enviable few who are privileged to exhibit their magnificence in that exclusive haunt of fashion and foolery. Aspiring young ladies, who read flaming

accounts of some "fancy fair in high life," suddenly grow desperately charitable; visions of admiration and matrimony float before their eyes; some wonderfully meritorious institution, which, by the strangest accident in the world, has never been heard of before, is discovered to be in a languishing condition... [*SB* 116–117].

Although the tone of the piece is one of mock condescension, there is an element of truth in the observation that there are class distinctions and that the lower classes, while jealous of those above them, tend to mimic the tastes and affectations of the higher classes. Unfortunately, in the highly stratified society of Dickens's time, the ability to climb the social ladder is limited. Dickens himself, although admired and respected, never quite felt that he had arrived in polite society. In an article appearing in *History Workshop* entitled "Cruikshank and Early Victorian Caricature," Louis James offers this assessment of Dickens's sense of estrangement in Victorian society: "In the text [of the *Sketches*], Dickens offers us London as experienced by a sensitive but lonely and estranged onlooker" (114).

The "London Recreations" sketch continues, with a discussion of gardens, and the use of gardens by the middle and upper classes to either impress or intimidate those of the lower classes. Dickens imagines a scene where the father of a young lady, who is being courted by a suitor, gives a tour of his garden to the young couple. The young man reflects on the scene: "This is to impress you—who are a young friend of the family— with a due sense of the excellence of the garden, and the wealth of its owner; and when he has exhausted the subject, he goes to sleep" (*SB* 118). One cannot help but wonder if Dickens was thinking of the father of Maria Beadnell, his first love, when he wrote this passage; the Beadnells were a middle-class family whose station was several rungs up the social ladder than the Dickens family at the time. Maria's father objected to her seeing Dickens because of the distance in their social standing, an objection which seems to have contributed to ending Maria's relationship with Dickens.[8]

The sense of the divide between those of the upper classes of society and those of the lower classes is also noted in the sketch "Shabby-genteel People." Dickens begins the sketch by describing the lower classes of people who inhabit the city:

There are certain descriptions of people who, oddly enough, appear to appertain exclusively to this metropolis. You meet them every day in the streets of London, but no one ever encounters them elsewhere; they seem to be indigenous to the soil, and to belong exclusively to London as its own smoke, or the dingy bricks and mortar. We could illustrate the remark by a variety of examples, but in our present sketch we will only advert to one class as a specimen—that class which is so aptly and expressively designated as "shabby-genteel."

> Now shabby people, God knows, may be found any where, and genteel people are not articles of greater scarcity out of London than in it, but this compound of the two—this shabby-gentility—is as purely local as the statue at Charing-cross, or the pump at Aldgate [SB 303–304].

The passage makes clear that Dickens recognizes the divide between the various classes of society and has sought to combine the classes in the person of the shabby-genteel man, who exhibits characteristics of both the upper and lower classes. Ultimately, the gap between the two classes is too great to bridge; the shabby portion of the characterization rings true but the attempt of the man to borrow an aura of gentility falls short. What Dickens hints at in this passage is that the isolation of individuals in London will continue; the sense of being different is too great to be overcome. Dickens ends the sketch with the following observation:

> Whether our readers have noticed these men in their walks as often as we have, we know not; this we know—that the miserably poor man (no matter whether he owes his distresses to his own conduct, or that of others) who feels his poverty and vainly strives to conceal it, is one of the most pitiable objects in human nature. Such objects, with few exceptions, are shabby-genteel people [SB 307].

The *Sketches* were an important step in the writing career of Charles Dickens, making him an instant celebrity and offering him new publishing opportunities. He would return to a number of themes which he introduced in the *Sketches:* themes like naming, identity and self; dreams and dreaming; society and social pretension; ineffective institutions; and prisons.

J. Hillis Miller and David Borowitz sum up the *Sketches* and their relationship to Dickens's later work:

> In spite of some youthful crudities and some self-conscious awkwardness of style the *Sketches by Boz* are a characteristic expression of Dickens's genius. Moreover, they contain all of Dickens's later work in embryo—the comedy, the sentimentality, the respect for the vitality of his characters, however foolish or limited they are, the habit of hyperbole, the admirable gift for striking linguistic transformations, the notion of an irresistible social determinism in which the urban environment causes the sad fate of the unlucky people living within it. The *Sketches* provide an excellent opportunity to watch the development of a great writer and to see his characteristic ways with words at the level of emergence, where they may be more easily identified. The full implications of the *Sketches* are only visible in the light of their relations to the later work of Dickens [8–9].

Dickens would expand on these themes, developed in his early career and beginning with the publication of *Dombey and Son*, would focus on a single aspect of Victorian life that he wished to highlight as a means of informing his readers on a particular area that he believed was ripe for change.

CHAPTER TWO

Naming, Identity and Self

Chapter 3 of *A Tale of Two Cities* begins with the following paragraph:

A wonderful fact to reflect upon, that every human creature is constituted to be that profound secret and mystery to every other. A solemn consideration, when I enter a great city by night, that every one of those darkly clustered houses encloses its own secret; that every room in every one of them encloses its own secret; that every beating heart in the hundreds of thousands of breasts there, is, in some of its imaginings, a secret to the heart nearest it! Something of the awfulness, even of Death itself, is referable to this.... My friend is dead, my neighbor is dead, my love, the darling of my soul, is dead; it is the inexorable consolation and perpetuation of the secret that was always in that individuality, and which I shall carry in mine to my life's end. In any of the burial places of this city through which I pass, is there a sleeper more inscrutable than its busy inhabitants are, in their innermost personality, to me, or than I am to them? [*TTC* 10]

It is unclear if the paragraph is a direct address by the author to his readers, or if it is a glimpse into the mind of one of its characters, perhaps Dr. Manette or Mr. Jarvis Lorry. Perhaps it is best that the attribution of the paragraph is left unsaid.

Before proceeding to a discussion of the themes of naming, identity and self it might be helpful to define these terms. John Locke, in "An Essay Concerning Human Understanding," provides a definition of identity that is dependent on consciousness, as well as a sense of time, both of which provide a basis for understanding the self:

For, since consciousness always accompanies thinking, and it is that which makes every one to be what he calls self, and thereby distinguishes himself from all other thinking things, in this alone consists personal identity, i.e. the sameness of a rational being: and as far as this consciousness can be extended backwards to any past action or thought, so far reaches the identity of that person; it is the same self now it was then; and it is by the same self with this present one that now reflects on it, that that action was done [222].

The notion of consciousness itself, which is central to an understanding of identity, has been debated over the years, and the advent of a theory of modern psychology has attempted to shed light on what constitutes consciousness. Sigmund Freud defines consciousness as "the *superficies* of the mental apparatus; that is, we have allocated it as a function to the system which is situated nearest to the external world" (700). In other words, consciousness is the system which processes sensory input. Although this definition attempts to state what consciousness is or does, there is no sense of how it integrates into the workings of the mind, into a human being as a distinct being. Freud proposes that the integrative agent is the ego: "We have formulated the idea that in every individual there is a coherent organization of mental processes, which we call his *ego*. This ego includes consciousness, and it controls the approaches to motility, i.e., to the discharge of excitations into the external world" (699). Another function of the ego is to block painful or unwanted memories from entering into consciousness. Freud terms this function repression: "The state in which the ideas existed before being made conscious is called by us *repression*" (698). Repression is triggered when memories become too painful to recollect. These memories are not forgotten, however, they are stored in the unconscious.

The discussion of the ego and consciousness seems necessary to understand how Dickens viewed identity, as well as to understand some of the questions which are raised by Dickens's treatment of identity in his writings. Among the questions to be raised are the following: Do character names in Dickens adequately describe the notion of identity in a character? Is identity stable in a constantly changing society, and if so, how does Dickens portray this concept? A third question arises about Dickens's use of repressed ideas in his personal life and the lives of his characters.

Turning to the question of identity in his characters, Dickens has been accused of drawing one-dimensional characters by a number of critics, and his habit of having character names act as a sort of representation or emblem of a character trait is often cited as an example of this lack of an inner life in his characters. Peter Ackroyd, in his book, *The Life and Times of Charles Dickens*, discusses the oft-repeated criticism that Dickens merely created caricatures, and not three-dimensional people:

> It is sometimes suggested that he merely created caricatures. But they are more like figures from eighteenth-century cartoons, where a single trait or characteristic is so extended that it takes on a life of its own; it represents a theatrical view of reality, perhaps, but one immeasurably deepened by Dickens's own art. The people *are* their behaviour, *are* their words, *are* their gestures; they inhabit some expansive world where the truth lies in appearances.

There is, however, another element of his strident characterization that merits reflection. In many instances he outlines one particular trait: Pecksniff is remarkable for his hypocrisy, for example, and Scrooge for his miserliness, Mr. Micawber is memorable for his orotund phraseology, to the extent that he *becomes* his language ... [56–57].

The list of characters whose names seem to express their personality or an aspect of their personality is quite extensive and a few examples will serve to illustrate this point. Alfred Jingle in *The Pickwick Papers* speaks in a rapid-fire staccato that seems to confirm the jingle-jangle nature of his personality: "Ah! You should keep dogs—fine animals—sagacious creatures—dog of my own once—pointer—surprising instinct—out shooting one day—entering enclosure—whistled—dog stopped—whistled again—Ponto—no go..." (*PP* 34). Yet, despite his lack of verb usage, Jingle manages to convey his meaning in an amusing manner. The character of Sally Brass in *The Old Curiosity Shop* is distinguished more by her outward appearance and mannerisms than through her dialogue. Miss Brass is described as being angular, gaunt and bony. She closely resembles her brother, Sampson Brass, an attorney on retainer to Daniel Quilp, the evil dwarf who persecutes everyone he meets. Dickens ironically refers to Miss Brass as being lovely when in reality her figure was like that of a man: "In face she bore so striking a resemblance to her brother Sampson ... that had it consorted with Miss Brass's maiden modesty and gentle womanhood to have assumed her brother's clothes ... it would have been difficult for the oldest friend of the family to determine which was Sampson and which Sally..." (*OCS* 245).[1]

Although the list of characters whose names seem to express their personality is quite extensive, it is but a small sample of the hundreds of characters created by Dickens. It is also worth noting that although the names seem to be suggestive or emblematic of the nature of the characters this is true of the minor characters such as Pluck and Pyke in *Nicholas Nickleby*, or Tony Jobling in *Bleak House*. The characters in the early novels, such as Serjeant Buzfuz and Mr. Fogg in *Pickwick Papers* and the Cheerybles in *Nicholas Nickleby* also have names that seem to express their natures. The characters in the later novels tend to be more developed, although they are sometimes portrayed by their outward characteristics. As an example, Captain Cuttle's name conjures up images of a sea creature (cuttlefish) in *Dombey and Son*. Miss Flite in *Bleak House* suggests her bird-like nature and connects her character with the birds she keeps in her apartment.

What some critics tend to forget is that a number of the characters developed by Dickens have attained an iconic status, much like a number of characters in Shakespeare's plays, and these characters become, in some sense, representatives of a certain type of person. Consider for example the character of Mr. Micawber, in *David Copperfield*, who has become representative of a person possessed of an overflowing verbosity and expectations of personal fortune which are in stark contrast to his actual impecunious situation. Similarly, the character of Uriah Heep in the same novel has become a touchstone for an unctuous, servile, and villainous person whose words are incongruous with his vile temperament and fraudulent actions. Little Nell, in *The Old Curiosity Shop*, is another character that has become synonymous with an angelic goodness untouched by the squalid conditions which surround her; and Quilp, her tormentor, has become associated with lewd, vicious, and monstrous personages.

One of the ways in which Dickens portrays character identity is through the use of dialogue to add complexity to his characters, even when the dialogue is sometimes repetitive. Take the case of Wilkins Micawber in *David Copperfield*, as an example: one of his favorite sayings is that "Something will turn up." Although this phrase is repeated throughout *David Copperfield*, there are other flourishes which accompany the saying some of which are quite profound and which define Wilkins Micawber as a three-dimensional character. Micawber's advice to David about his personal finances, which is eminently practical, is taken directly from John Dickens's advice to his son: "Annual income twenty pounds, annual expenditure nineteen nineteen six, result happiness. Annual income twenty pounds, annual expenditure twenty pounds ought and six, result misery"; but Dickens is not finished with Micawber's advice and adds a small flourish at the end: "The blossom is blighted, the leaf is withered, the God of day goes down upon the dreary scene, and—and in short you are for ever floored. As I am!" (*DC* 175).[2]

It is this sense of individual narrative, a sense of cohesiveness, which helps to define the character of Wilkins Micawber. Another character in the same novel, Uriah Heep, makes us of repetitive phrases to declare his humility. Heep uses these phrases to disguise his avarice; yet behind the catch phrases expressing his humbleness there is a sense on the part of the reader that Uriah Heep is not what he appears to be. It becomes apparent in the course of the novel that the expressions of humility uttered by Uriah Heep are a sort of mask to conceal the real person behind it. Similarly, the character of Quilp in *The Old Curiosity Shop* professes to be harmless and to express his love for Nell in tender terms. Yet in Quilp's violent interactions with his wife, Betsy, it is apparent that he harbors the same misogynistic tendencies towards Nell as he does towards his wife.

The dialogue which Quilp utters is in direct contrast to his real feelings; like Uriah Heep, Quilp uses words to disguise his real intentions.

Dickens's use of dialogue as one of the ways to portray an inner narrative, in an attempt to define character, is insightful and psychologically accurate. In *The Man Who Mistook His Wife for a Hat*, Oliver Sacks comments on the use of a cohesive, inner narrative, to construct a sense of self:

> ... We have, each of us, a life-story, an inner narrative—whose continuity, whose sense, *is* our lives. It might be said that each of us constructs and lives, a "narrative," and that this narrative *is* us, our identities.
>
> If we wish to know about a man, we ask "what is his story—his real, inmost story?"— for each of us *is* a biography, a story. Each of us *is* a singular narrative, which is constructed, continually, unconsciously, by, through, and in us—through our perceptions, our feelings, our thoughts, our actions; and, not least, our discourse, our spoken narrations. Biologically, physiologically, we are not so different from each other; historically, as narratives—we are each of us unique.
>
> To be ourselves we must *have* ourselves—possess, if need be re-possess, our life-stories. We must "recollect" ourselves, recollect the inner drama, the narrative, of ourselves. A man *needs* such a narrative, a continuous inner narrative, to maintain his identity, his self [110].

It seems from the foregoing that Dickens uses dialogue to establish an inner narrative that helps to forge an identity for his characters in a way that echoes the comments made by Oliver Sacks.

The next point to consider in Dickens's writing is whether personal identity can be maintained in times of rapid societal change. William James speculates that consciousness requires a sense of stability and that thought requires a perception of the continuous flow of time:

> The proposition that within each personal consciousness thought feels continuous, means two things:
>
> 1. That even when there is a time-gap the consciousness after it feels as if it belonged together with the consciousness before it, as another part of the same self;
>
> 2. That the changes from one moment to another in the quality of the consciousness are never absolutely abrupt [154].

Where one of the two elements James discusses is missing—either the element of consciousness or the element of the continuity of time through the function of memory—the stability required for a notion of self is also missing. Oliver Sacks provides insight into one of his patients, Greg F., in *An Anthropologist on Mars*. Greg seemed to lack a mental picture of time, and his consciousness and inner life suffered as a result:

> I had already had some sense of this [apparent lack of self in Greg F.] when testing his memory, finding his confinement, in effect, to a single moment—"the present"— uninformed by any sense of a past (or a future). Given this radical lack of connection

and continuity in his inner life, I got the feeling, indeed, that he might not *have* an inner life to speak of, that he lacked the constant dialogue of past and present, of experience and meaning, which constitutes consciousness and inner life for the rest of us [49–50].

This passage by Sacks demonstrates that the notions of time and consciousness can be altered by disease, trauma or a number of other psychological events. It does not provide an answer to the question of whether the perception of time can be altered by external events which lead to a feeling of dissociation in individuals. Sigmund Freud addresses the notion of the breakdown of cultural norms in "Thoughts for the Times on War and Death." During times of war, he speculates that people lose faith in a government which attempts to impose a moral order on its citizens, but demonstrates a lack of moral rectitude in its relations with opposing governments. Freud notes that the trauma of war results in disruption to people's lives as well as their sense of identity. In other writings, Freud attempts to understand the disruption to a person's identity caused by modern society. In *Civilization and its Discontents,* Freud posits that "Life as we find it is too hard for us; it entails too much pain, too many disappointments, impossible tasks" (771).

Dickens wrestles with the same notion of the breakdown of society in *Barnaby Rudge* and *A Tale of Two Cities* where he examines individual and group behavior during the Gordon Riots and the French Revolution. In both of these novels, the breakdown of civilization results in an alteration in the notion of self. Barnaby Rudge, the main character for whom the novel is named, is portrayed as mentally handicapped; his character acts as a mirror to society which has itself become unstable, as social norms break down amid the chaos that ensues as the riot proceeds. Dr. Manette, one of the main characters in a *Tale of Two Cities,* undergoes a regression during his years of captivity in prison, going from a highly respected surgeon to a shoe cobbler as a result of the chaos introduced by the French Revolution. The scenes of violence and hysteria that Dickens narrates in the chapters concerning the destruction of Paris emphasize his concern that a similar breakdown in society might occur in Britain.

As noted, Dickens was keenly aware of the issues which arose as a result of the rapid changes in Victorian society and that people sometimes found it difficult to cope with these changes, much as Freud postulated. For Dickens, the nuclear family was the foundation of society; to the extent that the family had become fractured is an indication that society itself was becoming unstable. In his political beliefs, Dickens was conservative and viewed the function of government as being patriarchal. He believed that government should act to protect its people from harm and should endeavor to promote the welfare of its citizens. Viewed in this manner, the orphan stands as a symbol for the people who have been abandoned by an uncaring, inefficient, parental figure represented by the government.[3] Dickens's attitude toward the government as being an uncaring parent may also be the result of his own upbringing as a child, and having been abandoned at the age of twelve in the teeming city of London.[4]

In his non-fictional writings, particularly in *Household Words*, Dickens attempts to portray family life as idyllic. The introduction to the first number reads as follows:

> We aspire to live in the Household affections, and to be numbered among the Household thoughts, of our readers. We hope to be the comrade and friend of many thousands of people, of both sexes, and of all ages and conditions, on whose faces we may never look. We seek to bring into innumerable homes, from the stirring world around us, the knowledge of many social wonders, good and evil, that are not calculated to render any of us less ardently persevering in ourselves, less tolerant of one another, less faithful in the progress of mankind, less thankful for the privilege of living in this summer-dawn of time [*HW* 1].

Dickens's personal life, particularly his early childhood, was far from idyllic. It is striking that Dickens attempted to portray an idealized family life in his non-fictional work as well as in a number of his novels yet his early personal life and the portrayal of dysfunctional families in his books, belie this attempt, as did his unsuccessful marriage. Edgar Johnson comments on the discrepancy between Dickens's attempts to portray idealized families in his fiction, and the absence of such happiness in his fictional works and personal life:

> This dearth of happy homes and good parents is startling in a writer whose warm celebration of family life and fireside has created a glow in which readers overlook how relatively seldom he portrays what he praises. The dark pit of the blacking warehouse had made the bright and vanished safety of loving parents and protective hearth infinitely precious to Dickens by revealing it as dreadfully fragile. As he was to write to his friend Thompson in 1844, the greater part of the parents who came under his observation seemed to him selfish in their behavior to their children. Even after he was freed from the bondage of the warehouse and sent back to school again, the security of the happy time in Chatham was gone forever. The home which he had known and lost became for his heart a radiant center in his vision of the good life. And its loss, of which he reveals the very essence in the weeping child washing the bottles in his tears, molded his entire response to all the unhappy and misused of the world [II: 685].

Like Edgar Johnson, Arthur Adrian, in *Dickens and the Parent-Child Relationship*, discusses Dickens's recurrent theme of orphaned children in his novels. Adrian comments:

The largest cluster of orphans or demi-orphans appears in *David Copperfield* (1849–1850). Without either parent are David, Ham, Little Emily, the Micawber's "Orfling," Traddles, Clara Copperfield, Martha Endell, Rosa Dartle and Dora Spenlow. Anne Strong, Steerforth and Uriah Heep have lost their fathers; Agnes Wickfield has been motherless since early childhood.... That orphans and half-orphans figure in every novel from first to last (in *Pickwick Papers* Sam Weller is motherless) clearly indicates Dickens's obsession with the theme of the homeless child cast adrift in an alien world [80].

In writing about dysfunctional families, Dickens emphasizes the connection between improper upbringing and personal development. He asks how an ineffective family structure can provide an environment which leads to a healthy notion of self. Equally important to Dickens, he wonders how an unstable family situation can lead to a stable society. For Dickens, the stability of society depends upon the stability of the family.[5]

Dickens employs a technique known as doubling to illustrate the loss of identity in a number of characters in his novels.[6] Perhaps the most obvious example of the loss of identity that occurs in Dickens's characters can be seen when a split in consciousness occurs within a character. In *Martin Chuzzlewitt*, the notion of a split personality can be seen in Montague Tigg and Tigg Montague, who are one and the same person, but are seen as mirror images of each other. Although the underlying personality of the character is little changed, the multiplication of personalities points to a lack of definition of personhood; it is noteworthy that the other characters in the novel do not notice that Tigg Montague and Montague Tigg are one and the same person until they have been let in on the secret.

Another example of a split personality is that of Sairey Gamp and her alter ego, Mrs. Harris, who are also present in the novel *Martin Chuzzlewitt*. The fictional character Mrs. Harris constantly praises Sairey and is allowed to make utterances which would seem self-serving if uttered by Mrs. Gamp. Eventually, the other characters in the novel discover that Mrs. Harris is a fictional character (how ironic, and ultimately Dickensian, that there should be a fictional character within a work of fiction), and she eventually exits stage left. The personality splits in *Martin Chuzzlewitt* are portrayed comically; but later splits are less comical and more troubling.

Although Mr. Dick is portrayed as being eccentric in *David Copperfield*, flying his kites when he is unable to remove references to Charles I in his memoirs, there is a note of sadness in the portrayal of Mr. Dick. He is a lost soul who struggles with his purpose in life and is mistakenly portrayed as a species of genius by Betsey Trotwood, who is herself something of a split being. The venerable Miss Trotwood is portrayed as being a determined, ferocious woman early in the novel when she appears to Clara

Copperfield and insists that Clara's baby will be a girl, and therefore should be named after her. She accepts David Copperfield into her home and rechristens him "Trotwood," recalling her original intention to name his "sister." Later, she stands up to Mr. Murdstone and his sister and dismisses them, having bested these two self-righteous people, who have sadistically attempted to browbeat others into submission to their will. Despite her outward toughness Dickens manages to convey an inner sensitivity to the character of Betsey Trotwood who not only provides a home for the tortured Mr. Dick but provides a stable, comforting home for David Copperfield.

By the time of *Little Dorrit* and *A Tale of Two Cities*, the personality split is more disturbing. Mr. Dorrit undergoes a complete mental breakdown as a result of his attempt to reconcile his prior life in the Marshalsea with his new-found celebrity in the outside world. Similarly, Dr. Manette in *A Tale of Two Cities* alternates between his life as a respected doctor and that of a shoe cobbler after being buried alive for eighteen years in prison. The reader is left with the impression that the two halves of Dr. Manette's personality, as well as the two halves of Mr. Dorrit, can never be joined together into a complete human being.

The doubling of characters is not limited to a single novel. Characters which appear to be similar are found in different novels. As an example, the verbosity of Micawber in *David Copperfield* is repeated in the character of Mr. Dorrit in the novel *Little Dorrit*, and both are a reflection of the non-fictional personality of John Dickens, father to Charles Dickens.[7] Similarly, the female characters of Agnes Wickfield (*David Copperfield*), Little Dorrit, Little Nell (*The Old Curiosity Shop*), and Esther Summerson (*Bleak House*) are eerily alike in their goodness, domesticity, and self-effacement and have been seen by a number of critics as a reflection of Dickens's sister-in-law, Mary Hogarth.[8] Similarly, the waifs Oliver Twist and David Copperfield are alike, so much so, that they both overcome an orphaned existence to achieve success later in life. The characters of Quilp (*The Old Curiosity Shop*) and Bill Sikes (*Oliver Twist*) are equally at home with their villainy and ability to terrorize the women in their lives, and Chadband (*Bleak House*), Pecksniff (*Martin Chuzzlewitt*), and Uriah Heep (*David Copperfield*) are equally adept at projecting a false sense of humility which they all lack. While some of the doublings which occur are fairly straight-forward, and easy for the reader to follow, they all lead to a proliferation of characters within the novels. As a result, the personal identity of a number of characters becomes confusing, and true self-knowledge on the part of the characters is problematic.

The doubling of characters, along with the high incidence of dysfunctional families in Dickens's works is due, in part, to changes in society at large. Peter Ackroyd notes the presence of the themes of orphans and single parent families, as well as Dickens's concerns with the breakdown of society:

> There was something of an obsession with thwarted or threatened innocence in nineteenth-century England, primarily because it represented an overwhelming and unsettling reality; the number of child prostitutes in the streets, and of child labourers in the mines and factories, was a terrible indictment of Victorian "civilization," which seemed to have built upon the shuddering backs of oppressed innocents [64].

There was also an autobiographical element to the appearance of the theme of personal identity in Dickens's work. Philip Hobsbaum alludes to some of the recurring themes in Dickens's work in *A Reader's Guide to Charles Dickens*: "Certain topics recur with the force of obsession: the substitute or inadequate father, the debtors' prison, the deprived child, the buried past, the Calvinist heritage: these are familiar properties throughout the books" (15). Forster offers an additional insight into Dickens's personal life, and the manner in which it found expression in his fictional works:

> To what in the outset of his difficulties and trials gave the decisive bent to his genius, I have already made special reference; and we are to observe, of what followed, that with the very poor and unprosperous, out of whose sufferings and strugglings, and the virtues as well as vices born of them, his not least splendid successes were wrought, his childish experiences had made him actually one. They were not his clients whose cause he pleaded with such pathos and humour, and on whose side he got the laughter and tears of all the world, but in some sort his very self [I: 41].

Although Dickens expressed concerns about the problems facing Victorian society and the impact that changes in society had on personal identity, he does not give in to despair in his novels. Not all of Dickens's characters were helpless or consigned to a fate which they cannot change. In some cases, the characters engage in a form of Bildungsroman, a search for identity which leads to some degree of happiness.[9] Oliver Twist is adopted by his patron, Mr. Brownlow, and is able to leave the company of Fagin and his gang of pickpockets. Nicholas Nickleby is befriended by the Cheeryble brothers and retires with his wife and sister to Devonshire. David Copperfield overcomes the hostility of the Murdstones, his inauspicious marriage to Dora and later marriage to the more compatible Agnes, and becomes a successful writer. Esther Summerson learns about her true identity as the illegitimate daughter of Lady Dedlock and the legal scribe Mr. Hawdon and lives quietly with her husband Allan Woodcourt in a Bleak House that is restored to light and sunshine, far away from the city of London. Little Dorrit and Arthur Clenham manage to overcome the effects of bad parenting and imprisonment to lead "a modest life of usefulness and happiness," while separated from the "Marshalsea and all its blighted fruits" (*LD* 826).

In some respects, the endings of these novels resemble a fairy-tale, with all problems pushed aside and a happy ending achieved for the protagonists. This was due, in part, to Dickens's love of adventure stories he read as a youth: *The Arabian Nights, Roderick Random, Tom Jones,* and *Don Quixote*. It was an effort by Dickens to compensate for the forces he saw at work in Victorian England, and the individual greed, selfishness and hostility that he witnessed firsthand. Despite the problems that he portrayed in his novels, problems he wished to have corrected, Dickens did not initially despair when the correction did not arrive in a timely manner as Edgar Johnson attests:

> They [the people] were Dickens's only real hope for the world. He had no panacea to solve all problems. In his own day he worked piecemeal within limited areas for every particular improvement that seemed to him attainable. Though he understood how external circumstances could twist and ruin men's lives, and hoped to make the opportunities for human fulfillment available on the widest scale, he was not an economic determinist and did not believe that people were only the products of environment. Though he saw that Government agencies were corrupted by powerful influences, he did not believe that it was an intrinsic defect in the potentiality of government. He never ceased to demand that government continually remake itself into the instrument of human welfare. Unlike those who worry about "creeping socialism," he was no opponent of centralization. But he was not an abstract theorist. He never formulated any blueprints of systematic social reform or any constitution for the ideal political state. Instead of trying to elaborate the entire machinery for the improvement of the world, he sought to portray its human goals [II: 1136].

If novels such as *Oliver Twist* or *David Copperfield* portray a romanticized view of the world in which the protagonist finds his calling and all problems are resolved by the end of the novel, Dickens labored under no false pretenses that such happy endings were bound to occur in life. He was also a realist who understood that hard work and effort were required to become successful or to advance in life. In a speech he gave at the Athenaeum in Manchester on October 5th, 1842, which marked the opening of an educational facility for working men, Dickens touched on the effort required to procure an education and the effects of that education on the self-esteem and character of such men:

> And this I know, that the first unpurchasable blessing earned by every man who makes an effort to improve himself in such a place as the Athenaeum, is self-respect— an inward dignity of character, which, once acquired and righteously maintained,

nothing—no, not the hardest drudgery, nor the direst poverty—can vanquish. Though he should find it hard for a season even to keep the wolf—hunger—from his door, let him but once have chased the dragon—ignorance—from his hearth, and self-respect and hope are left him.

... The man who lives from day to day by the daily exercise in his sphere of hands or head, and seeks to improve himself in such a place as the Athenaeum, acquires for himself that property of soul which has in all times upheld struggling men of every degree, but self-made men especially and always [*SP* 22].

These two views, the traditional happy ending of the novel and the clear-eyed view of the man of the world who spoke at the Athenaeum, reflect different sides of Dickens's own personality. On the one hand, he was an idealist who labored tirelessly for those less fortunate members of Victorian society in the hope of effecting lasting changes which would improve that society. On the other hand, he was a realist who was influenced by the events of his youth and adolescence and who realized as he grew older, that the reforms he wished to institute were less and less likely to become reality. These two seemingly contradictory views, that of the idealist and that of the realist, also represent the efforts of a man who attempted to fashion an identity for himself. During his life, Dickens worked as a factory operative, a Parliamentary reporter, a writer of sketches, an amateur actor, novelist, reformer, amateur playwright, and successful performance artist who read his novels throughout the U.K. and the United States.

As he developed his identity, he also repressed certain feelings and the knowledge of his past life from his family and friends. Jane Smiley touches upon Dickens's secretive nature, and his efforts to conceal his past from family and friends: "Charles Dickens was a secretive man. Acquaintances, friends, relatives, and children always commented upon the fact that he could withdraw as readily as he could extend himself, that while he was so eagerly observing others he was also resisting observation himself" (74). The two views that Dickens embraced, that of an idealist and that of a realist, lead to the question of repression in Dickens's novels and life.

The effort to resist observation can also be seen as an act of repression on the part of Dickens. At some level, while Dickens was keenly aware of the effects of his childhood and how those events influenced him throughout his life, he made a conscious effort to downplay those events, and even at times, to forget them. Repression, however, has consequences as Freud notes: "*the essence of repression lies simply in the function of rejecting and keeping something out of consciousness*" (422). Freud also notes that repression is a continual process and not a one-time event. The extent of the effort needed to repress an emotion is severe, and repressed emotions in most people, find release in sleep and dreams. Repression is also released through substitute formations such as anxiety or through various neurotic tendencies. Freud posits that there is a way of avoiding repression which can be found through the formation of an ideal. Freud indicates that ideal formation leads to sublimation by means of art. It is likely that Dickens was able to overcome his feelings of neglect and betrayal which he suffered as a child through his art but that it required a constant effort on his part. Towards the end of his life, the effort required to repress his early childhood experiences was made more difficult by the strains associated with his readings as well as the separation from his wife which caused a public stir. Edgar Johnson alludes to Dickens's struggles to balance the conflicting emotions of his early childhood against the success he experienced later in life:

> Beneath the blare of applause there is the heartbreak of his father's imprisonment, the terror of butcher and baker raising angry voices, of insufficient meals choked down with tears, of rooms pawned bare of household goods. Beneath the later fame there is the weeping of a child taken out of school and delivered to toil, all his early ambition of growing up to be a learned and distinguished man crushed within his breast [I: 4].

If, as proposed, Dickens indeed coped with the repressed feelings of his childhood through sublimation, the repressed emotions surfaced in the portrayal of his fictional characters. Perhaps the best example of the effect which repression can have on a person's identity can be seen in the fictional character of Miss Havisham in *Great Expectations*. As a result of her canceled marriage, she has, in effect, stopped time. Every clock in the house is set to the time of the aborted marriage ceremony; the table is set just as it was on the wedding day, complete with disintegrating marriage cake; she is attired in her now yellowing, moldy, wedding dress. In her pain, she has attempted to halt all progress, all emotional growth. The one emotion she feels toward the outside world is that of revenge. She raises her ward, Estella, to act as her avenger, as a tool to exact revenge for the harm she, Miss Havisham, has endured. Miss Havisham's desire for revenge is based upon the hurt she experienced as a result of her being jilted at the marriage altar; it is a hatred that has its seeds in a lack of reciprocal love. The psychological accuracy of this portrayal is verified by Freud, who writes that such an obsessional neurosis "rests on the premise of a regression by means of which a sadistic trend has been substituted for a tender one" (426).

Ultimately, Dickens's search for identity led to his great success as a

Pip with Miss Havisham, illustration by John McLenan, which appeared in *Great Expectations*. Miss Havisham, whose marriage was canceled, has attempted to preserve her house in the same state it was in at the time of the canceled marriage. As a result, she has repressed her feelings, resulting in a stunted emotional life (British Library, London).

novelist and his struggle to cope with and overcome his childhood experiences. As he portrays the attempts that his characters make to forge their own identities, he is at the same time struggling to form his own identity, and that struggle appears in his writing. One of the commonplace notions that resonate with people is that of the self-made man. In many ways, Dickens is the embodiment of the notion of the self-made man. He overcame early personal hardship, boring hack-work as a legal clerk, undertook a methodical approach to learning shorthand and then emerged as a celebrated reporter, journalist and novelist. Ultimately, he emerged to become the most celebrated novelist in the English language. Yet despite his success, Dickens remained conflicted.

Edgar Johnson sums up the contradiction that lies within the personality of Charles Dickens:

> In this tension between his splendid public success and his deep-rooted dissatisfaction with the world that heaped rewards upon him lies the drama and the pity of his life. Its tragedy grows out of the way in which the powers that enabled him to overcome the obstacles before him contained also the seeds of his unhappiness [I: 5].

As Johnson's quotation makes clear, Dickens's ambivalent attitude towards society and personal growth is rooted in the tension between his early, neglected childhood and his later successful personal life. He struggled with the concept of identity both personally and in the construction of his fictional characters. It is this ambivalence which led to the portrayal of orphans and fatherless children, dysfunctional families, social conventions which no longer seem to reflect traditional values and the plight of the urban poor which allowed him to construct characters that attempted to forge stable personal identities. At the same time these characters exhibited the struggle that was required to achieve personal stability.

Dickens was aware of and was interested in the power of names in forming the identity of his characters and in exploring how naming denotes possession and ownership of that which is named.[10] Dickens's efforts at naming characters leads to the question of whether or not a name can somehow identify the underlying nature of a person. The notion that a person's name is, in some way, representative of that person has been debated since the fifth century B.C., if not before. In the Socratic dialogue, *Cratylus*, Plato entertains the notion that names represent the true character of a person. The dialogue considers two extreme positions in the debate on naming. The first position, held by Hermogenes, is that names are merely conventions adopted at a certain time and place and that the name assigned to something does not represent the nature or essence of the thing named. The opposite position is held by Cratylus, who asserts that the name of something identifies the essence or nature of the thing named. Socrates, ever the skeptic, entertains both positions in turn and ultimately takes an intermediate position, that the "name is an imitation of the thing" (108), and that "names rightly given are the likenesses and images of the things they name" (113).[11]

If the position espoused by Socrates is a starting point for a discussion about whether a name can somehow represent the inner character of a person, then a corollary to this question can be posed about Dickens's use of names. Did Dickens use names to imitate actual personages and attempt to determine if names were assigned properly or improperly to his fictional constructs? By the proper assignment of a name we mean is the name faithful to the portrayal of a character. An improper assignment of a name means that a characteristic is assigned to a character who did not warrant that characteristic. Of course, the unstated implication is that Dickens intended to develop fictional characters which were consistent in their behavior, motives and actions; a requirement which is essential in establishing believable characterizations.

This question of naming is more easily answered in a fictional work than in everyday life, since an author can select names for his/her characters. If the author wishes to select a name for a character which denotes a particular trait or habit, the author is free to do so. The novel *David Copperfield* can be used as an example of the way in which Dickens viewed the inter-relationship of names and personal identity in his characters. The principal character in *David Copperfield* is assigned dozens of names throughout the course of the novel, which leads to questions of authenticity and identity, questions which Dickens attempts to resolve by the end of the novel.

The notion that naming somehow confers identity is not limited to early philosophers; it is a subject which continues to interest scholars and social scientists in the present day. Joseph Bottum argues in his paper "The Gentleman's True Name: *David Copperfield* and the Philosophy of Naming," that David progresses to an understanding of "true" names, that is, he learns that names signify a person's character: "The characters themselves feel the tension of naming and explore with the author what their names are for" (437). Bottum provides examples of the attempts of various characters to impose a name upon Copperfield, attempts which he must overcome: "Murdstone's disinheriting 'David,' Micawber's premature 'Copperfield,' Steerforth's diminishing 'Daisy,' Dora's cloying 'Doady'" (437). By the end of the novel, Bottum asserts that Copperfield has learned to understand the true nature of the characters in the novel, and that he has forged his own identity. Jonathan Potter in "Constructing Social and Personal Identities in Dickens' *David Copperfield*," notes that Dickens explores the relationship between self-expression and the formation of identity in the novel: "The concern for authorship that pervades the entire novel marks the importance of the idea of self-expression as a way of confirming or creating one's self-identity" (2).

Sociologists have attempted to understand the significance of naming in the development of personal and familial identity. Janet Finch explores the relationship between naming and identity in "Kinship, Individuality and Personal Names." According to Finch, naming denotes both the individual and the individual's role within society: "The role of names in the construction of social identities has been very little explored, but one could argue that the possession of the same name throughout life provides a continuity in one's public persona which contributes to a stable sense of the self, that coherence of personal narrative which Giddens regards as 'at the core of self-identity in modern social life' (1991: 76)" (712).

The notion of naming is of interest to linguists as well. Ferdinand de Saussure explores the relationship of names and meaning in *Course in General Linguistics*. Saussure holds that the linking of a name with a thing is arbitrary; that is, there is no implicit connection between a name and the thing named. Every name is a combination of a concept (idea) and a sound-image. At first glance, this position appears to be like that of Hermogenes in Plato's dialogue, yet Saussure adds a twist which distances it from the position taken by Hermogenes. Language does not exist in a vacuum; it is modified by conventions which are established by society in a place and at a particular point in time. Without this convention, the arbitrary name would have no meaning: "In fact, every means of expression used in society, is based, in principle, on collective behavior or—what amounts to the same thing—on convention" (68).

It follows then that names are arbitrary unless the concept of the name and the sound-image are generally accepted by society through the means of convention. In other words, people agree on the name of a thing; without this agreement, all that remains is an arbitrary series of sounds and ideas without meaning. If a name is assigned by one person it does not mean that it will be accepted by society at large. Saussure believes, in fact, that no one person can assign names that will be universally accepted; language is a social, not individual construct. To relate this back to the names given to David Copperfield in the novel, it is apparent that each person who attempts to impose a name on David is doing so individually, that is, without a general consensus that the name is understood and accepted by every other character in the novel much less the main character in the novel, David Copperfield. It is this lack of consensus and the proliferation of names that contributes to a lack of identity in the main character, David Copperfield.

In the early chapters of the novel (chapters 1 through 18), David Copperfield is assigned a series of names which are an attempt to identify him as a boy and young man. Most of the early names assigned to him are employed on his personal name, not his surname. That these names are given to him by other people is important to the development of the novel, and in some respects the given names are antithetical to his development as a fully functioning character. The first instance of a name being imposed upon him comes at the hands of his Aunt, Betsey Trotwood, who attempts to append a name to him before he was born. "'I tell you I have a presentiment that it must be a girl,' returned Miss Betsey. 'Don't contradict. From the moment of this girl's birth, child, I intend to be her friend. I intend to be her godmother, and I beg you'll call her Betsey Trotwood Copperfield'" (Dickens, *DC* 7). Of course, Miss Trotwood is disappointed when Betsey turns out to be David and she departs, never to return, leaving Betsey Trotwood Copperfield "for ever in the land of dreams and shadows" (Dickens, *DC* 12). That the name Trotwood is resurrected when David appears at his aunt's door after his unsuccessful work at Murdstone and Grinby's, the reader is not so much surprised as admitting the inevitability of the name given his aunt's insistence at his birth that his "sister" be named Trotwood.

The naming of David continues throughout the early parts of the work: he is called by various names by other characters in the novel, yet in the case of each name, it is imposed on him; he has no choice in the selection of the names he is called. Perhaps the most insulting name appended to him is not a name at all, but a mere sign which read "*Take care of him. He bites,*" (*DC* 78). That these attempts to identify him had an effect on David Copperfield is demonstrated in his confession at the beginning of chapter 11:

> I know enough of the world now, to have almost lost the capacity of being much surprised by anything; but it is a matter of some surprise to me, even now, that I can have been so easily thrown away at such an age. A child of excellent abilities, and with strong powers of observation, quick, eager, delicate, and soon hurt bodily and mentally, it seems wonderful to me that nobody should have made any sign in my behalf. But none was made; and I became, at ten years old, a little laboring hind in the service of Murdstone and Grinby" [*DC* 154].

These early chapters illustrate how the use of names which are improperly assigned to David impede his development as a fully realized character in the novel. In effect, each of the people in the novel who append a name to David attempt to define him for his/her own purpose (a form of possession), and in so doing, violate the notion that a name is an attempt to develop the identity of the person. Rather, each character who assigns a name to David is in some way revealing something about him/herself.

As an example, Peggoty, Mr. Peggoty and Ham all assign names to David which reveal a class distinction. Their names for David always indicate a deference in addressing him, due to their lower social standing. Steerforth, Murdstone and Miss Murdstone, on the other hand, reveal a disregard for David; each of these characters address David as an inferior because of their perceived class distinction and as an expression of their superiority to him. Clara Copperfield and Dora name David in ways that indicate affection and possession, but it is an affection that is more akin to dependency. In the case of both his mother and wife, the affection each one exhibits toward David is not the affection of equals but that of a person who relies on someone else to fulfill her own emotional needs. The names imposed on David by Mr. Murdstone's friends, his acquaintances at Murdstone & Grinby, and the schoolmaster, Mr. Creakle display a callous indifference bordering on cruelty; each is an attempt to place David in a servile position. Uriah Heep's usage of "Master Copperfield" is an attempt by Uriah to establish his "umble" superiority over David. The reader learns early on that Uriah Heep is playing a clever game; he is trying to out-humble everyone he meets in order to insinuate himself into taking over the affairs of his employer, Mr. Wickfield. The Micawber's naming of David by his surname of "Copperfield" can be seen as an extension of their wish to see him as a fully developed, mature individual, and thus relieve them of any responsibility they might have toward him even though he is only a child.[12]

In each case the name reveals an important fact about the person naming David, but ultimately, the name each person attempts to impose upon him does not capture the spirit or identity of David. That these attempts to define David are examples of improper naming is made explicit by Joseph Bottum, "Dickens shows how a name imposed in the economy of power and desire pushes a person into an expression of that name. But he also shows how the essence to which a true name refers pushes back on that economy with the moral force of truth," (438).[13] Similarly, Jonathan Potter notes the attempt of other characters in the novel to define David:

> Names and naming create David's identities throughout the novel as different characters each impose different names and labels upon him: He is called "Davey" by his mother, "David" by Mr. Murdstone, "Trotwood" by Aunt Betsy, and "Doady" by Dora. These names all represent an identity externally applied to David to which other characters expect him to conform [3].

David's struggle to form his personal sense of identity, and therefore to grow, is not an isolated event in the novel. Indeed, one of the notable issues in the novel is the lack of growth of several of the primary characters. Among the characters who remain trapped in their roles and therefore do not grow in the novel, are: Steerforth, Dora, Mr. and Miss Murdstone, the Micawbers, Clara Copperfield and Little Emily. Steerforth remains a spoiled, petulant, destructive person from the time he is introduced at

Mr. Creakle's boarding school until his death during a storm in chapter 55. Mr. Murdstone remains a fierce, puritanical figure until the end of the novel; he continues his habit of marrying recently widowed young women whom he proceeds to browbeat while pretending to "improve" them. Mr. Micawber continues his improvident ways until he is surprisingly announced as magistrate in his adopted home of Australia. Little Emily is seen only fleetingly after her seduction by Steerforth; she and Mr. Peggoty are whisked off to Australia along with the Micawbers. The reader is told that she attempts to redeem herself in her new homeland but is never provided with evidence that she has in fact been reformed. Despite their lack of growth, or perhaps because of it, each of these characters attempts to impose his/her views on David. Throughout the novel, David must reject each attempt to define him as a person; his growth must be authentic in order for him to achieve his own identity.

To a certain extent, the lack of growth in the characters portrayed in the novel may be the result of the broken familial relationships creating a sense of isolation that pervades the work. The number of orphans in the novel is disconcerting and to this list can be added the number of widows and widowers. Clearly, the world of *David Copperfield* is blighted and isolation from other figures within society is the norm, not the exception.[14] The lack of stable families is not isolated to the novel *David Copperfield*; very few of Dickens's novels exhibit stable familial relationships.

The notion that naming and identity are somehow related to stable family relationships is vindicated by recent sociological studies. Janet Finch writes extensively on the connection between naming, individuality, and familial relationships, noting that names act as a means to view relationships within families: "As well as their power to symbolize social connection, names provide a potential set of tools with which family relationships can be constituted and managed. Thus, names and naming can provide a lens through which family relationships can be viewed and their characteristics more fully understood" (713). Hayley Davies makes the argument that names, in particular surnames, provide a sense of stability in otherwise fluid familial relationships; an argument which resonates in the chaotic world of broken relationships that characterize *David Copperfield*. According to a study of the effects of naming on young children, Davies notes that: "...surnames were experienced by the children as identifiers for others to interpret in making sense of who children were, and to whom they were related" (567).

If naming is seen as a vital link in establishing personal as well as familial identity, what is to be made of the world populated by the characters in *David Copperfield*? Rather than names which establish a fixed personal and familial identity the novel is populated by broken families, imposed or improper names, and strained social relationships. Furthermore, the attempts to define David by imposed names are responsible, in part, for David's struggle to find an authentic identity for himself in the early portions of the novel. The progress of the novel can therefore be seen as David's struggle to forge an identity for himself and it should be noted that there is a parallel struggle on the part of Dickens to forge his own identity in nineteenth century London. That Dickens identified with the character of David Copperfield has been acknowledged by a number of writers, beginning with his biographer John Forster. Gwen Watkins in *Dickens in Search of Himself*, provides insight into Dickens's writing about his personal childhood experiences in his fictional work:

> Dickens's preoccupation with childhood no doubt had its roots in the fact that he had never left his own childhood behind—that in his inner self he remained always a child deprived of natural growth by the lack of early parental love. We can see easily enough how often the actual happenings of his own life appear in his writings, but we can only feel intuitively—and never know if we are right—when he is writing, under the guise of fiction, about inner experiences of his childhood and the feelings which, perhaps unknown to himself, derive from them [83–4].

The progress of the novel is not straightforward due in part to David's attempts to form a coherent narrative of his early life. Virginia Carmichael notes the tension involved in the character of David who attempts to develop his identity, while at the same time reconstructing his past: "Dickens's protagonists however, and especially David Copperfield, are often preoccupied with 'that old unhappy loss,' and appear to be as involved with attempting some sort of recovery from their pasts as with achieving an identity in the present" (653).

Dickens acknowledged in the preface to *David Copperfield* that "Of all my books, I like this the best. It will be easily believed that I am a fond parent to every child of my fancy, and that no one can ever love that family as dearly as I love them. But, like many fond parents, I have in my heart of hearts a favourite child. And his name is DAVID COPPERFIELD" (*DC* xii). This admission bolsters the argument that Dickens, like David Copperfield, struggled to forge his personal identity early in life. That this book is autobiographical in nature is given further credence by the comments Dickens made in his unpublished biography which he gave to Forster:

> It is wonderful to me how I could have been so easily cast away at such an age. It is wonderful to me, that, even after my descent into the poor little drudge I had been

since we came to London, no one had compassion enough on me—a child of singular abilities, quick, eager, delicate, and soon hurt, bodily or mentally—to suggest that something might have been spared, as certainly it might have been, to place me at any common school [I: 25].

The similarity of Copperfield's lament at being abandoned in London at an early age to that of Dickens's own anguish which was poured out to Forster is striking. Perhaps more striking is the similarity of David Copperfield's attempts at an early age to find solace in reading his father's collection of books to that of Dickens, who also found refuge in his father's book collection. The passage described by Copperfield when he learns that his mother has married and that he has acquired a stepfather is an example of a boy who escaped from his changed condition by immersing himself in fictional works:

My father had left a small collection of books in a little room up-stairs, to which I had access (for it adjoined my own) and which nobody else in our house ever troubled. From that blessed little room, Roderick Random, Peregrine Pickle, Humphrey Clinker, Tom Jones, the Vicar of Wakefield, Don Quixote, Gil Blas, and Robinson Crusoe, came out, a glorious host, to keep me company. They kept alive my fancy, and my hope of something beyond that place and time,—they, and the Arabian Nights, and the Tales of the Genii,—and did me no harm; for whatever harm was in some of them was not there for me; I knew nothing of it. It is astonishing to me now, how I found time, in the midst of my porings and blunderings over heavier themes, to read those books as I did. It is curious to me how I could ever have consoled myself under my small troubles (which were great troubles to me), by impersonating my favourite characters in them— as I did—and by putting Mr. and Miss Murdstone into all the bad ones—which I did too. I have been Tom Jones (a child's Tom Jones, a harmless creature) for a week together. I have sustained my own idea of Roderick Random for a month at a stretch, I verily believe [DC 55–56].

Dickens attempted to relieve the pain he experienced in early childhood by retreating into a fictional world. He transformed the pain he lived through as a child into the fictional scene described in *David Copperfield,* as Foster attests:

It is one of the many passages in *Copperfield* which are literally true, and its proper place is here [repeating the above quotation from David Copperfield].... Every word of this personal recollection has been written down as fact, some years before it found its way into *David Copperfield*; the only change in the fiction being his omission of the name of a cheap series of novelists then in course of publication, by means of which his father had become happily the owner of so large a lump of literary treasure in his small collection of books [I: 9, 10].

Virginia Carmichael echoes Forster's view that Dickens wrote as a means of coming to grips with the events of his own life: "At this point we need to consider Charles Dickens writing David's writing and recognize the fictive resolution he was attempting on David's behalf as a compensation for a felt insufficiency in his own life" (666). Looked at in this manner the assumption is that the role of a fictional character, David Copperfield, satisfied a deeper need in Dickens's childhood—that of escaping a present reality which was intolerable—into a realm of fantasy where he could become someone else. Edgar Johnson, in *Charles Dickens: His Tragedy and Triumph*, provides further insight into Dickens's use of personal recollection in the writing of *David Copperfield*: "All these things have their roots in Dickens's personal experience, and derive their depths from the intensity of his feeling about his own childhood and days of youth. Above all, they are steeped in his childhood unhappiness and sense of rejection..." (II: 677).

The need to establish a fictional world is not uncommon in young children; in fact, assuming different roles is normal and aids in childhood development. It is only when the natural impulses of a child to role play are repressed, as in the case of Copperfield and Dickens, that the escape becomes an impediment to further childhood development. Arthur Adrian observes that Dickens understood the need for a child living in an intolerable role to escape into fantasy: "At this point Dickens introduces a development that shows his grasp of an important principle in child psychology: when harsh reality becomes unbearable a sensitive child seeks escape in fantasy" (102).

That Dickens keenly felt his isolation is demonstrated in another passage from Forster's *Life of Charles Dickens*: "Many many times has he spoken to me of this [his feelings of isolation at relocating to Camden Town], and how he seemed at once to fall into a solitary condition apart from all other boys of his own age, and to sink into a neglected state at home which had been always been quite unaccountable to him" (I: 15).

The imposition of tasks normally relegated to grown-ups also weighed heavily on young Dickens and no doubt contributed to his growing sense of isolation and insecurity. Mary Ainsworth, prior to her research on attachment theory, studied the need for parental support in establishing a feeling of security in children: "Clinical experience suggests that if primary insecurity continues—that is, if the young child is unable to count on his parents or parent surrogates for the basic support, both material and emotional, that he needs for his development—a very disturbed and highly defensive pattern of adjustment ensues" (17).

Forster writes that Dickens often assumed duties normally assigned to grown-ups and that he witnessed struggles with finances at home:

> Then, at home, came many miserable daily struggles that seemed to last an immense time, yet they did not perhaps cover many weeks. Almost everything by degrees was

sold or pawned, little Charles being the principal agent in those sorrowful transactions. Such of the books as had been brought from Chatham, *Peregrine Pickle, Roderick Random, Tom Jones, Humphrey Clinker*, and all the rest, went first. They were carried off from the little chiffonier, which his father called the library, to a bookseller in the Hampstead-road, the same that David Copperfield describes as in the City-road; and the account of the sales, as they actually occurred and were told to me long before David was born, was reproduced word for word in his imaginary narrative [I: 21].

There is a passage in *David Copperfield* which imitates Dickens's actual employment as pawn shop conveyancer:

> I understood Mrs. Micawber now, and begged her to make use of me to any extent. I began to dispose of the more portable articles of property that very evening; and went out on a similar expedition almost every morning, before I went to Murdstones and Grinby's.
> Mr. Micawber had a few books on a little chiffonier, which he called the library; and those went first. I carried them, one after another, to a bookstall in the City Road— one part of which, near our house, was almost all bookstalls and bird-shops then— and sold them for whatever they would bring [*DC* 164].

The connection between the fictional work of *David Copperfield* and the actual circumstances of Dickens's own childhood cannot be overstated. Forster commented on Dickens's intention to write an autobiography and notes that he abandoned this project and chose rather to use his early life experiences in writing *David Copperfield*:

> Very shortly afterwards, I learnt in all their detail the incidents that had been so painful to him, and what then was said to me or written respecting them revealed the story of his boyhood. The idea of *David Copperfield*, which was to take all the world into his confidence, had not at this time occurred to him; but what it had so startled me to know, his readers were afterwards told with only such change or addition as for the time might sufficiently disguise himself under cover of his hero.... It had all been written, as fact, before he thought of any other use for it; and it was not until several months later, when the fancy of *David Copperfield*, itself suggested, by what he had so written of his early troubles, began to take shape in his mind, that he abandoned his first intention of writing his own life [I: 23].

The psychological impact of isolation, neglect, and feelings of worthlessness had a profound impact on Dickens, as well as on his fictional character, David Copperfield. Here is Copperfield's account of his days at Murdstone and Grinby:

> No words can express the secret agony of my soul as I sunk into this companionship; compared these henceforth everyday associates with those of my happier childhood— not to say with Steerforth, Traddles, and the rest of those boys; and felt my hopes of growing up to be a learned and distinguished man crushed in my bosom. The deep remembrance of the sense I had, of being utterly without hope now; of the shame I felt in my position; of the misery it was to my young heart to believe that day by day what I had learned, and thought, and delighted in, and raised my fancy and my emu-

lation up by, would pass away from me, little by little, never to be brought back any more; cannot be written [*DC* 155].

The fictional narrative again matches the actual events in Dickens's life, as related to Forster, almost exactly:

> No words can express the secret agony of my soul as I sunk into this companionship [at the blacking house]; compared these every day associates with those of my happier childhood; and felt my early hopes of growing up to be a learned and distinguished man, crushed in my breast. The deep remembrance of the sense I had of being utterly neglected and hopeless; of the shame I felt in my position; of the misery it was to my young heart to believe that, day by day, what I had learned, and thought, and delighted in, and raised my fancy and my emulation up by, was passing away from me, never to be brought back any more; cannot be written. My whole nature was so penetrated with grief and humiliation of such considerations, that even now, famous and caressed and happy, I often forget in my dreams that I have a dear wife and children; even that I am a man; and wander desolately back to that time of my life [I: 26–27].

Dickens never quite recovered from his experiences in early childhood, just as David never quite recovered from his fictional experiences growing up. At one point in his discussions with Forster, Dickens related his reaction to inadvertently walking towards Hungerford-stairs, the site of the old blacking factory in which he labored: "Until old Hungerford-market was pulled down, until old Hungerford-stairs were destroyed, and the very nature of the ground changed, I never had the courage to go back to the place where my servitude began. I never saw it. I could not endure to go near it" (I: 38).

Along with the sense of isolation that pervaded the fictional settings in *David Copperfield* and the real-life experiences of Charles Dickens was the development of a keen eye which was able to discern "cant," one of Dickens's favorite words to describe hypocrisy. Dickens's powers of observation allowed him to understand and commiserate with those who experienced broken familial relationships, to identify with abandoned children and those who struggled with a seemingly indifferent society. Claire Tomalin, in her book *Charles Dickens: A Life*, notes that Dickens possessed an understanding that children observe the actions of adults, and judge them based on those actions:

> He tells us that even very young children observe adults critically and judge them, not only the ones they dislike but also ones they love, in David's case his mother, whose faults of vanity and pettishness he notices even before she betrays him by marrying a stepfather against whom she will fail to protect him.... Before Freud or any of the child experts arrived on the scene the voice of childhood was truly rendered by Dickens out of his own experience ... [217].

As the book progresses the attempts to label David continue, yet as

Lithograph of the Hungerford Market by George Harly, 1822. Warren's Blacking Factory was located adjacent to Hungerford Stairs, and Dickens related to his biographer, John Forster, that he was so ashamed of his employment as a "drudge" at the factory that he could not bear to pass it, even as a full-grown man (London Metropolitan Archives).

the protagonist of the novel, he attempts to find his own identity and to create his own name. Chapter 19 marks a division in the novel; it is in this chapter that David begins his journey towards developing his own identity. Leaving the company of Doctor Strong, David resolves to journey to London and at the same time embarks on a journey of self-discovery. Like Dickens, Copperfield's search for his identity begins with a search for a vocation, a search which leads him to the legal offices of Spenlow and Jorkins where here is apprenticed as a proctor in the firm. He later learns shorthand and becomes a Parliamentary reporter, and then a novelist; the career trajectory that Copperfield follows is the same one that Dickens himself followed.

The character of David Copperfield, like that of Dickens, immerses himself in his work in an attempt to erase his past. The effort required to successfully expunge the past is enormous and, is made clear in this passage from *David Copperfield*:

> I felt as if it were not for me to record, even though this manuscript is intended for no eyes but mine, how hard I worked at that tremendous shorthand, and all improvement appertaining to it, in my sense of responsibility to Dora and her aunts. I will only add, to what I have already written of my perseverance at this time of my life, and of a patient and continuous energy which then began to be matured within me, and which I know to be the strong part of my character, if it have any strength at all, that there, on looking back, I find the source of my success.... My meaning simply is, that whatever I have tried to do in life, I have tried with all my heart to do well; that whatever I have devoted myself to, I have devoted myself to completely; that in great aims and small, I have always been thoroughly in earnest [*DC* 606].

Commenting to Forster, about his own struggles to learn shorthand which led to his later success as newspaper and Parliamentary reporter, Dickens noted:

> ... [that] he took sudden determination to qualify himself thoroughly for what his father was lately become, newspaper parliamentary reporter. He set resolutely therefore to the study of short-hand; and, for the additional help of such general information about books as a fairly educated youth might be expected to have, as well as to satisfy some higher personal cravings, he became an assiduous attendant in the British-museum reading room.... Of the difficulties that beset his short-hand studies, as well as of what first turned his mind to them, he has told also something in *Copperfield* [I: 53–54].

Despite Copperfield's attempts to develop his own identity in the middle portions of the novel, he realizes that he has not yet arrived at adulthood. After his first bacchanal at his apartment in London, David encounters his childhood companion, Agnes, at a play which he and his friends attended while they were inebriated. The next morning, he receives a letter from Agnes addressed to "T. Copperfield, Esquire." David's remarks on receiving the letter attest to his own doubts about his identity and self-sufficiency: "I could scarcely lay claim to the name [of esquire]: I was so disturbed by the conviction that the letter came from Agnes. However, I told him [the ticket-porter] I was T. Copperfield, Esquire, and he believed it, and gave me the letter, which he said required an answer" (*DC* 365). Upon opening the letter, Copperfield was relieved that it contained no mention of the prior night's episode at the theater. Clearly, Copperfield himself has doubts about reaching a mature level of development.

Later, when David visits Steerforth at his house and before he learns of Steerforth's seduction of Little Emily, Steerforth addresses David in his usual manner: "'Daisy,' he said, with a smile—'for though that's not the name your godfathers and godmothers gave you, it's the name I like best to call you by—and I wish, I wish, I wish, you could give it to me!'" (*DC* 436). This time, however, the name "Daisy" is tinged with a note of regret or longing. No longer is the appellation a term of condescension, as when Steerforth says "you are a very Daisy. The daisy of the field, at sunrise, is not fresher than you are," (*DC* 288). The term "Daisy" now takes on an almost biblical connotation of innocence; an innocence that Steerforth has lost and which David, despite his attempts at finding his identity, still retains.

The naming continues throughout the middle course of the novel, and by this time Copperfield believes that he has at last attained his true identity and his status as a man. The opening passage in chapter 43 begins with an assertion that "I have come legally to man's estate. I have attained the dignity of twenty-one. But this is a sort of dignity that may be thrust upon one" (*DC* 626).

Of course there is a realization that David has not yet achieved his true identity. This point is made clear some pages later when Dora, his child-wife, gives him the name "Doady" which is meant to be a term of endearment. David struggles against this attempt at naming him, imagining at the time that he has at last found his true identity and name. He embarks on a series of improvements that he wishes to make in Dora and in the process attempts to define her role, just as he has had his role defined for him. Yet, Dora, for all her childishness and simplicity, addresses the issue of naming in perhaps the most direct manner of any character in the book when she asks David to call her his "child-wife."

David, taken aback by her request, seems puzzled prompting Dora to explain: "I don't mean, you silly fellow, that you should use the name instead of Dora. I only mean that you should think of me that way. When you are going to be angry with me, say to yourself, 'it's only my child-wife!'" (*DC* 644). In a moment of true introspection David admits to Dora that he has not yet attained manhood, and that he too is in need of further improvement: "'I must teach myself first, Dora,' said I. 'I am as bad as you, love'" (*DC* 643).

The first real revelation Copperfield has concerning his true nature and that of all married people comes during a scene in which he witnesses the reconciliation of Doctor Strong and his wife Annie, facilitated by the ministrations of Mr. Dick, of all people. It is surprising that Mr. Dick can facilitate anything as complicated as a reconciliation between a married couple since Mr. Dick possess a deeply divided personality himself; but he manages to perform the feat and the doctor and his wife are reconciled. As Annie explains her unhappiness to Dr. Strong, her family and friends, she confides that she was wounded by suspicions that she loved her cousin Mr. Maldon but that she could not love him because "There can be no disparity in marriage like unsuitability of mind and purpose" (*DC* 660). David was struck by these words, but could not initially understand their import:

> I pondered on those words, even while I was studiously attending to what followed, as if they had some particular interest, or strange application that I could not divine. "There can be no disparity in marriage like unsuitability of mind and purpose"—"no disparity in marriage like unsuitability of mind and purpose" [*DC* 661].

As David contemplates these words, he realizes that they apply to himself and Dora yet he realizes, perhaps too late, that their marriage must continue. No doubt, Dickens realized that an unsuitability of mind and temperament existed between himself and his wife, Catherine, and like David he also realized that the marriage must continue. John Forster comments on Dickens's own domestic life and speculates that for David Copperfield, his dreams of domestic happiness are realized, but marital happiness did not exist for Dickens:

> This was among the reproductions of personal experience in the book; but it was a sadder knowledge that came with the conviction some years later, that David's contrasts in his earliest married life between his happiness enjoyed and his happiness once anticipated, the "vague unhappy loss or want of something" of which he so frequently complains, reflected also a personal experience which had not been supplied in fact so successfully as in fiction [II. 134].

The marriage between Dickens and Catherine Hogarth continued for a number of years but Dickens, unlike David Copperfield, had no means of officially dissolving the marriage, eventually choosing to abandon his wife and children.[15]

It was the long illness and eventual death of Dora that provided the impetus for change in David's character. And Dora, seen as the embodiment of childhood and simplicity, once again surprises David with her insight, when she told him on her deathbed that perhaps it was best that she die: "'I was very happy, very. But, as years went on, my dear boy would have wearied of his child-wife. She would have been less and less a companion for him. He would have been more and more sensible of what was wanting in his home. She wouldn't have improved. It is better as it is" (*DC* 767).

After Dora's death David embarked on a European tour, ostensibly to heal from the wounds experienced by his wife's death and the departure of Mr. Peggoty, Little Emily and the Micawbers to Australia as the following passage attests:

> The desolate feeling with which I went abroad, deepened and widened hourly. At first it was a heavy sense of loss and sorrow, wherein I could distinguish little else. By imperceptible degrees, it became a hopeless consciousness of all that I had lost—love, friendship, interest; of all that had been shattered—my first trust, my first affection, the whole airy castle of my life; of all that remained—a ruined blank and waste, lying wide around me, unbroken, to the dark horizon [*DC* 813].

In fact, David's journey follows the outlines of the traditional Bildungsroman where the main character undertakes a journey for a number of reasons but in the end, finds himself. So it is with David, who, in an attempt to escape the loss associated with his past life finds his true nature. He also comes to the realization that his true nature is somehow inextricably linked with that of Agnes:

> I cannot so completely penetrate the mystery of my own heart, as to know when I began to think that I might have set its earliest and brightest hopes on Agnes. I cannot say at what stage of my grief it first became associated with the reflection that, in my wayward boyhood, I had thrown away the treasure of her love. I believe I may have heard some whisper of that distant thought, in the old unhappy loss or want of something never to be realised, of which I had been sensible. But the thought came into my mind as a new reproach and new regret, when I was left so sad and lonely in the world [*DC* 817].

His return home was marked by further introspection and a resolution of the last remaining major plot development—his marriage to Agnes. Prior to this final resolution, David meets with Mr. Chillip the doctor who delivered him and provided comfort for him at his mother's burial. The recognition scene between an older, white haired Mr. Chillip and the mature David is notable for the emphasis placed on naming, as Mr. Chillip informs David: "'I have a kind of an impression that something in your countenance is familiar to me, sir; but I couldn't lay my hand upon your name, really,' [to which David replies]: 'And yet you knew it, long before I knew it myself'" (*DC* 831).

On one level, this discussion about names between Mr. Chillip and Copperfield is merely the superficial small talk which is made to conceal the fact that a person cannot recall the name of an acquaintance who has gone unseen for a long time. On the other hand, David's admission that Mr. Chillip "knew it, long before I knew it myself," is an admission that for most of his life David's name was given to him by others. The discovery of his true name and nature was revealed after many years of struggle.

David's courtship of Agnes is the centerpiece of the final chapters of the novel. It is approached in a circular manner in a sort of wary, timid, fashion. The reticence on the part of David is ascribed to his decision to have a more disciplined heart and to direct his affections in a manner which was different from his puppy-love of Dora. This reticence is also due, in part, to David's growing understanding of who he is as a person. Just prior to making his true affection known to Agnes he recalls that: "I tried to show her how I had hoped I had come into a better knowledge of myself and of her; how I had resigned myself to what that better knowledge brought; and how I had come there, even that day, in my fidelity to this" (*DC* 862).

After declaring his love for Agnes and receiving her assurances of mutual affection, David describes a reverie he had: "Long miles of road then opened out before my mind; and, toiling on, I saw a ragged way-worn boy forsaken and neglected, who should come to call even the heart now beating against mine, his own" (*DC* 863). It is at the moment of the realization of his greatest joy that he recognizes the journey he has undertaken a journey which not only resulted in finding his true love but of finding his true identity.

The last chapter of the novel is a retrospective, a journey backward but also forward in time. It is only now after David had forged his own identity as a writer, husband, and person, that he can confront his past and look forward to the future. The novel began with a failed naming and ends with the proper bestowal of a long-forgotten name: "My aunt's old disappointment is set right, now. She is godmother to a real living Betsey Trotwood; and Dora (the next in order) says she spoils her" (*DC* 874). Similarly, having overcome his many tribulations, the mature Copperfield can look back upon his earlier life with a sense of equanimity: "I find it very curious to see my own infant face, looking up at me from the Crocodile stories; and to be reminded by it of my old acquaintance Brooks of Sheffield" (*DC* 874).

Dickens, unlike David Copperfield, was unable to find happiness in a stable marriage and an ideal family life. As he looked back upon his life he was not able to achieve the equanimity that his fictional character, David Copperfield, achieved.

CHAPTER THREE

Dreams and Dreaming

Before beginning a discussion on dreams and dreaming, it is necessary to address Dickens's understanding of psychology and its influence on character development. Both the notion of Dickens's method of character development and his use of psychology have undergone a transformation in the twentieth and twenty-first centuries. Dickens's works were originally thought to lack character development and psychological insight by a number of Victorian critics who maintained that he did not delve into the psyche of his characters; that is, he did not provide a sense of interiority, a sense of the way their minds function through internal dialogue. This method of character exposition was made popular by the novels of George Eliot and Thomas Hardy, among others, in the mid to late Victorian era and is a technique that continues to the present day.

Criticism of Dickens's understanding of the psychology of his characters began in his own lifetime and is perhaps best expressed by George Eliot (Mary Ann Evans) as follows:

> We have one great novelist who is gifted with the utmost power of rendering the external traits of our town population; and if he could give us their psychological character—their conceptions of life and their emotions—with the same truth as their idiom and manners, his books would be the greatest contribution Art has ever made to the awakening of social sympathies ["Natural History" 71].

George Lewes, a friend of Dickens and associate of George Eliot, with whom he lived, admired Dickens's style as well as his attempts at social reform although he did not believe that Dickens's characters were psychologically believable. In "George Henry Lewes as a Critic of the Novel," Morris Greenhut maintains:

> Because he [Dickens] could not transcend the purely perceptual, he had no conception of the complexity of character. Lewes points out that "his characters have nothing fluctuating and incalculable in them, even when they embody true observations." In

such "monstrous failures" as Mantalini, Rosa Dartle, Mr. Dick, Arthur Gude, Edith Dombey, Mr. Carker, we are "distressed" to observe the substitution of mechanisms for minds, puppets for characters [503–504].

Opinions regarding Dickens's use of psychology began to change with the development of psychological theory in the twentieth century, driven primarily by the writings of Sigmund Freud. Although Dickens did not have knowledge of Freud's theories, in many ways, he intuited a number of Freud's theories on dreams, the use of analysis to understand psychological problems, and repression.

Dickens's understanding of psychology is rooted in three areas: (1) his observation of people and events; (2) his study and practice of mesmerism; (3) his reflection on the nature of dreams and dreaming.

Dickens's powers of observation were formed during his early career as law clerk, journalist and Parliamentary reporter. These occupations afforded him first hand views of ordinary people, criminals, and members of Parliament. In a speech delivered on May 20, 1865, to the Newspaper Press Fund, Dickens described his work as Parliamentary reporter in adverse conditions which required great accuracy:

> I went into the gallery of the House of Commons as a parliamentary reporter when I was a boy not eighteen, and I left it—I can hardly believe the inexorable truth—nigh thirty years ago.... I have often transcribed for the printer, from my shorthand notes, important public speeches in which the strictest accuracy was required, and a mistake in which would have been to a young man severely compromising, writing on the palm of my hand, by the light of a dark lantern, in a post-chaise and four, galloping through a wild country, and through the dead of the night, at the then surprising rate of fifteen miles an hour. The very last time I was at Exeter, I strolled into the castle yard there to identify, for the amusement of a friend, the spot on which I once "took," as we used to call it, an election speech of my noble friend Lord Russell, in the midst of a lively fight maintained by all the vagabonds in that division of the country, and under such a pelting rain, that I remember two goodnatured colleagues, who chanced to be at leisure, held a pocket-handkerchief over my notebook, after the manner of a state canopy in an ecclesiastical procession [*SP* 102–103].

Dickens often walked ten to twenty miles a night visiting the affluent sections of London such as Grosvenor Square, the area around Regent's Park and Hyde Park, and Belgravia. He also visited the area of the city frequented by the less fortunate including St. Giles, the areas surrounding the Newgate and Fleet prisons, Seven Dials as well as the Hungerford Market area near the Thames (although he avoided Hungerford Stairs because he associated this area with Warren's Blacking factory). Dickens's first-hand observation of life in London provided him with a knowledge of the city that he believed was possessed by few people. Alan R. Burke, in "The Strategy and Theme of Urban Observation in *Bleak House*," comments on Dickens's knowledge of London, a knowledge that the author used to effect in his novels:

> That Dickens was a brilliant observer of the urban milieu which figures in his novels has long been a critical concern. In 1858, Walter Bagehot wrote that Dickens possessed a marvelous "power of observation in detail" which enabled him to describe London "like a special correspondent for posterity." Although the London which Dickens observed was, in Bagehot's words, as multitudinous and as disconnected as a "newspaper" containing various unrelated stories, Dickens could "go down a crowded street, and tell you all that is in it, what each shop was, what the grocer's name was, how many scraps of orange-peel there were on the pavement" [659].

In addition to his powers of observation, Dickens became interested in mesmerism, a form of medical practice that has fallen into disrepute in the present day. Mesmerism was developed by the German physician, Franz Mesmer, and was based on principles of "animal magnetism" or the aligning of the magnetic impulses of the body to effectuate cures of the psyche and to relieve pain. Edgar Johnson, in *Charles Dickens: His Tragedy and Triumph*, relates that Dickens became acquainted with the practice of mesmerism through the auspices of Dr. John Elliotson, one of the founders of University College in London:

> Around this time, also, Dickens met Dr. John Elliotson and first became interested in mesmerism. Professor of the Practice of Medicine at London University, Elliotson was the first physician to use the stethoscope and was one of the founders of University College Hospital. He was also a daring innovator in unorthodox realms of knowledge and, as the first president of the Phrenological Society, one of the pioneers in experimenting with the use of mesmerism to relieve pain [I: 221].

While the principle of "animal magnetism" has been debunked, the actual process of effectuating a psychic cure is similar in practice to the use of hypnotism, and later the practice of psychotherapy developed by Freud. In order to effectuate the trance-like state necessary for the application of a cure, the mesmerist talked to the patient and applied pressure to the patient's head, much like the practice Freud used in performing psychotherapy. Dickens, in a letter written to his friend Frederick Evans dated September 25, 1849, describes his use of mesmerism on their mutual friend, John Leech, who was struck by a wave on the Isle of Wight and was incapacitated:

> He was more like a ship in distress, in a sea of bedclothes, than anything else. In the difficulty of getting at him, and of doing the thing with any reasonable effect, at first, in a dark room, it was more than half an hour before I could so far tranquillize him (by the magnetism I mean) as to keep him composed, awake for five minutes altogether. Then, that effect began, and he said he felt comfortable and happy [*SL* 198].

During a trip to Genoa in the mid-eighteen-forties Dickens made the acquaintance of Emile de la Rue, a Swiss banker, and his wife, Augusta, who was born in England. Augusta suffered from an anxiety disorder which manifested itself in tics, facial spasms, insomnia and convulsions. Dickens offered to mesmerize her and succeeded in relieving her symptoms for short periods of time. Eventually, Dickens suggested that Augusta undergo a more involved type of mesmerism which involved a trance-like state and he described a session in which Augusta identified a phantom, who troubled her and led to her illness. Augusta's mesmeric session was discussed in a letter written to Emile de la Rue on January 27, 1845.

Illustration by Ebenezer Sibley entitled *A Key to Physic, and the Occult Sciences,* which depicts mesmerism. Dickens practiced mesmerism and believed it was effective in eliminating certain hysterical symptoms. Although the principle of animal magnetism has been debunked, mesmerism bears certain affinities to a form of hypnotism used by Freud to treat his patients (British Library, London).

She has now no secret in connexion with the devilish figure; for that chain is utterly broken. That it bound her to the disease, and the disease to her, and that it must have linked her (she says so) in the course of time to Madness, I have no earthly doubt. I cannot yet quite make up my mind, whether the phantom originates in shattered nerves and a system broken by Pain; or whether it is the representative of some great nerve or set of nerves on which her disease has preyed—and begins to loose its hold now, because the disease of those nerves is itself attacked by the inexplicable agency of the Magnetism. I think upon the whole, I incline to this last opinion; but I could not make up my mind without more observation of, and more conversation with, herself [*SL* 156].

Dickens's use of mesmerism to relieve Madame de la Rue's symptoms, which appear to be hysterical in nature, by inducing a trance-like state and having Augusta relate her dreams in the form of pictures is similar to the therapeutic process described by Freud:

I inform the patient that in the next moment I will exert pressure on his forehead. I assure him that during this pressure he will see some reminiscence in the form of a picture, or some thought will occur to him, and I obligate him to communicate to me this picture or this thought, no matter what it might be [66].

Dickens's interest in dreams can be seen in a letter he sent to his biographer, John Forster. In a letter dated September 30 (?), 1844, Dickens describes to Forster a dream he had which involved his sister-in-law, Mary Hogarth, who died at the age of seventeen in the year 1837. In the letter, Dickens indicates that he mingled events from the current day with his past remembrances of Mary and that Mary appeared to him in something like a visionary state. Dickens believed that Mary's appearance in a dream was brought about by three factors: Dickens's request that Forster provide assistance for his wife's family, the presence of an altar in the room in which the Dickens family was staying on holiday in Italy, and the presence of convent bells which Dickens heard nearby (SL 144–145).

In a letter to Dr. Thomas Stone dated February 2, 1851, Dickens once again touches on his theories of dreaming. In the letter, Dickens notes that he dreams of events which occurred in the present and that when these occur "the incidents are usually of the most insignificant character—such as made no impression, of which we were conscious, at the time—such as present themselves again, in the wildest eccentricity" (SL 225). He goes on to write that he believes dreams are of an allegorical nature and that both allegory and myth may be operative in the formation of dreams: "I sometimes think that the origin of all fable and Allegory—the very first conception of such fictions—may be referable to this class of dreams" (SL 225). According to Dickens, dreams are often not conscious, and are similar to myth and allegory.

Dickens's musings on the nature of dreams led him to believe that certain dreams were common to all men. In the same letter to Dr. Stone of February 2, 1851, Dickens provides the doctor with a summary of the type of dreams common to everyone:

And how many dreams are common to us all, from the Queen to the Costermonger! We all fall off that Tower—we all skim above the ground at a great pace and can't keep on it—we all say "this *must* be a dream, because I was in this strange, low-roofed, beam-obstructed place, once before, and it turned out to be a dream"—we all take unheard-of trouble to go to the Theatre and never get in—or to go to a Feast, which can't be eaten or drunk—or to read letters, placards, or books, that no study will render legible—or to break some Thraldom or other, from which we can't escape—or we all confound the living with the dead, and all frequently have a knowledge or suspicion that we are doing it—we all astonish ourselves by telling ourselves, in a dialogue with ourselves, the most astonishing and terrific secrets—we all go to public places in our night dresses, and are horribly disconcerted lest the company should observe it [SL 226].

Although Dickens died before Freud developed his theory of dream formation, Freud's work on dreams provides a method for understanding Dickens's use of dreams in his works. Freud's theory of dream formation continued throughout his life, although his most extensive writing on the subject can be found in *The Interpretation of Dreams*. Freud describes the workings of dreams and defines the method of content selection in dreams as follows:

> 1. That the dream clearly prefers the impressions of the last few days...
> 2. That it makes a selection in accordance with principles other than those governing our waking memory, in that it recalls not essential and important, but subordinate and disregarded things;
> 3. That it has at its disposal the earliest impressions of our childhood, and brings to light details from this period of life, which, again, seem trivial to us, and which in waking life were believed to have been long since forgotten [205–206].

Freud notes that there are four sources of stimuli which may affect sleep and the formation of dreams. The first is composed of external sensory stimuli such as light, odors, sounds, heat or cold. The second set of stimuli listed by Freud are internal sensory stimuli, which he claims are harder to verify and are composed of hypnogogic hallucinations. Freud defines the third category of stimuli as internal physical stimuli which include derangements and excitations of the internal organs, sexual excitation, muscular, gastric and pneumatic excitations. The final category commented on by Freud involves the psychic sources of excitation which are usually composed of sensory impressions from the current day (145–155).

Freud describes the way in which dreams are presented during sleep: "Dreams, then, think preponderantly, but not exclusively, in visual images. They make use also of auditory images, and, to a lesser extent, of the other sensory impressions ... we may say, with every well-informed authority, that the dream hallucinates—that is, that it replaces thoughts by hallucinations" (157). Later, Freud notes the similarity of dreams and visions: "And we must here reflect that this transformation of ideas into visual images does not occur in dreams alone, but also in hallucinations and visions, which may appear spontaneously in health, or as symptoms in the psychoneuroses" (351).

Freud also noted that there are certain dreams which appear common to all people: "...there are a number of dreams which almost every one has dreamed in the same manner, and of which we are accustomed to assume that they have the same significance in the case of every dreamer" (237). Among the common dreams he lists are ones relating to flying, falling, missed appointments, being inappropriately dressed for an occasion, and visits by loved persons who are dead.

In another passage, Freud draws the conclusion that dreams are similar to allegory and myth when he writes:

> The relation of our typical dreams to fairy-tales and other fiction and poetry is neither sporadic nor accidental. Sometimes the penetrating insight of the poet has analytically recognized the process of transformation of which the poet is otherwise the instrument, and has followed it up in the reverse direction; that is to say, has traced a poem to a dream [239].

He continues his discussion of dreams, myth and symbols, writing:

> In this connection it should be noted that symbolism does not appertain especially to dreams, but rather to the unconscious imagination, and particularly to that of the people, and it is to be found in a more developed condition in folklore, myths, legends, idiomatic phrases, proverbs, and the current witticisms of a people than in dreams [282].

Freud's definition of dreams and dream content corresponds to Dickens's ideas about dreaming to a remarkable degree. Dickens's dreams of his sister-in-law, which he related to Forster, contain all the elements Freud specified for the content of a dream: Dickens mingled the events from the current day with past remembrances of Mary; the dream contained trivial as well as important items; and it referred to an earlier period in Dickens's life when Mary was still alive. Freud's theory of visual presentation in dreams is well suited to Dickens's powers of observation and explains the preponderance of visual imagery when Dickens records the dream activities of his characters. Dickens also makes use of visual presentations in his narration of reveries and visions in his novels. Similarly, Dickens's letter to Dr. Stone mentions the dreams common to all men and contains many of the elements which Freud discusses in common dreams. Finally, Dickens's notion that dreams are akin to fairy-tales and myths is similar to Freud's notion that dreams, fairy-tales and myth are somehow joined together in the unconscious.

Broadly speaking, Dickens makes use of dreams in several ways including using dreams as reveries or images; as symbols, fairy-tales or fables; as a means of introducing sickness or illness where the dream provides insight to earlier events in the novel; to convey a particular feeling, or to evoke a mood. In each case the dream acts as a means of advancing the narrative, stressing a point, or revealing the inner state of a character. This latter use involving a way to reveal a character's inner consciousness, serves as a further counterpoint to those critics who contend that Dickens made use of one-dimensional characterization.

The first category to be discussed is that of reveries or visions. Technically, a reverie or vision is not the same as a dream. For dreaming to occur, the person dreaming must lose consciousness and enter into a state where the outside world is suspended for a period of time, although some sensory impressions from the outside world will continue in sleep. In *The Old Curiosity Shop*, Nell and her grandfather journey to escape their tormentor, Quilp, and arrive at a church located in Shropshire. Here, Nell reflects on the graves of the dead whose resting places lay in the churchyard outside her casement window; she gradually slips into a reverie where she imagines the fate of the dead souls buried outside her window. She proceeds from reverie to outright sleep, and:

> ... dreams of the little scholar; of the roof opening, and a column of bright faces, rising far away into the sky, as she had seen in some old scriptural picture once, and looking down on her, asleep. It was a sweet and happy dream. The quiet spot, outside, seemed to remain the same, saving that there was music in the air, and a sound of angel's wings. After a time the sisters came there, hand in hand, and stood among the graves. And then the dream grew dim, and faded [*OCS* 388–389].

This passage is significant in a number of ways. In the first place, it begins with a reverie, a series of reminiscences about Nell's past experiences and thoughts about death. Secondly, it is expressed in visual terms and contains auditory elements as well, "music in the air and a sound of angel's wings." Thirdly, it provides a connection to earlier events in the novel in the case of both the little scholar and the sisters. In the case of the young scholar, the passage foreshadows Nell's declining health and ultimate death. The mention of the little scholar harkens back to chapters 25 and 26, which introduces the character. He is an orphan, like Nell, and is raised by his grandmother, just as Nell is raised by her grandfather. The little scholar dies, after suffering for a period of time, just as Nell is destined to die after her period of suffering. By referring back to the little scholar, Dickens is reminding his reader of the parallel between the scholar and Nell, and preparing the way for Nell's death. The reference to the two sisters is meant to remind the reader of passages in chapters 31 and 32, in which Nell meets two sisters, the Misses Edwards. They are also orphans, and like Nell, are set apart from polite society due to the circumstances of their birth. For a while, Nell follows the sisters, hoping to form a bond with them—and for some sort of human companionship from people nearer to her own age. That wish was broken by her grandfather's decision to steal money from Nell's employer, Mrs. Jarley, in order to finance his gambling addiction. Nell, through the use of a false dream, persuades her grandfather to leave the area near Mrs. Jarley and thereby avoid the theft of money.

Finally, the reference to the angel's wings is both a look backward to chapter 26, and the little scholar and a look forward to chapter 71, in which Nell dies. In chapter 26, Dickens prepares the reader for the later reference to angels in the following passage: "Her dreams were of the little scholar: not coffined and covered up, but mingling with angels..." (194). The passage in book 71 ties together the references to the angels, Nell's death, and the little scholar:

> And still her former self lay there, unaltered in this change. Yes. The old fireside had smiled upon that same sweet face; it had passed, like a dream, through haunts of misery and care; at the door of the poor schoolmaster on the summer evening, before the furnace fire upon the cold wet night, at the still bedside of the dying boy, there had been the same mild lovely look. So shall we know the angels in their majesty, after death [*OCS* 539].[1]

The character of Kit is also the subject of a reverie in the novel. Kit, friend to Nell and her grandfather, is falsely imprisoned through the machinations of Quilp. While in jail, Kit slips into a reverie in which he imagines times spent with Nell and her grandfather around the supper table warmed by the fire, and then falls asleep. While asleep, he dreams of his freedom:

> It was a long night, which seemed as though it would have no end; but he slept too, and dreamed—always of being at liberty, and roving about, now with one person and now with another, but ever with a vague dread of being recalled to prison; not that prison, but one which was in itself a dim idea—not of a place, but of a care and sorrow: of something oppressive and always present, and yet impossible to define. At last, the morning dawned, and there was the jail itself—cold, black, and dreary, and very real indeed [*OCS* 454].

Kit's reveries and dream repeat a number of themes which occur in Dickens: the prison, the visual images, the repetitive dream sequences, the indistinct dread of something which is just beyond the realm of consciousness and understanding.

The technique of reverie and dream sequence is explored once again in *A Tale of Two Cities*, in chapter 3, when Jarvis Lorry, an employee of the Tellson's Bank, is sent to France to retrieve Dr. Alexander Manette, who has been in jail for the past eighteen years. During his coach ride through the countryside prior to his departure for France, Mr. Lorry enters a reverie in which he imagines Dr. Manette after a period of eighteen years in prison; the reverie is then followed by a dream:

> Now, which of the multitude of faces that showed themselves before him was the true face of the buried person, the shadows of the nights did not indicate; but they were all the faces of a man of five-and-forty by years, and they differed principally in the passions they expressed, and in the ghastliness of their worn and wasted state.

Pride, contempt, defiance, stubbornness, submission, lamentation, succeeded one another; so did varieties of sunken cheek, cadaverous colour, emaciated hands and figures. But the face was in the main one face, and every head was prematurely white. A hundred times the dozing passenger inquired of this spectre:

"Buried how long?"

The answer was always the same: "Almost eighteen years."

"You had abandoned all hope of being dug out?"

"Long ago."

"You know that you are recalled to life?"

"They tell me so."

"I hope you care to live?"

"I can't say" [*TTC* 12].

The technique of following a reverie with a dream is repeated in the same manner as the reverie and dream sequence in *Old Curiosity Shop* and points to other events in the novel. In the case of Mr. Lorry and Dr. Manette, the dream sequence points to Dr. Manette's actual condition upon being released from prison which is worse than envisaged by Mr. Lorry in his dream. It also foreshadows the dream-like, disjointed, and disturbing images of the French Revolution that form the backdrop to the story of Dr. Manette and his unjust imprisonment.

Dickens weaves the story of Dr. Manette's imprisonment throughout the novel; whenever the doctor meets with an unexpected or traumatic experience, he reverts to the condition he was in after his release from prison. His occupation becomes that of a shoe cobbler and

Dr. Manette in prison; illustration by H.K. Browne (Phiz) for *A Tale of Two Cities*. In the novel, Dr. Manette, who was wrongfully imprisoned for eighteen years, loses all sense of his prior existence, and dreams of being buried alive (Wikimedia Commons).

he forgets that he previously was a successful physician. The triggering of anxiety by a traumatic event (in this case Dr. Manette's imprisonment) is consistent with Freud's theories of trauma: "Now in the traumatic neuroses the dream life has this peculiarity: it continually takes the patient back to the situation of his disaster, from which he awakens in renewed terror" (641). It was in this condition that Mr. Lorry discovered Dr. Manette, after being released from prison, cobbling shoes and avoiding human contact. Later, when Dr. Manette's daughter Lucie is engaged to marry Charles Darnay, Dr. Manette discusses the reveries he had about her while in prison:

> In that more peaceful state, I have imagined her, [his daughter, Lucie who was born while he was imprisoned, and whom he had never seen] in the moonlight, coming to me and taking me out to show me that the home of her married life was full of her loving remembrance of her lost father. My picture was in her room, and I was in her prayers. Her life was active, cheerful, useful; but my poor history pervaded it all.
> "I was that child, my father. I was not half so good, but in my love, that was I."
> "And she showed me her children," said the Doctor of Beauvais, "and they had heard of me, and had been taught to pity me. When they passed a prison of the State, they kept far from its frowning walls, and looked up at its bars, and spoke in whispers. She could never deliver me; I imagined that she always brought me back after showing me such things. But then, blessed with the relief of tears, I fell upon my knees, and blessed her" [TTC 181].

The reverie and dream sequence in which Dr. Manette relates his experiences in prison to his daughter Lucie, is motivated, in part, by the discovery that Charles Darnay is actually Charles St. Evremonde, son of Marquis St. Evremonde, one of the brothers responsible for unjustly imprisoning Dr. Manette. The discovery of the actual identity of Charles Darnay brings back the memories of Dr. Manette, and causes the doctor to relive the anguish and anxiety of his time in prison. Here, Dickens has captured the repetitive nature of a traumatic event in just the same way that Freud posited in his theory of trauma.

The final series of reveries appears in *Great Expectations*, when Pip is first introduced to Miss Havisham and Estella. Venturing out into the brewery attached to Miss Havisham's estate, Pip enters into a reverie in which he has a vision of Miss Havisham:

> It was in this place, and at this moment, that a strange thing happened to my fancy. I thought it a strange thing then, and I thought it a stranger thing long afterwards. I turned my eyes—a little dimmed by looking up at the frosty light—towards a great wooden beam in a low nook of the building near me on my right hand, and I saw a figure hanging there by the neck. A figure all in yellow white, with but one shoe to the feet; and it hung so, that I could see that the faded trimmings of the dress were like earthy paper, and that the face was Miss Havisham's, with a movement going over

the whole countenance as if she were trying to call to me. In the terror of seeing the figure, and in the terror of being certain that it had not been there a moment before, I at first ran from it, and then ran towards it. And my terror was greatest of all, when I found no figure there [*GE* 64].

The vision of Miss Havisham is based upon her appearance in the story, attired as she was, in her faded wedding dress and in a house where everything was halted at the exact time when Miss Havisham learned that her wedding ceremony would not be held. Moreover, Dickens uses the technique of reverie to advance the plot of the story, and to prefigure later events in the novel.

In chapter 44, Pip returns to visit Miss Havisham and asks her for money to assist his friend, Herbert Pocket. As he took his leave from Miss Havisham, Pip approached the brewery where he had the vision of Miss Havisham years before and the vision reappeared, "A childish association revived with wonderful force in the moment of the slight action, and I fancied that I saw Miss Havisham hanging to the beam. So strong was the impression, that I stood under the beam shuddering from head to foot before I knew it was a fancy—though to be sure I was there in an instant" (*GE* 401). This final reverie is a prelude to the events later in the novel which led to Miss Havisham's setting fire to her wedding dress and to her eventual death.

Dickens makes use of the technique of dreams as a means of introducing sickness or illness in several of the novels including *Little Dorrit*, and *Great Expectations;* each of these works contains valuable psychological insights into the nature of dreaming. In *Little Dorrit*, the notion of a dream which originates in sickness occurs in chapter 29, book 2, when Arthur Clenham has been confined to the Marshalsea and falls into a sickness induced by the environment of the prison:

Light of head with want of sleep and want of food (his appetite, and even his sense of taste, having forsaken him), he had been two or three times conscious, in the night, of going astray. He had heard fragments of tunes and songs in the warm wind, which he knew had no existence. Now that he began to doze in exhaustion, he heard them again; and voices seemed to address him, and he answered, and started.

Dozing and dreaming, without the power of reckoning time, so that a minute might have been an hour and an hour a minute, some abiding impression of a garden stole over him—a garden of flowers, with a damp warm wind gently stirring their scents. It required such a painful effort to lift his head for the purpose of inquiring into anything, that the impression appeared to have become quite an old and importunate one when he looked round. Beside the tea-cup on his table he saw, then, a blossoming nosegay: a wonderful handful of the choicest and most lovely flowers [*LD* 384].

Here the pattern that was noted in the reverie/dream sequence occurs again: a reverie lapses into a dream and harkens back to earlier events in the novel. In the case of Arthur Clenham's dream sequence, the flowers refer back to chapter 16, book 1, when he witnesses flowers drifting down the river. In this sequence, Clenham reflects that the best days of his life have passed him by and that his longing for love would be denied forever. The aural quality of the reveries is also highlighted: Clenham hears tunes and songs as he drifts in and out of consciousness.

Pip, in *Great Expectations,* also has a dream during his recuperation from the events surrounding the aborted escape and subsequent care of Magwitch, the man responsible for Pip's fortune:

> That I had a fever and was avoided, that I suffered greatly, that I often lost my reason, that the time seemed interminable, that I confounded impossible existences with my own identity; that I was a brick in the house-wall, and yet entreating to be released from the giddy place where the builders had set me; that I was a steel beam of a vast engine, clashing and whirling over a gulf, and yet that I implored in my own person to have the engine stopped, and my part in it hammered off; that I passed through these phases of disease, I know of my own remembrance, and did in some sort know at the time. That I sometimes struggled with real people, in the belief that they were murderers, and that I would all at once comprehend that they meant to do me good, and would then sink exhausted in their arms, and suffer them to lay me down, I also knew at the time. But, above all, I knew that there was a constant tendency in all these people—who, when I was very ill, would present all kinds of extraordinary transformations of human face, and would be much dilated in size—above all, I say, I knew that there was an extraordinary tendency in all these people sooner or later to settle down into the likeness of Joe [*GE* 462–463].

The apparent changing of faces and people in Pip's dreams is an effect described by Freud as dream condensation, "The construction of collective and composite persons is one of the principal methods of dream-condensation." (258). According to Freud, condensation is one of the primary attributes of dreaming and condensation is a way in which the dream content may escape censorship. Dream censorship opposes the primary function of a dream, which is wish-fulfillment, and censorship acts through distortion or disguise. In the case of Pip's dream, the changing faces and people are condensed, distorted and combined. This condensation is an attempt to escape the guilt Pip feels for the poor treatment of his brother-in-law, Joe Gargery and is a form of wish fulfillment. Ultimately, Joe's face is reconstructed from the myriad faces Pip sees in his dream. Pip's guilt is resolved some eleven years later, when he returns home after serving as a partner in a trading company located somewhere in the Far East (Dickens never actually gives an indication of where the trading house is located), and discovers that Joe's son has been named after him. Pip then realizes that the prospects for the baby's future will be different than his own. Further analysis of the dream reveals that Pip's wish is to escape from the exhausting work of suppressing his guilt, work which made him feel like a brick in the wall of a house or a steel beam in a vast engine.

Another dream distortion appears in *Martin Chuzzlewitt*, when Tigg Montague has a dream after arriving at an inn near Salisbury. Montague, Jonas Chuzzlewitt, and Bailey Junior were passengers in a coach that crashed near Salisbury, where they were bound for a meeting with Seth Pecksniff. The meeting was arranged in order to induce Pecksniff to invest in their sham enterprise, the Anglo-Bengalee Disinterested Loan and Life Assurance Company. After arriving at an inn near Salisbury, Montague falls into an uneasy sleep in his room and has the following dream:

> After examining his chamber, and looking under the bed, and in the cupboards, and even behind the curtains, with unusual caution (although it was, as has been said, broad day), he double-locked the door by which he had entered, and retired to rest. There was another door in the room, but it was locked on the outer side; and with what place it communicated he knew not.
>
> His fears or evil conscience reproduced this door in all his dreams. He dreamed that a dreadful secret was connected with it: a secret which he knew, and yet did not know, for although he was heavily responsible for it, and a party to it, he was harassed even in his vision by a distracting uncertainty in reference to its import. Incoherently entwined with this dream was another, which represented it as the hiding-place of an enemy, a shadow, a phantom; and made it the business of his life to keep the terrible creature closed up, and prevent it from forcing its way in upon him. With this view Nadgett, and he, and a strange man with a bloody smear upon his head (who told him that he had been his playfellow, and told him, too, the real name of an old schoolmate, forgotten until then), worked with iron plates and nails to make the door secure; but though they worked never so hard, it was all in vain, for the nails broke, or changed to soft twigs, or what was worse, to worms, between their fingers; the wood of the door splintered and crumbled, so that even nails would not remain in it; and the iron plates curled up like hot paper. All this time the creature on the other side—whether it was in the shape of a man, or beast, he neither knew nor sought to know—was gaining on them. But his greatest terror was when the man with the bloody smear upon his head demanded of him if he knew this creature's name, and said that he would whisper it. At this the dreamer fell upon his knees, his whole blood thrilling with inexplicable fear, and held his ears. But looking at the speaker's lips, he saw that they formed the utterance of the letter "J"; and crying out aloud that the secret was discovered, and they were all lost, he awoke [*MC* 652–653].

Tigg Montague's secret, which was referenced in the dream, concerned Jonas Chuzzlewitt's involvement in the death of his father, Anthony Chuzzlewitt. Montague learned of Jonas's involvement in his father's death and attempted to blackmail Jonas with this knowledge. Montague's vacillation between knowing and not knowing a secret in the dream refers to Jonas's involvement in his father's death, and Tigg's hesitation in exposing Jonas's secret. The enemy referenced in the dream (who is also Jonas) was to remain behind doors in captivity but his bonds were constantly being broken. The entire sequence is an example of what Freud calls dream distortion. Freud explains the presence of composite faces and situations in dream, much like those situations which occur in Tigg Montague's dream, in the following passage: "The possibility of creating composite formations is one of the chief causes of the fantastic character so common in dreams, in that it introduces into the dream-content elements which could never have been objects of perception" (270). Seen in light of Freud's theory, Tigg's composite creations are an act of dream censorship; they are an attempt by Montague to expiate his guilt at having contemplated the blackmailing of Jonas. The final portion of the dream ends with the speaker forming the letter "J" (for Jonas) and crying out that the secret (of the blackmail) was discovered.

Prior to arriving at the inn near Salisbury, Tigg Montague and Jonas Chuzzlewitt were involved in a coach crash. In the crash, Tigg Montague was thrown from the coach and passed out. Jonas Chuzzlewitt attempted to kill him while Montague was unconscious but was prevented from doing so. Shortly after the coach disaster, while Jonas Chuzzlewitt was sleeping, he has a dream which contains several distortions:

> He dreamed at one time that he was lying calmly in his bed, thinking of a moonlight night and the noise of wheels, when the old clerk put his head in at the door, and beckoned him. At this signal he arose immediately: being already dressed in the clothes he actually wore at that time: and accompanied him into a strange city, where the names of the streets were written on the walls in characters quite new to him; which gave him no surprise or uneasiness, for he remembered in his dream to have been there before. Although these streets were very precipitous, insomuch that to get from one to another it was necessary to descend great heights by ladders that were too short, and ropes that moved deep bells, and swung and swayed as they were clung to, the danger gave him little emotion beyond the first thrill of terror: his anxieties being concentrated on his dress, which was quite unfitted for some festival that was about to be holden there, and in which he had come to take a part. Already, great crowds began to fill the streets, and in one direction myriads of people came rushing down an interminable perspective, strewing flowers and making way for others on white horses, when a terrible figure started from the throng, and cried out that it was the Last Day for all the world. The cry being spread, there was a wild hurrying on to Judgment; and the press became so great that he and his companion (who was constantly changing, and was never the same man two minutes together, though he never saw one man come or another go) stood aside in a porch, fearfully surveying the multitude; in which there were many faces that he knew, and many that he did not know, but dreamed he did; when all at once a struggling head rose up among the rest—and denounced him as having appointed that direful day to happen. They closed together. As he strove to free the hand in which he held a club, and strike the blow he had so often thought of, he started to the knowledge of his waking purpose and the rising of the sun [MC 721].

The elements of dream distortion are evident in this passage: the street names change constantly; he is unable to attain his destination because of a series of ladders, ropes and bells which change shape as he attempts to scale them; his dress in not appropriate for the festival that was proceeding; he encounters a companion whose face was constantly changing; the faces in the crowd change as they await the Judgment Day. All these changing events point to an anxiety, a fear that something will not be accomplished. That something, of course, is the murder of Tigg Montague which Jonas failed to accomplish when the coach overturned, and which would have kept his secret safe. The dream also points to Jonas's guilt for plotting Tigg's murder; he is accused by the mob of bringing about the final Judgment Day, in other words, for attempting to murder Tigg.

As noted earlier, there is a connection between dreams, myth, fables, fairy-tales and symbols both in the writings of Sigmund Freud, and in Dickens. Myths, fables and fairy-tales attempt to construct a world-view that makes sense of the seemingly chaotic events that occur in our daily lives.[2] Dickens attempts, through the use of dreams, symbols and myth-making to develop a world-view that makes sense of the seeming chaos that permeates life in Victorian England.

In *Little Dorrit*, Dickens makes use of a fairy-tale, one which Little Dorrit told to Maggy, her friend ravaged by fever at the age of ten, a fever which left Maggy mentally limited. In the tale, a tiny woman sits by her spinning wheel and is befriended by a princess. The princess is admitted to the tiny woman's house and asks to see the tiny woman's secret; the secret turns out to be the shadow of a man who passed by once and the shadow has assumed a kind of life as a memory of that man. Upon the death of the tiny woman, the shadow was buried along with her. This particular tale is an allegory for Little Dorrit, who is also a seamstress, and who is prepared to carry her love for Arthur Clenham, who represents the shadow in the fairy-tale, with her to the grave. In a letter written to Arthur Clenham after her family's departure from Venice, Little Dorrit confesses that she has "always dreamed of myself as a child learning to do needlework," and that she dreams more in the outside world than she did while in the Marshalsea Prison (*LD* 281). Dickens uses the reference of the tale of the little seamstress to connect Little Dorrit to the tiny woman. Both Little Dorrit and the tiny woman are seamstresses and both suffer from unrequited love. Both have names which denote their small stature: Little Dorrit, and the tiny woman. Dickens's use of the fairy tale reinforces Freud's claim that fairy tales play a role in the collective unconscious of people, because neither Maggy nor Little Dorrit consciously acknowledge the connection between the figure of the tiny woman and Little Dorrit.

Illustration by H.K. Browne (Phiz) of Little Dorrit and Maggy in the novel *Little Dorrit*. In this illustration, Little Dorrit tells Maggy a fairy-tale of a little seamstress and her hidden love of a man who passes by her house. The tale is a metaphor for Little Dorrit's love for Arthur Clenham (Wikimedia Commons).

A more traditional form of fairy-tale or fable appears in *Pickwick Papers*, Dickens's first novel. The dream occurs after the Eatanswill election incidents in chapter 13, and is meant as an interlude between the continuing adventures of Mr. Pickwick and his friends. The story concerns a stagecoach bagman, who at the beginning of the story is alone in a driving rainstorm. He stops at an inn, where he meets a tall man vying for the affections of the inn's mistress, who is a widow. Retiring for the night, the bagman dreams that an antique chair tells him of the tall man's existing marriage, providing the means for the bagman to end the relationship between the tall man and the widow. The bagman, having disposed of his rival, marries the widow and settles in as the proprietor of the inn, a position which the bagman desired to occupy since his earliest days. The tale harkens back to the traditional fairy-tale, in which a wish is granted and the characters live happily ever after. The dream itself appears as a simple wish fulfillment, as noted by Freud "...frequently, and under the most complex conditions, dreams may be noted which can be understood only as wish-fulfillments, and which present their content without concealment" (191).

Dickens, in addition to using dreams as narrative devices, also used dreams as a form of social commentary. Smiley offers a perspective on Dickens's use of fairy-tales as an antidote to the mechanization that he saw gaining a foothold in Victorian London: "Dickens often told his friends that he had loved fairy tales as a child and that he still approved of them as an adult for their antidote to the dead, commercial, mechanical life that seemed to be taking over all around him" (30). A further example of the use of fairy-tales and allegory as an antidote to mechanization and commercialism is made in *Christmas Carol*. The story is so well known by now, with the appearance of the three spirits on Christmas Eve to save Ebenezer Scrooge, that it is taken for granted by many readers and is sometimes dismissed as being an overly sentimental paean to Christmas festivity. In the story, the spirits appear to Scrooge in dreams and are allegories for Scrooge's past, present and future; the tale itself contains elements of morality common to such folk stories. Yet there are a number of serious themes which appear in the work including the poverty of the working classes; the rise of utilitarianism which relegated the poor to work houses or prisons where they could be put to good use; the incidence of broken families and the lack of effective sanitary conditions for a large segment of the populace of Victorian London.

Scrooge's replies to the gentlemen seeking funds for the poor illustrates Dickens's feelings regarding the treatment of those less fortunate by the more affluent members of Victorian society; feelings which were espoused by practitioners of utilitarianism:

> "Are there no prisons?" asked Scrooge.
> "Plenty of prisons," said the gentleman, laying down the pen again.
> "And the Union workhouses?" demanded Scrooge. "Are they still in operation?"
> "They are. Still," returned the gentleman, "I wish I could say they were not."
> "The Treadmill and the Poor Law are in full vigour, then?" said Scrooge.
> "Both very busy, sir."

> "Oh! I was afraid, from what you said at first, that something had occurred to stop them in their useful course," said Scrooge. "I'm very glad to hear it" [Dickens, *CC* 12].

The charitable collectors, appalled by Scrooge's sentiments, reply that the workhouses and prisons are full and that many people would rather die than be consigned to such a fate, to which Scrooge replies: "'If they would rather die ... they had better do it, and decrease the surplus population'" (*CC* 12).

As a result of the visits by the first two spirits and his visit to the Cratchit family, where he witnesses the ill health of Tiny Tim, Scrooge begins to relent in his opinions concerning the poor. He inquires about Tim's health to the second spirit and is told that unless "'these shadows remain unaltered by the Future, none other of my race,' returned the Ghost, 'will find him here. What then? If he be like to die, he had better do it, and decrease the surplus population'" (47). The theme of poverty continues when the second spirit, the Spirit of Christmas Present, shows Scrooge mankind's two children brought forth by selfishness and want:

> From the foldings of its robe, it brought two children; wretched, abject, frightful, hideous, miserable. They knelt down at its feet, and clung upon the outside of its garment.
>
> "Oh man! Look here. Look, look, down here!" exclaimed the Ghost.
>
> They were a boy and a girl. Yellow, meagre, ragged, scowling, wolfish; but prostrate too, in their humility. Where graceful youth should have filled their features out, and touched them with its freshest tints, a stale and shriveled hand, like that of age, had pinched, and twisted them, and pulled them into shreds. Where angels might have sat enthroned, devils lurked, and glared out menacing. No change, no degradation, no perversion of humanity, in any grade, through all the mysteries of wonderful creation, has monsters half so horrible and dread.
>
> Scrooge started back, appalled. Having them shown to him in this way, he tried to say they were fine children, but the words choked themselves, rather than be parties to a lie of such enormous magnitude.
>
> "Spirit! Are they yours?" Scrooge could say no more.
>
> "They are Man's," said the Spirit, looking down upon them. "And they cling to me, appealing from their fathers. This boy is Ignorance. This girl is Want. Beware them both, and of all their degree, but most of all beware this boy, for on his brow I see that written which is Doom, unless the writing be erased. Deny it!" cried the Spirit, stretching out its hand towards the city. "Slander those who tell it ye! Admit it for your factious purposes, and make it worse. And bide the end!" [*CC* 56–57]

The Spirit ends the conversation with a reminder to Scrooge of his own advice given to the charitable collectors early in the tale: "'Are there no prisons?' said the Spirit, turning on him for the last time with his own words. 'Are there no workhouses?'" (*CC* 57).

In addition to the references to the workhouse and poverty made throughout the novel, there is the presence of broken families so common

Illustration of the Ghost of Christmas Present, by John Leech, used in *A Christmas Carol*. In the story, Scrooge is confronted by two children, who represent Ignorance and Want, and is admonished by the Ghost that the two children are mankind's creation (British Library, London).

in Dickens's writings. Scrooge is left at a boarding school early in the tale and is rescued by his sister, Fanny, in Stave II. Fanny dies in childbirth, leaving her son Fred, who is rejected by Scrooge at the beginning of the tale, an orphan. The Cratchits live in poverty, barely able to make ends meet, in Camden Town. The twin specters of Ignorance and Want are universalized to become exemplars of all victimized and orphaned children. Commenting on the presence of these broken families, Peter Ackroyd notes that, "In the phantoms of Ignorance and Want he glimpsed his own helpless and hopeless childhood, but he saw also the outline of Victorian civilization" (93).

Dickens's powers of observation, his grasp of mesmeric practice and his understanding of and use of dreams in his novels indicates his knowledge and use of psychology in developing three dimensional fictional characters. Further, his grasp of psychological concepts anticipates many of Freud's theories regarding dreams, reveries and the relationship between dream and myth. In his desire to reconcile himself to Victorian culture, Dickens uses dreams, fairy-tales and myths to make sense of a rapidly changing society that marginalized those who were somehow different or "other" than those in power.

CHAPTER FOUR

Society and Social Pretension

Dickens's concern with the social values of Victorian society began in the 1840s. By the time he finished *David Copperfield* in 1850 he was ready to embark on the writing of his greatest novels. He chose the themes for these novels carefully and wished to make a statement about the state of Victorian society and what he perceived to be its shortcomings. By the time he began work on *Little Dorrit*, his frustration with the state of affairs in England had reached a boiling point. In a letter to Austen Layard written on April 10, 1855, he expressed his wish that the people of England would "array themselves peacefully, but in vast numbers, against a system they know to be rotten altogether—make themselves heard like the Sea, all round the Island—I for one would be in such a movement, heart and soul..." (*SL* 42–43).

Dickens's ire was stirred by a society which placed great emphasis on misguided philanthropic endeavors, hypocritical religious practices and the reliance of money as a social panacea and a measure of the worth of individuals. His dislike of Parliament increased as he realized that there was little interest in that quarter in relieving the ills that were rampant in society. Edgar Johnson summarizes Dickens's views on the social system prevalent in Victorian Society in *Charles Dickens: His Tragedy and Triumph*:

> More and more, in fact, he found himself deeply and bitterly skeptical of the whole system of respectable attitudes and conventional beliefs that cemented all of society into a monolithic structure stubbornly resistant to significant change. He derided the pompous self-assurance of the aristocracy and hated the cold-hearted selfishness of the men of wealth. He despised the subservient snobbery of the middle class, which was "nothing but a poor fringe on the mantle of the upper." He was contemptuous of the corruption and inefficiency of the Government and bitter over the brutal workings of an economic system that condemned the masses of the people to ignorance, suffering, and squalor [I: 858].

The notion of philanthropic causes which concerned themselves with distant lands while ignoring the plight of the poor in England was particularly galling to Dickens. For Dickens, it was more important to address the poor educational systems, unsanitary conditions in London and the squalid working conditions of the factories and workhouses than to be concerned with the "telescopic philanthropy" of a Mrs. Jellyby in *Bleak House*. Upon making the acquaintance of Mrs. Jellyby, Esther, Guppy, Richard and Ada, Mrs. Jellyby declaimed about the importance of her mission in aiding the natives of Africa:

> ... "you find me, my dears, as usual, very busy; but that you will excuse. The African project at present employs my whole time. It involves me in correspondence with public bodies, and with private individuals anxious for the welfare of their species all over the country. I am happy to say it is advancing. We hope by this time next year to have from a hundred and fifty to two hundred healthy families cultivating coffee and educating the natives of Borrioboola Gha, on the left bank of the Niger" [*BH* 38].

That estimable lady, whose sole concern was the aid of the inhabitants of Borrioboola Gha (a fictional state located in Africa), was at the same time completely insensible of the welfare of her own children. The introduction of Esther Summerson, Mr. Guppy, Richard Carstone and Ada Clare to Mrs. Jellyby was punctuated by the discovery that one of the Jellyby children, Peepy, managed to get his head lodged in one of the railings surrounding the entrance to the Jellyby domicile. Another of the children managed to fall down a stairway leading to the same entrance, a total of seven stairs; neither of these incidents aroused the least bit of concern in the breast of Mrs. Jellyby who was at the time immersed in her efforts on behalf of the Borrioboola Ghanians.

But Mrs. Jellyby's project never advances and she continues her correspondence to no avail. Nor does she ever pay attention in the least to her neglected children causing her oldest daughter, Caddy, to exclaim: "I wish Africa was dead!" (*BH* 44). In the next chapter of the novel, Esther Summerson attempts to upbraid Caddy Jellyby, intimating that she should be more cognizant of her duty as a child, when Caddy exclaims: "O! don't talk of duty as a child, Miss Summerson; where's Ma's duty as a parent? All made over to the public and Africa, I suppose! Then let the public and Africa show duty as a child; it's much more their affair than mine" (49). Dickens is at his finest here—using satire to point out Mrs. Jellyby's, and by extension all those who practice a similar form of philanthropy, obsession with projects that seek to provide education, a fair living, and sanitary conditions in a distant part of the world while neglecting to provide the same conditions at home or to provide basic care to their own children.

When Esther, Richard, and Ada return to their guardian, Mr. John Jarndyce, he inquires about their visit to the Jellyby house and asks their opinion of Mrs. Jellyby's enterprise. Esther answers for the three wards as follows:

> "We rather thought," said I, glancing at Richard and Ada, who entreated me with their eyes to speak, "that perhaps she was a little unmindful of her home."
> "Floored!" cried Mr. Jarndyce.
> I was rather alarmed again.
> "Well! I want to know your real thoughts, my dear. I may have sent you there on purpose."
> "We thought that perhaps," said I hesitating, "it is right to begin with the obligations of home, sir; and that, perhaps, while those are overlooked and neglected, no other duties can possibly be substituted for them."
> "The little Jellybys," said Richard, coming to my relief, "are really—I can't help expressing myself strongly, sir—in a devil of a state" [*BH* 65].

That Dickens was contemptuous of those who pretended to be concerned with philanthropy in distant places while neglecting the needs of those closer to home is noted by Edgar Johnson who writes about *Bleak House*: "Many other readers were disturbed and bewildered by Dickens's bitter ironies on the missionary zeal that worried about savages abroad and felt no concern for its own homeless waifs ... and then ignored them [England's needy children] or made benevolence a device for bullying the poor" (II: 760–761). The juxtaposition of "telescopic philanthropy" and the needs of the residents of London is made more pronounced by the suit of Jarndyce versus Jarndyce in Chancery Court. Embroiled in the heart of the suit is a property known as "Tom-All-Alones," where contagion and plague are bred, where people live in abject poverty and where light itself seems to be reticent to penetrate. "Tom-All-Alones" is therefore the visible manifestation of the workings of "telescopic philanthropy," a place where the residents of Borrioboola Gha would be loath to enter.

But the number of philanthropic personages in *Bleak House* was not limited to Mrs. Jellyby. As Esther and Ada began to help Mr. Jarndyce with his correspondence, they discovered that he was petitioned for money from all sides, and were astonished that:

> ... the great object of the lives of nearly all of his correspondents appeared to be to form themselves into committees for getting in and laying out money. The ladies were as desperate as the gentlemen; indeed, I think they were even more so. They threw themselves into committees in the most impassioned manner, and collected subscriptions with a vehemence quite extraordinary. It appeared to us that some of them must pass their whole lives in dealing out subscriptions-cards to the whole Post-office Directory—shilling cards, half-crown cards, half-sovereign cards, penny cards. They wanted everything. They wanted wearing apparel, they wanted linen rags, they wanted money,

they wanted coals, they wanted soup, they wanted interest, they wanted autographs, they wanted flannel, they wanted whatever Mr. Jarndyce had—or had not. Their objects were as various as their demands. They were going to raise new buildings, they were going to pay off debts on old buildings, they were going to establish in a picturesque building (engraving of proposed West Elevation attached) the Sisterhood of Mediaeval Marys; they were going to give a testimonial to Mrs. Jellyby; they were going to have their Secretary's portrait painted, and presented to his mother-in-law, whose deep devotion to him was well known; they were going to get up everything, I really believe, from five hundred thousand tracts to an annuity, and from a marble monument to a silver tea-pot. They took a multitude of titles. They were the Women of England, the Daughters of Britain, the Sisters of all the Cardinal Virtues separately, the Females of America, the Ladies of a hundred denominations [BH 100].

Into the midst of this collected multitude strode Mrs. Pardiggle, whom Dickens portrays as being possessed of a "rapacious benevolence." She was an associate of Mrs. Jellyby, and she, like Mrs. Jellyby, presided over a tribe of children. Each of Mrs. Pardiggle's children practiced a form of her own brand of "telescopic philanthropy." One of the children donated his funds to a band of Tockahoopoo Indians; another to the Great National Smithers Testimonial; the next to the fund for Superannuated Widows; the youngest enrolled himself into the Infant Bonds of Joy, whose mission was to eliminate the use of "tobacco in any form." Esther, upon meeting Mrs. Pardiggle and the little practitioners of "rapacious benevolence" remarked that:

We had never seen such dissatisfied children. It was not merely that they were weazen and shrivelled—though they were certainly that too—but they looked absolutely ferocious with discontent. At the mention of the Tockahoopoo Indians, I could really have supposed Egbert to be one of the most baleful members of that tribe, he gave me such a savage frown. The face of each child, as the amount of his contribution was mentioned, darkened in a peculiarly vindictive manner, but his was by far the worst. I must except, however, the little recruit into the infant Bonds of Joy; who was stolidly and evenly miserable [BH 101].

One imagines Dickens grinding his pen into the paper on which he wrote as he enumerates the ridiculous and wasteful practices of these misguided philanthropists. Not only were these philanthropists ignoring the intolerable conditions which existed in England for those less fortunate, they were coercing their children into endorsing their own misguided charitable efforts.

Dickens's disdain for these moralizing but ineffectual philanthropists is matched by his loathing of organized religion, which professed to obey the teachings of Jesus with regard to the poor and less fortunate but which in reality is too often intent on making life pleasant for the practitioners of the various religious institutions. In a letter to David Macrae, a United Presbyterian Minister sent in 1861, Dickens replies to Macrae's charge that he does not provide Christian guidance in his novels. Dickens, in his response, refers to his attempt to inculcate the teachings of the New Testament in his novels and objects to the use of the Bible to justify men's actions:

> I have so strong an objection to *mere* professions of religion, and to the audacious interposition of vain and ignorant men between the sublime simplicity of the New Testament and the general human mind to which our Saviour addressed it, that I urge that objection as strongly and as positively as I can. In my experience, true practical Christianity has been very much obstructed by the conceit against which I protest.... With a deep sense of my great responsibility always upon me when I exercise my art, one of my most constant and most earnest endeavours has been to exhibit in all my good people some faint reflections of the teachings of our great Master, and unostentatiously to lead the reader up to those teachings of the great source of all moral goodness. All my strongest illustrations are derived from the New Testament: all my social abuses are shown as departures from its spirit; all my good people are humble, charitable, faithful, and forgiving. Over and over again, I claim them in express words as disciples of the Founder of our religion; but I must admit that to a man (or woman) they all arise and wash their faces, and do not appear unto men to fast. Furthermore, I devised a new kind of book for Christmas years ago (which has since been imitated all over England, France, and America), absolutely impossible, I think, to be separated from the exemplification of the Christian virtues and the inculcation of the Christian precepts. In every one of those books there is an express text preached on, and the text is always taken from the lips of Christ [*SL* 364].

There are two characters in his novels who stand in stark contrast to Dickens's belief in embodying the principles of Jesus and who are meant to portray the antithesis of Christian virtue: The Reverend Chadband in *Bleak House*, and Mrs. Clenham in *Little Dorrit*. The reader is acquainted with the Reverend Chadband in chapter 19 of the novel, when, during the course of the long vacation in Chancery Court, Mr. Snagsby, a law-stationer, holds a get together at his house. Mr. Chadband is introduced as follows:

> The expected guests are rather select than numerous, being Mr. and Mrs. Chadband, and no more. From Mr. Chadband's being much given to describe himself, both verbally and in writing, as a vessel, he is occasionally mistaken by strangers for a gentlemen connected with navigation; but he is, as he expresses it "in the ministry." Mr. Chadband is attached to no particular denomination... [*BH* 258–259].

Dickens goes on to write that Mr. Chadband "is rather a consuming vessel—the persecutors say a gorging vessel; and can wield such weapons of the flesh as a knife and fork, remarkably well" (*BH* 259). Continuing in his description of the good Reverend, Dickens relates that "Mr. Chadband is a large yellow man, with a fat smile, and a general appearance of having a good deal of train oil in his system" (*BH* 260). The sarcasm is piled on thickly in these passages: Mr. Chadband is a "vessel," which is ordinarily meant to denote a person filled with the presence of grace; in the case of the yellow Mr. Chadband his vessel is filled with train oil and foodstuffs. Rather than wielding his virtue as a weapon against the wages of sin, the Reverend Mr. Chadband wields the knife and fork, the better to suffuse his body with the comestibles he favors.

The meal at Snagsby's is interrupted by a constable, who delivers Jo, a poor street sweeper in the vicinity of "Tom-All-Alones," into Mr. Snagsby's custody. Jo, the illiterate orphan, is clearly out of his element in Snagsby's house and under the best of circumstances, barely able to eke out a living sweeping the filthy, disease plagued streets of Tom-All-Alone's. Mr. Chadband, having finished his dinner and being a paragon of morality, delivers an impromptu speech meant to suffuse Jo with a sense of his own place in society:

> "My friends" says Chadband, "we have partaken, in moderation" (which was certainly not the case so far as he was concerned), "of the comforts which have been provided for us. May this house live upon the fatness of the land; may corn and wine be plentiful therein; may it grow, may it thrive, may it prosper, may it advance, may it proceed, may it press forward! But, my friends, have we partaken of anything else? We have. My friends, of what else have we partaken? Of spiritual profit? Yes. From whence have we derived that spiritual profit? My young friend, stand forth!"
>
> Jo, thus apostrophized, gives a slouch backward, and another slouch forward, and another slouch to each side, and confronts the eloquent Chadband, with evident doubts of his intentions.
>
> "My young friend," says Chadband, "you are to us a pearl, you are to us a diamond, you are to us a gem, you are to us a jewel. And why, my young friend?"
>
> "*I* don't know," replies Jo. "I don't know nothink."
>
> "My young friend," says Chadband, "it is because you know nothing that you are to us a gem and jewel. For what are you, my young friend? Are you a beast of the field? No. A bird of the air? No. A fish of the sea or river? No. You are a human boy, my young friend. A human boy. O glorious to be a human boy! And why glorious, my young friend? Because you are capable of receiving the lessons of wisdom, because you are capable of profiting by this discourse which I now deliver for your good, because you are not a stick, or a staff, or a stock, or a stone, or a post or a pillar" [*BH* 267–268].

Chadband's words to Jo are a mockery of the Gospel of Matthew.[1] As a religious man, Chadband should be aware of the meaning of this passage. Instead, he perverts its meaning with his references to foodstuffs which he consumes while at the same time making Jo, who should be the beneficiary of his kindness, feel uncomfortable.

Chadband does not really care for Jo, although he apostrophizes him as a creature of God. Jo is left to wander the desolate streets of "Tom-All-Alone's" and eventually dies of a pestilence that sweeps through the section of town mired in the Chancery Court case of Jarndyce versus Jarndyce.

Chadband acts as a symbol of all that is wrong with organized religion in Victorian society, a religion that prided itself on implementing the message of the New Testament on behalf of the poor and less fortunate but, in reality, ignored the spirit of that message which was to assuage the sufferings of the poor. He also acts as a symbol of the materialism that pervades Victorian society; a consumerism that is manifest in his insatiable appetite and his comparison to a steam engine that requires constant oiling to function properly. Chadband is the embodiment of what Carlyle terms the "Mechanical Age" in "Signs of the Times," and his religion "is found, on inquiry, to be altogether an earthly contrivance" (7).

If Chadband is the symbol of the failure of organized religion to implement Christian virtue, then Mrs. Clenham is the symbol of all that is wrong with attempting to impose the harshness of the Old Testament onto Victorian society. Dickens describes Mrs. Clenham's religion in the following passage:

> Great need had the rigid woman of her mystical religion, veiled in gloom and darkness, with lightnings of cursing, vengeance, and destruction, flashing through the sable clouds. Forgive us our debts as we forgive our debtors, was a prayer too poor in spirit for her. Smite Thou my debtors, Lord, wither them, crush them; do Thou as I would do, and Thou shalt have my worship: this was the impious tower of stone she built up to scale Heaven [*LD* 24].

She is a woman for whom vengeance was more important than love, her will more important than that of her Creator. The words Dickens uses to describe her all resonate with those contained in the darkest passages of the Old Testament: cursing, vengeance, retribution, destruction. The tower of stone that is referenced in the passage is meant to remind the reader of the Tower of Babel, and is a foreshadowing of the fate of Mrs. Clenham's house, which at the end of the novel, comes crashing down, just as the Tower of Babel crashed in Genesis.

The depth of Mrs. Clenham's belief in a rigid system of vengeance, a system in which there is no shred of compassion, becomes apparent in a meeting with the villain Blandois and Mr. Flintwinch, who is a partner of Mrs. Clenham's. The meeting was arranged by Blandois in preparation for an attempt to blackmail Mrs. Clenham with secrets about her past. During the meeting, Blandois reminds Mrs. Clenham of a family motto which appears on a watch given to her by her late husband; the motto reads "Do Not Forget." Mrs. Clenham gathers herself up and replies as follows to Blandois:

> "No, sir, I do not forget. To lead a life as monotonous as mine has been during many years, is not the way to forget. To lead a life of self-correction is not the way to forget.

> To be sensible of having (as we all have, every one of us, all the children of Adam!) offenses to expiate and peace to make, does not justify the desire to forget. Therefore I have long dismissed it, and I neither forget nor wish to forget.... I will say this much: that I shape my course by pilots, strictly by proved and tried pilots, under whom I cannot be shipwrecked—can not be—and that if I were unmindful of the admonition conveyed in those three letters [DNF, or do not forget], I should not be half as chastened as I am" [*LD* 182].

Mrs. Clenham invokes Adam as the father of the race and the originator of sin, forgetting that man was unable to redeem himself in the eyes of God and required Jesus to expiate man's sin. The pilots she refers to are ostensibly the Old Testament prophets but once again, she forgets that their prime purpose was to remind the children of Israel to adhere to the Lord's commandments, at times when they abandoned those commandments. In the Christian tradition, the prophets paved the way for the coming of Jesus who instituted a new commandment: to love thy neighbor.

Later in the novel, when Blandois is ready to spring his trap on Mrs. Clenham, she offers a glimpse into her childhood, a glimpse of the mind of a tortured woman whose repression has blighted everything around her: "Mine were days of wholesome repression, punishment, and fear. The corruption of our hearts, the evil of our ways, the curse that is upon us, the terrors that surround us—these were the themes of my childhood" (*LD* 394). Her comment that repression is wholesome indicates that she does not understand the nature of repression; in reality, repression is not wholesome and leads to serious psychological problems. This comment also suggests that she is not aware of the workings of her own psyche, for she has attempted to suppress any sympathetic human feeling and instead focus on the emotions of revenge and hatred. Her vitriol is saved for her husband, a man who turned away from her and sought love in another source; a source that provided him with a son, Arthur Clenham, and whose secret birth was source of the trap set by Blandois:

> No! "Do not forget." The initials of those words are within here now, and were within here then.... "Do not forget." It spoke to me like a voice from an angry cloud. Do not forget the deadly sin, do not forget the appointed discovery, do not forget the appointed suffering.... Yet, gone those more than forty years, and come this Nemesis now looking her in the face, she still abided by her old impiety—still reversed the order of Creation, and breathed her own breath into a clay image of her Creator [*LD* 394].

Mrs. Clenham's secret, finally disclosed, allows her to reveal the true nature of her anger: a husband who spurned her, a child not her own. As a result of this suppressed rage, she dares to dictate to God, to invoke His power to punish those who have opposed her; she has overturned the order of creation and has set herself up as a rival to her creator. Her pride is an echo of that of Lucifer who also set himself up as a rival to God.

In the characters of Chadband and Mrs. Clenham, Dickens exposes the hypocrisy of a social system that on the one hand attempts to promote Christian virtue and on the other hand does not attempt to ameliorate the suffering of the less fortunate members of society. For Dickens, the qualities of forgiveness, mercy, and compassion outweigh all the invective and cant surrounding organized religion in Victorian society.

Added to the list of social pretensions despised by Dickens is the notion that money is a panacea for all that is wrong with society. Dickens detested the men of business who cared nothing for the arts and "fancy," or imagination but who measured everything in terms of gain and profit. In a letter to Douglas Jerrold dated May 3, 1843, Dickens comments on a dinner he attended which marked the seventh anniversary of the founding of the Charterhouse Square Infirmary:

> Oh heaven, if you could have been with me at a Hospital Dinner last Monday! There were men there—your City aristocracy—who made such speeches, and expressed such sentiments, as any moderately intelligent dustman would have blushed through his cindery bloom to have thought of. Sleek, slobbering, bow-paunched, overfed, apoplectic, snorting cattle—and the auditory leaping up in their delight! I never saw such an illustration of the Power of Purse, or felt so degraded and debased by its contemplation, since I have had eyes and ears. The absurdity of the thing was too horrible to laugh at. It was perfectly overwhelming [*SL* 118].

The letter conveys Dickens's detestation of such events and the need for an ostentatious display of wealth which was felt by so many in polite society.

Dickens draws a picture of such a gentleman in the person of Mr. Merdle in *Little Dorrit*. Dickens is not content to merely scorn Mr. Merdle as he does the "City aristocracy" in his letter to Jerrold but emphasizes that viewing money as an end in itself, as a lifelong goal, leads to a sort of moral emptiness: " All people knew (or thought they knew) that he had made himself immensely rich; and, for that reason alone, prostrated themselves before him, more degradedly and less excusably than the darkest savage creeps out of his hole in the ground to propitiate, in some log or reptile, the Deity of his benighted soul" (*LD* 282).

If money is pursued long enough, moral emptiness ultimately turns into contagion, as the lust for money spreads through the populace:

> That it is at least as difficult to stay a moral infection as a physical one; that such a disease will spread with the malignity and rapidity of the Plague; that the contagion, when it has once made head, will spare no pursuit or condition, but will lay hold on people in the soundest health, and become developed in the most unlikely constitutions:

is a fact as firmly established by experience as that we human creatures breathe an atmosphere....

As a vast fire will fill the air to a great distance with its roar, so the sacred flame which the mighty Barnacles had fanned caused the air to resound more and more with the name of Merdle. It was deposited on every lip, and carried into every ear. There never was, there never had been, there never again should be, such a man as Mr. Merdle. Nobody, as aforesaid, knew what he had done; but everybody knew him to be the greatest that had appeared [*LD* 290].

The Merdle contagion spread to every district in town, from the Circumlocution Office to Bleeding Heart Yard, and infected everyone with the same effect: the desire for profit and easy money. Ultimately, Merdle is found out for what he is: a fraud, "...every servile worshipper of riches who had helped to set him on his pedestal, would have done better to worship the Devil point-blank.... For by that time it was known that the late Mr. Merdle's complaint had been simply Forgery and Robbery" (*LD* 362).

In these passages, Dickens makes it clear that the pursuit of money for its own sake leads to no good. As if the example of Mr. Merdle was not enough to convince his readers that money, by itself, cannot cure the ills of society, Dickens's later works, *Great Expectations* and *Our Mutual Friend*, hammer home the point so that it cannot be missed by even the most casual reader. As Edgar Johnson notes in his analysis of *Great Expectations*, the premise of Pip's expectations is founded on a bankrupt view of inheriting a fortune he did not earn:

There is a layer of criticism, however, in *Great Expectations* still deeper than this personal triumph over false social values. It pierces to the very core of the leisure-class ideal that lurks in the heart of a pecuniary society. This is symbolized in Pip's dream of becoming a gentleman living in decorative grandeur on money he has done nothing to earn, supported entirely on the labour of others.... Pip's "great expectations" were the great expectations of Victorian society, visions of a parasitic opulence of future wealth and glory, a materialistic paradise of walnut, plush, gilt mirrors, and heavy dinners.... And Dickens's analysis of the frivolity, falseness, emptiness, loss of honor, loss of manhood, and sense of futility that the acceptance of that ideal imposed upon Pip is a measure of the rottenness and corruption he now found in the society dominated by it [II: 989–990].

Pip is embarrassed by Joe Gargery, a man who labors honestly for his money and who provides the moral compass for the novel. Joe is the antithesis of everything Miss Havisham stands for: he is self-sacrificing, honest, kind, and humble; and yet, he is rejected by Pip as being too rustic, and therefore, not gentlemanly. Pip's idea of a gentleman is based upon the external trappings of dress, custom, and social grace. Joe possess none of these qualities yet in his manly love for Pip is the embodiment of true gentility, as Philip Hobsbaum notes: "The true gentleman is not recognized by varnish; certainly Joe has none. Instead, he has a deep consideration for others. More, he has his place in the world, and fulfills it admirably" (235).

Pip eventually learns Joe's true worth, but that appreciation comes at a cost. It is only after Pip realizes the effort that his real benefactor, Magwitch, went through in an attempt to transform Pip from a blacksmith's apprentice into a gentleman, that Pip experiences an epiphany. Magwitch ultimately loses his fortune by returning to England under penalty of death, a return motivated solely by his sense of gratitude for a kindness performed by a younger Pip. Magwitch also sees that his dream of transforming Pip into a gentleman was unsuccessful but he does not lose hope that somehow, Pip may become a true gentleman. It is only after Pip nurses Magwitch and performs true service without the prospect of recompense that Pip attains his place in the world, a sense of belonging that is not defined by money. At the end of the novel, Pip is chastened, a changed man. It is only by renouncing his goal of becoming a moneyed gentleman and man of substance that Pip discovers Joe's worth and his own place in society.

By the time he wrote his last complete novel, Dickens's vision of wealth as a transformative force in society reached its nadir. In *Our Mutual Friend*, wealth is symbolized by the dust piles of the Harmon fortune. Lest the reader think that dust was merely a collection of dirt, Dickens makes the point that the dust piles were composed of bones, rubbish, ordure, and decayed forms of every variety. Here, the garbage of human life was transformed into wealth, but it was a wealth that all aspired to but few would be fain to touch. Edgar Johnson notes the irony inherent in the image of the dust heap as both a source of wealth and a source of revulsion:

> The image of wealth as filth, the supreme goal of nineteenth-century society as dust and ordure, gave a deep and savage irony to Dickens's hatred for its governing values.... Ultimately the dust-heaps are magnified into an all-embracing metaphor of mistaken endeavor directed to the piling up rubbish, mounds marking the dust and ashes of buried aspiration [II: 1030–1031].

The dust heap is not the only means of making a living that is repulsive; Lizzie Hexam and her father, Jesse, act as watermen on the Thames, a euphemism for persons who make their living dragging dead bodies out of the river and retrieving valuables from the bodies or from selling the bodies for medical purposes. Here again, the concept of making money from human remains is seen as an indictment of a society that would sanction such methods, that would degrade the individual by forcing him/her to resort to such means to earn a living. Philip Hobsbaum comments on the notion of society in *Our Mutual Friend*, when he writes: "*Our Mutual*

Friend remains a trenchant attack upon that part of the System that most subjugates the needs of the individual: Money, and especially money for its own sake, the wrong use of money" (244).

In *Our Mutual Friend*, Dickens notes that wealth is derived from the very items men discard: the dust, bones and refuse that is unwanted, is transformed into wealth. Ultimately, the very bodies that men occupied in life are transformed after their death into a livelihood for other men. To Dickens, the ultimate end-game of a consumer driven society is that the society feeds upon itself and that its cast off garbage becomes more valuable once it is discarded. This is irony raised to the level of social invective—an indictment of the principle that money is an end in itself.

There is a common theme that runs through each of the subjects leading to a breakdown in society, according to Dickens; they are sanctioned, or at least tolerated, by the government. In a speech delivered at the Theatre Royal at Drury Lane on June 27, 1857, Dickens outlined his views on Parliament to those gathered for the occasion:

> I have not the least hesitation in saying that I have the smallest amount of faith in the House of Commons at present existing.... I was reading no later than yesterday the book of Mr. Pepys, which is rather a favourite of mine, in which he, two hundred years ago, writing of the House of Commons, says:
>
> > "My cousin Roger Pepys tells me that it is a matter of the greatest grief to him in the world that he should be put upon this trust of being a Parliament man; because he says nothing is done, that he can see, out of any truth and sincerity, but mere envy and design."
>
> Now, how it comes to pass that after two hundred years, and many years after a Reform Bill, the house of Commons is so little changed, I will not stop to inquire....
> I will merely put it to the experience of everybody here, whether the House of Commons is not occasionally a little hard of hearing, a little dim of sight, a little slow of understanding, and whether, in short, it is not in a sufficiently invalided state to require close watching, and the occasional application of sharp stimulants; and whether it is not capable of considerable improvement? I believe that, in order to preserve it in a state of real usefulness and independence, the people must be very watchful and very jealous of it; and it must have its memory jogged; and be kept awake when it happens to have taken too much Ministerial narcotic; it must be trotted about, and must be bustled and pinched in a friendly way, as is the usage in such cases [*SP* 57–58].

In *Little Dorrit*, he paints a picture of a system so derelict in its duties, so ossified in its structure, so caught up in its own self-importance, that it seems to exist for the sole purpose of conducting a business whose motto is "How not to do it." This venerable institution is known as the Circumlocution Office—literally the talking in circles office. Run by the Barnacle family, it is set up along the lines of an hereditary monarchy, complete with its own royalty and lines of succession. Like a poorly run monarchy, the spoils of government were distributed amongst the Barnacles, with little provision made for the public welfare: "Thus the Barnacles were all over the world, in every direction—despatch-boxing the compass ... on which there was nothing (except mischief) to be done and anything to be pocketed, it was perfectly feasible to assemble a good many Barnacles" (*LD* 203). Dickens begins chapter 10, book 1, by describing the Circumlocution Office:

> The Circumlocution Office is (as everybody knows without being told) the most important Department under Government. No public business of any kind could possibly be done at any time without the acquiescence of the Circumlocution Office. Its finger was in the largest public pie, and in the smallest public tart. It was equally impossible to do the plainest right and to undo the plainest wrong without the express authority of the Circumlocution Office. If another Gunpowder Plot had been discovered half an hour before the lighting of the match, nobody would have been justified in saving the parliament until there had been half a score of boards, half a bushel of minutes, several sacks of official memoranda, and a family-vault full of ungrammatical correspondence, on the part of the Circumlocution Office [*LD* 52].

Dickens's description of the functioning of the Circumlocution Office does not improve throughout the course of the novel; in fact, even the titular heads of government seem powerless to act contrary to the wishes of this august body: "It is true that every new premier and every new government, coming in because they upheld a certain thing as necessary to be done, were no sooner come in than they applied their utmost faculties to discovering How not to do it" (52–53).

A similar state of affairs exists in *Bleak House*, but in this novel, the non-functioning governmental body is the Chancery Court. As the novel opens, the reader is greeted with an unflattering view of the Chancery Court:

> The raw afternoon is rawest, and the dense fog is densest, and the muddy streets are muddiest, near that leaden-headed old obstruction, appropriate ornament for the threshold of a leaden-headed old corporation: Temple Bar. And hard by Temple Bar, in Lincoln's Inn Hall, at the very heart of the fog, sits the Lord High Chancellor in the High Court of Chancery [*BH* 4].

Later in the novel, when Esther, Richard and Ada have been introduced to their new home, Bleak House, Mr. John Jarndyce explains to Esther the basis of the case of Jarndyce versus Jarndyce and the workings of the Chancery Court:

> The lawyers have twisted it into such a state of bedevilment that the original merits of the case have long disappeared from the face of the earth. It's about a Will, and the trusts under a Will—or it was, once. It's about nothing but Costs, now. We are always appearing, and disappearing, and swearing, and interrogating, and filing, and cross-

filing, and arguing, and sealing, and motioning, and referring, and reporting, and revolving about the Lord Chancellor and all his satellites, and equitably waltzing ourselves off to dusty death, about Costs. That's the great question. All the rest, by some extraordinary means, has melted away [*BH* 95].

Here again is an institution running like some great perpetual motion machine. There is no rhyme or reason in the mechanism; it is built to run its course, indifferent to the needs of the people it was formed to serve. In the words of Horace Skimpole, the irresponsible friend to Mr. Jarndyce, "The universe makes rather an indifferent parent," and so does the Chancery Court.

The indifference of the Court eventually wears on the petitioners: there are no beneficiaries in the Jarndyce case; the money has been squandered by court costs and lawyer's fees. The harmless, addled Miss Flite awaits a judgment on the "Day of Judgment," and conflates a biblical resolution of justice with her long, drawn out, Chancery case. In her despair, she has named her birds as her Chancery case has dragged on. At the beginning of the case, the names of the birds are filled with optimism: "Hope, Joy, Youth, Peace, Rest, Life…" but as the case progresses, her hope for a settlement gives way to hopelessness, which is reflected in the names of her birds: "Dust, Ashes, Waste, Want, Ruin, Despair, Madness, Death, Cunning, Folly, Words, Wigs, Rags, Sheepskin, Plunder, Precedent, Jargon, Gammon, and Spinach" (*BH* 199).

Mr. Gridley, the Shropshire man, spends his entire life awaiting a judgment on a simple transfer of property, but that judgment is not forthcoming. As Mr. Gridley explains to Mr. Jarndyce, he is beset by a system which no longer answers to the needs of the people: "I have been in prison for contempt of Court. I have been in prison for threatening the solicitor. I have been in this trouble, and that trouble, and shall be again" (*BH* 213), all the while suffering because of the system.

Edgar Johnson provides an assessment of Dickens's views of the system which he believes permeates Victorian society:

No wonder, Dickens thought, that the mechanisms of society could not even serve their own masters efficiently, but were always breaking down—symbolic of their final collapse. Privilege could not function without corruption, and corruption undermined itself and the structure of which it was a rotten support [II: 821].

"The System! I am told, on all hands, it's the system," exclaims Mr. Gridley. It is a system which Dickens detests, a system which values social standing, wealth, and appearances and manifests disdain for the individual, the worker, and the poor. It is a system which places an honest man, like Mr. Gridley, in prison for questioning why the system no longer serves the people. It is a system Dickens experienced first-hand in Marshalsea Prison, and later witnessed as a law clerk. It is a system he reported on as a Parliamentary reporter, where much was said, but little actually was done or changed. It was a system that ran like a perpetual motion machine, but which accomplished nothing. It was a system which endorsed "telescopic philanthropy" while it neglected its own poor. It was a system that provided lip service to the notions of charity promulgated in the New Testament but failed to put those charitable notions into practice. It was a system that fed on its own waste, that valued human life at its end more than it valued the living man. It is a system that remains in place to the present day.

Beginning with the novel *Martin Chuzzlewitt*, Dickens arranged each of his books using an overarching theme, all of which addressed a particular ill which existed in Victorian society. His themed works emphasize Dickens's attempt to enact social, political, and personal reform in England. *Martin Chuzzlewitt* emphasized selfishness; *Dombey and Son* highlighted the effects of pride and greed on families and society at large. *David Copperfield*, although autobiographical in nature, emphasized the effects of bad parenting on the lives of children. Dickens returned to broad social themes with the publication of *Bleak House*, which pilloried the ineffective and outmoded workings of the Chancery Court. In *Hard Times*, Dickens criticized a school system that embraced the concepts of utilitarianism, while at the same time neglecting the arts, or as Dickens would say, "fancy." With the publication of *Little Dorrit*, Dickens envisaged a world transformed into a prison where society itself is incapable of escaping the bonds forged by the government, religious institutions, and the rigid class system of Victorian society. *A Tale of Two Cities* is a warning, a sort of parable and glimpse of what happens when class distinctions create a bifurcated society composed of those who possess wealth and power, and those who are powerless. *Great Expectations* inveighs against a society that values money and social standing over moral character and honor. *Our Mutual Friend* depicts a consumer society that feeds upon itself and ironically values its refuse more than the lives of its citizens.

In the case of *Martin Chuzzlewitt*, the theme Dickens wishes to portray is that of selfishness. As Philip Hobsbaum notes, Dickens was not entirely successful in realizing his goal of exposing selfishness in *Martin Chuzzlewitt*:

> From his various letters and comments, Dickens seems to have had the idea at first of exhibiting the vice of selfishness as manifested through all the branches of a large family. The scheme foundered in its very detail. Selfishness is an abstract concept,

and any attempts to make it concrete will take on many different forms. Moreover, the more compelling of those forms are liable to take over, in the shape of individual characters, and assert their independence vigorously [77].

Dickens must have sensed that *Martin Chuzzlewitt* did not adequately address the theme of selfishness and resolved that he would do a better job of addressing his organizing theme in his next novel. In the case of *Dombey and Son*, Dickens chose the theme of pride but allied that theme to the notion of commercialism and the ills of society that resulted from it. This choice led to a more coherent and successful novel; in fact, *Dombey and Son* was a commercial success and helped Dickens to gain back readers who were not pleased with *Martin Chuzzlewitt.*

The earlier novels, such as *Oliver Twist* and *Nicholas Nickleby*, while touching on the ills of society, were not organized under a central theme; moreover, they propounded a simpler view of society: if one worked hard and persevered, a person could achieve success and society's ills could be fixed. Richard A. Levine, in his article entitled "The Two Nations, and Individual Possibility," notes that as Dickens matured, his views of the complexity of society changed, as did his belief that personal effort alone could transform society: "Dickens came to perceive the intricate complexity of social and personal relationships which not only composed his culture but which militated against the significant change the early novels pointed toward" (174).

In a speech delivered on February 7, 1842 (on his 30th birthday) in Worcester Massachusetts, Dickens summed up his belief in the function of men in society:

Gentlemen, my moral creed—which is a very wide and comprehensive one, and includes all sects and parties—is very easily summed up. I have faith, and I wish to diffuse faith in the existence—yes, of beautiful things, even in those conditions of society, which are so degenerate, degraded, and forlorn, that, at first sight, it would seem as though they could not be described but by a strange and terrible reversal of the words of Scripture, "God said, Let there be light, and there was none." I take it that we are born, and that we hold our sympathies, hopes, and energies, in trust for the many, and not for the few. That we cannot hold in too strong a light of disgust and contempt, before the view of others, all meanness, falsehood, cruelty, and oppression, of every grade and kind. Above all, that nothing is high, because it is in a high place, and that nothing is low, because it is in a low one. This is the lesson taught us in the great book of nature. This is the lesson which may be read, alike in the bright track of the stars, and in the dusty course of the poorest thing that drags its tiny length upon the ground. This is the lesson ever uppermost in the thoughts of that inspired man, who tells us that there are "Tongues in the trees, books in the running brooks, /Sermons in stones, and good in everything" [*SP* 12].

As was the case in previous chapters the balance of the chapter focuses on a particular novel to illustrate the concept of social pretension in this case, *Dombey and Son*. In this novel, Dickens concentrates on arbitrary class distinctions, as well as the notion that money and materialism are more important than love and human relationships. His plan for *Dombey and Son* would explore the theme of societal ills and would focus, initially, on the figure of Paul Dombey, Sr., who was introduced to the reader early in the book:

> The earth was made for Dombey and Son to trade in, and the sun and the moon were made to give them light. Rivers and seas were formed to float their ships; rainbows gave them promise of fair weather; winds blew for or against their enterprises; stars and planets circled in their orbits, to preserve inviolate a system of which they were the centre. Common abbreviations took new meanings in his eyes, and had sole reference to them: A.D. had no concern with anno Domini, but stood for anno Dombei— and Son [*D&S* 2].

Here is a man so self-satisfied, so full of pride, that he would give Lucifer a run for his money—with the emphasis on money; perhaps in that regard, he should more readily be compared to Mammon in *Paradise Lost*. Dickens paints Paul Dombey, Sr., as being cold, aloof, and incapable of real love. Philip Hobsbaum notes Mr. Dombey's demeanor:

> Dombey is always represented in terms of snow, ice, marble; freezing into stone those who seek contact with him. Even the fire which is lit to warm his infant son retreats into distant feebleness in his presence. He represses emotion on all issues but one: his icy nature thaws for a moment to admit his son, then freezes with him into an unyielding block [102].

The love he professes for Paul Jr., is merely that of an extension of himself; he does not love little Paul for his own sake. Mr. Dombey's love of self and lack of love for Paul is demonstrated in the scene in which Paul Jr., is baptized. Here, Dickens apostrophizes the audience regarding the origin of baptism, and Mr. Dombey's lack of regard for that institution by indicating, "It might have been well for Mr. Dombey, if he had thought of his own dignity a little less; and had thought of the great origin and purpose of the ceremony in which he took so formal and so stiff a part, a little more. His arrogance contrasted strangely with its history" (*D&S* 57). Later in the novel, his employee, Mr. Carker the Manager, reveals the extent of his employer's pride when he informs Edith Skewton, second wife to Mr. Dombey, of the nature of his master:

> You do not know how exacting and how proud he is, or how he is, if I may say so, the slave of his own greatness, and goes yoked to his own triumphal car like a beast of burden, with no idea on earth but that it is behind him and is to be drawn on, over everything and through everything.... Mr. Dombey has had to deal, in short, with none but submissive and dependent persons, who have bowed the knee, and bent the

neck, before him. He has never known what it is to have angry pride and strong resentment opposed to him [*D&S* 628–629].

Mr. Dombey's lack of love extends to his daughter Florence, who is excluded from his life, presumably since she can offer him nothing that he values; that is, she cannot participate in the family business and perpetuate the family name. Yet, despite the lack of affection from her father, Florence remains true in her devotion to him, even when she is banished later in the novel. It is the family business that is important to Dombey Sr., and everything is viewed through the lens of the money to be made by the family business. Florence's introduction to the reader is inauspicious: she sneaks into the room to see her newborn brother, while Mr. Dombey contemplates his family and determines that he had no other children,

> —To speak of; none worth mentioning. There had been a girl some six years before, and the child, who had stolen into the chamber unobserved, was now crouching timidly, in a corner whence she could see her mother's face. But what was a girl to Dombey and Son! In the capital of the House's name and dignity, such a child was merely a piece of base coin that couldn't be invested—a bad Boy—nothing more [*D&S* 3].

Jane Smiley comments on the notion that value in the world of Mr. Dombey is based upon monetary gains and that people are also valued as a form of transaction: "*Dombey and Son*, like several other nineteenth-century works (*Vanity Fair*, for example, which was published at the same time, and *A Doll's House*, and "The Death of Ivan Ilyich") concerns the commodification of familial relationships" (68). This is the nexus of the book, the valuation of everyone and everything on the basis of their worth, not as human beings, but as commodities to be bought or sold. Indeed, the notion of trading in commodities extends to Mr. Dombey's wife who died giving birth to Paul; Mr. Dombey, at her death, expressed great sorrow for her loss: "...he would find a something gone from among his plate and furniture, and other household possessions, which was well worth the having, and could not be lost without sincere regret" (*D&S* 5); one wonders if he would have given as much thought to the breaking of a plate. Note too, the reference to Florence as a "piece of base coin that couldn't be invested" as a further indication of Mr. Dombey's value system. The fate of his second wife, Edith Skewton, was not much better; she was paraded around at parties for her beauty but was also unloved. She, however, applied tit-for-tat and gave back what she received to Mr. Dombey, with perhaps a little more gall and wormwood, when she ran off with Mr. Dombey's office manager, Mr. Carker.

Paul Jr., having been told by his father that money can purchase anything, asks why it could not purchase his mother's health, and is told that:

> ... money, though a very potent spirit, never to be disparaged on any account whatever, could not keep people alive whose time was come to die; and how that we must all die, unfortunately, even in the City, though we were never so rich. But how that money caused us to be honoured, feared, respected, courted, and admired, and made us powerful and glorious in the eyes of all men; and how that it could, very often, even keep off death, for a long time together [*D&S* 93].

In Mr. Dombey's eyes, money is all important; it forms the basis of every connection in society and defines a person's place within society. Love and sympathy have no place in a society governed by money; people are merely extensions of one's possessions, like plate or furniture. Mr. Dombey's explanation to Paul about the value of money points to an outward manifestation of its power—honor, fear, respect, admiration—it is never to be used to effect good. Angus Wilson, in his book *The World of Charles Dickens*, notes that in *Dombey and Son*, Dickens was finally able to integrate all rungs of society into his novel, and present in them the conflict of values based on money:

> ... it is well to say that in *Dombey and Son* he first achieves that complete social panorama towards which he seems to have been moving from the beginning of his career. For the first time, and with one stroke, he introduces the upper classes with complete success into this novel; and, what is more, makes their representatives stand for that very conflict of values which are the novel's total concern [208].

Of course, in a man as blind as Paul Dombey, Sr., is to anything not related to money, he is easily deceived by people who would flatter and appeal to his exaggerated sense of self-importance. Major Joseph Bagstock is one such fawning, servile character. In his unctuous, fawning, attitude he is similar to that later creation of Dickens, Uriah Heep. His greeting to Mr. Dombey prior to their taking a holiday after the death of the first Mrs. Dombey reveals a great deal about his character, "'Dombey,' said the Major, 'I'm glad to see you. I'm proud to see you. There are not many men in Europe to whom J. Bagstock would say that—for Josh is blunt. Sir: it's his nature—but Joey B. is proud to see you, Dombey'" (*D&S* 271). For his part, Mr. Dombey is quite unaware that Joey B. is a fawning toady: "He [Major Bagstock] was a man of the world, and knew some great people. He talked much, and told stories; and Mr. Dombey was disposed to regard him as a choice spirit who shone in society, and who had not that poisonous ingredient of poverty with which choice spirits in general are too much adulterated" (*D&S* 272). Joey B.'s appeal to Dombey, like everything else, is based on money—he was no poor spirit, meaning that he was not impecunious and therefore would not ask for money, which was the only thing that mattered to Dombey.

Richard A. Levine equates Major Joseph Bagstock to a parasite, an apt comparison for a man who latches on to the pompous and unaware merchant, Mr. Dombey:

> His selfishness is more akin to self-preservation, and given the nature of the society in which he operates (and which, indeed, went into the shaping of old J. Bagstock) he can translate self-preservation into a parasitic emulation of people like Dombey. But he is a human parasite and obviously will seek a new host when the present one loses the power to nourish. The parasite is bound to the host in accordance with a set of simple, rudimentary laws; loyalty, friendship, and faith are alien, if not fatal, qualities for the parasite. I chose the metaphor of the parasite, for the society Dickens is coming to describe in painfully sharp lines is, finally, parasitic [158].

Joey B. is not the only parasitic creature in this novel; so are Edith Skewton (later the second Mrs. Dombey) and Mr. Carker the Manager. Both prey upon Dombey, and in the end, abandon him for other prospects. Edith, as was mentioned previously, leaves Dombey for Mr. Carker, the Manager. She is a complex character who openly resents her mother for attempting to secure a favorable marriage for her and tells Dombey that she will not love him. In the following scene, prior to her marriage to Mr. Dombey, mother and daughter argue over the life Mrs. Skewton has arranged for her daughter:

> "What do you mean?" returned the angry mother. "Haven't you from a child—"
>
> "A child!" said Edith, looking at her, "when was I a child? What childhood did you ever leave to me? I was a woman—artful, designing, mercenary, laying snares for men—before I knew myself or you, or even understood the base and wretched aim of every new display I learnt. You gave birth to a woman. Look upon her. She is in her pride to-night."
>
> And as she spoke, she struck her hand upon her beautiful bosom, as though she would have beaten down herself.
>
> "Look at me," she said, "who have never known what it is to have an honest heart, and love. Look at me, taught to scheme and plot when children play; and married in my youth—an old age of design—to one for whom I had no feeling but indifference. Look at me, whom he left a widow, dying before his inheritance descended to him— a judgment on you! Well deserved!—and tell me what has been my life for ten years since" [*D&S* 394].

The themes in the novel are well represented in this scene: the valuing of money before everything else; the lack of love; the predatory, mercenary quality of mother and daughter; the poor parenting that Dickens was to return to in his novels. Dickens makes it clear that this is just the sort of woman that Dombey should marry: a woman who does not love him, is adept at appearing fair when in fact, she is foul; a woman who at the same time loathes herself for what she is doing. In Edith Skewton, Dombey has met his match.

Mr. Carker the Manager—his name and position are intertwined and inseparable—is another of the parasitic creatures in the novel, although his parasitic nature is different than that of Joey B. and is more akin to that of Mrs. Skewton (called Cleopatra in the novel with obvious sarcasm), Edith's mother. Dickens introduces Mr. Carker the Manager, in chapter 22, portraying the man at work:

> The general action of a man so engaged—pausing to look over a bundle of papers in hand, dealing them round in various positions, taking up another bundle and examining its contents with knitted brows and pursed-out lips—dealing, and sorting, and pondering by turns—would easily suggest some whimsical resemblance to a player at cards. The face of Mr. Carker the Manager was in good keeping with such a fancy. It was the face of a man who studied his play, warily: who made himself master of all the strong and weak points of the game: who registered the cards in his mind as they fell about him, knew exactly what was on them, what they missed, and what they made: who was crafty to find out what the other players held, and who never betrayed his own hand [*D&S* 298].

Mr. Carker the Manager, like Mrs. Skewton, is a scheming, predatory creature. He is Dombey's right hand and although he is allowed free rein in the office, he is never admitted into the social circles in which Dombey moves, and is, as a result, jealous of Mr. Dombey's possessions, including his second wife. The extent of Mr. Carker the Manager's hatred of Mr. Dombey is expressed in a passage in which Mr. Carker the Manager discusses the dislike of his employer with his brother, who is also an employee of the firm of Dombey and Son:

> "There is not a man employed here, standing between myself and the lowest in place (of whom you are very considerate, and with reason, for he is not far off), who wouldn't be glad at heart to see his master humbled: who does not hate him, secretly: who does not wish him evil rather than good: and who would not turn upon him, if he had the power and boldness. The nearer to his favour, the nearer to his insolence; the closer to him, the farther from him. That's the creed here!" [*D&S* 643]

The portrait of Mr. Carker the Manager is almost finished; Dickens gives the canvas one last touch when he adds the following paragraph:

> And although it is not among the instincts wild or domestic of the cat tribe to play at cards, feline from sole to crown was Mr. Carker the Manager, as he basked in the strip of summer-light and warmth that shone upon his table and the ground as if they were a crooked dial-plate, and himself the only figure on it. With hair and whiskers deficient in colour at all times, but feebler than common in the rich sunshine, and more like the coat of a sandy tortoise-shell cat; with long nails, nicely pared and sharpened; with a natural antipathy to any speck of dirt, which made him pause sometimes and watch the falling motes of dust, and rub them off his smooth white hand or glossy

linen: Mr. Carker the Manager, sly of manner, sharp of tooth, soft of foot, watchful of eye, oily of tongue, cruel of heart, nice of habit, sat with dainty steadfastness and patience at his work, as if he were waiting at a mouse's hole [D&S 299].

As it turns out, the mouse he was stalking was Edith Skewton but she was playing a game of her own. Mr. Dombey, blissfully unaware of the attentions of his underling for both his money and wife, continued in his own secluded world, grieving for the loss of his other self in the form of his son and believing that the world was indeed meant for the firm of Dombey and Son to exploit as a matter of right. But Mr. Dombey goes further than this; in his pride and arrogance and in an attempt to force his wife to his will, he appoints Mr. Carker the Manager as a mediator between Mrs. Dombey and himself:

"Mrs. Dombey has expressed various opinions," said Mr. Dombey, with majestic coldness and indifference, "in which I do not participate, and which I am not inclined to discuss, or to recall. I made Mrs. Dombey acquainted, some time since, as I have already told you, with certain points of domestic deference and submission on which I felt it necessary to insist. I failed to convince Mrs. Dombey of the expediency of her immediately altering her conduct in those respects, with a view to her own peace and welfare, and my dignity; and I informed Mrs. Dombey that if I should find it necessary to object or remonstrate again, I should express my opinion to her through yourself, my confidential agent" [D&S 595].

Mr. Carker is only too willing to accept the appointment as a means of laying his own trap for both Mr. and Mrs. Dombey. And so, a game of cat and mouse ensues; but this is a three-way game, with Mr. Carker the Manager, Mr. Dombey and Mrs. Dombey all participating. Later, when Mr. Dombey confronts his wife at dinner and informs her that her presence is required for a dinner party on the morrow, she refuses to attend the dinner and instead suggests that she and Mr. Dombey should become separated. Mr. Dombey rejects her suggestion with the following reproach:

"Good Heaven, Mrs. Dombey!" said her husband, with supreme amazement, "do you imagine that I could ever listen to such a proposition? Do you know who I am, Madam? Do you know what I represent? Did you ever hear of Dombey and Son? People to say that Mr. Dombey—Mr. Dombey!—was separated from his wife! Common people to talk of Mr. Dombey and his domestic affairs! Do you seriously think, Mrs. Dombey, that I would permit my name to be handed about in such connexion? Pooh, pooh, Madam! Fie for shame! You're absurd." Mr. Dombey absolutely laughed [D&S 658–659].

Mr. Dombey's arrogance is plain to see; he considers his wife's suggestion to be ridiculous, to say nothing of the fact that it would make his affairs a subject of gossip among common people. That he should be in any way associated with common people is Mr. Dombey's worst fear; he believes that his station is far above the common crowd, and as such, he should be deferred to on every possible occasion. This passage highlights Dickens's distaste for arbitrary class distinctions. Dombey, in his arrogance, is more worried about his standing in the eyes of the common people than in his wife's request to be excused from a dinner party designed to impress Mr. Dombey's associates. Mrs. Dombey's refusal to defer to him is unacceptable but she has her own game to play. She walks out of the house, never to return.

Edith's resentment of Mr. Dombey leads her to run away to Dijon, France, with Mr. Carker the Manager. She does this, not to please Mr. Carker, as he believes but in order to shame Mr. Dombey. At their meeting at an apartment in France, Mrs. Dombey informs Mr. Carker the Manager of her true nature, and of her position in society, a position which she does not covet. It forms the basis for her rejection of her husband, and of Mr. Carker himself:

> "I am a woman," she said, confronting him steadfastly, "who from her very childhood has been shamed and steeled. I have been offered and rejected, put up and appraised, until my very soul has sickened. I have not had an accomplishment or grace that might have been a resource to me, but it has been paraded and vended to enhance my value, as if the common crier had called it through the streets. My poor, proud friends, have looked on and approved; and every tie between us has been deadened in my breast. There is not one of them for whom I care, as I could care for a pet dog. I stand alone in the world, remembering well what a hollow world it has been to me, and what a hollow part of it I have been myself. You know this, and you know that my fame with it is worthless to me" [*D&S* 760–761].

The speech by Mrs. Dombey ties up several of the themes of the novel: the lack of love and respect for other human beings; the mercenary quality of Victorian society; the falseness of friends like Major Bagstock and Mr. Carker himself; the notion that value lies not within a person but in the external trappings of a person that can be used as a commodity; the lack of proper parental love and respect for children.

The novel winds down inexorably to an unhappy conclusion for the three principles in the game of cat and mouse. Mr. Carker the Manager is pursued by his employer, Mr. Dombey, for the damage done to the firm of Dombey and Son and secondarily for the seduction of his wife. After a series of chases involving Mr. Dombey and Mr. Carker, the latter is killed by a speeding train. The firm of Dombey and Son sinks into ruin through a series of bad moves orchestrated by Mr. Carker before abandoning the firm and Mr. Dombey is left bankrupt and alone. He is eventually helped by one of his former employees and a portion of his funds are restored to help him live, although at a greatly reduced standard of living. His daughter Florence, once banished from his sight, cares for him in his old age. Edith, with her cousin Feenix, moves to Italy but not before attempting to make some small show of reconciliation to Mr. Dombey for the love of Florence.

In this, his first novel to successfully integrate an overarching theme that was to permeate the entire work, Dickens chose to show how pride, along with commercialization and lack of love or human interaction, led to a corrupt society. That society is portrayed as being more concerned with outward appearances than with inner character, with viewing people as commodities to be consumed, than as unique individuals, worthy of respect and love. It is a society that is sharply divided into two groups: those who are wealthy and privileged, and those who are forced to rely on their cunning, servility, or ruthlessness to achieve their living in a society dominated by those more powerful than they. Jane Smiley comments on Dickens's view of society in his mature novels as follows: "Dickens's social vision is formed by the recognition that in the world around him there are few bonds of social responsibility or generous humanity linking class to class or individual to individual..." (54).

Yet, there is some sort of redemption in the novel. Mr. Dombey, after suffering a series of financial and personal setbacks, is nursed back to health by his formerly rejected daughter, Florence. The final scene in the novel is one in which Mr. Dombey, now old and white-haired, sits with his daughter, grandson and granddaughter. The boy's name is Paul, the girl, Florence.

> But no one, except Florence, knows the measure of the white-haired gentleman's affection for the girl. That story never goes about. The child herself almost wonders at a certain secrecy he keeps in it. He hoards her in his heart. He cannot bear to see a cloud upon her face. He cannot bear to see her sit apart. He fancies that she feels a slight, when there is none. He steals away to look at her, in her sleep. It pleases him to have her come, and wake him in the morning. He is fondest of her and most loving to her, when there is no creature by. The child says then, sometimes:
> "Dear grandpapa, why do you cry when you kiss me?"
> He only answers, "Little Florence! Little Florence!" and smooths away the curls that shade her earnest eyes [*D&S* 878].

Dickens was still relatively young when he wrote this novel. He still believed, as he did through the writing of *David Copperfield*, that good works and individual effort could transform society and the world. As he matured, his belief in good works remained, but his hope that they could transform society no longer existed.

CHAPTER FIVE

Ineffective Institutions

Dickens began *Hard Times for These Times* in 1854, and the novel was published serially in his magazine *Household Words*. The serial publication of the novel was not unique; Dickens preferred this method of publication.[1] His decision to publish the novel in *Household Words* was taken to boost sales of the magazine, which had recently declined.[2] The publication of the novel came after that of *Bleak House*, which looked at social ills through the lens of Chancery Court, and before that of *Little Dorrit*, which viewed social ills as permeating everything, much as prison life permeated the lives of the characters in *Little Dorrit*.

Like the novel preceding it, and the novel succeeding it, *Hard Times* takes aim at the social ills of Victorian society. In the case of *Hard Times*, that aim takes three separate, but related approaches: the notion that facts, and not imagination, are required in life; the ineffectiveness of government, and Parliament in particular to resolve society's problems; and finally, that Utilitarianism and unbridled capitalism are harmful to society. Jane Smiley offers an insight into the events which led Dickens to write *Hard Times*:

> The immediate inspiration for this shortest of Dickens's novels seems to have been a twenty-three-week-old millworkers' strike in Preston, where Dickens traveled for a look; he then wrote a long piece about the strike for *Household Words* at the beginning of February. Dickens had a long-standing interest in working conditions and workers' protests—he had, of course, touched on lower-class unrest in *Barnaby Rudge* and had intended to write about factories in *Nicholas Nickleby*. He set out his principles clearly in his essay: "that into the relations between employers and employed, as into all the relations in this life, there must enter something of feeling and sentiment; something of mutual explanation, forbearance, and consideration ... otherwise those relations are wrong and rotten to the core and will never bear sound fruit" [105–106].

In addition to *Hard Times* being the shortest novel Dickens wrote, it is also what some consider to be the most overtly moralizing novel. Smiley comments on the tendency of the novel to be didactic when she writes:

"A novel such as *Hard Times*, where the characters are acting as examples of ideas, always has the air of a cautionary tale or a parable and relies upon a set of beliefs shared between author and readers" (107). Edgar Johnson echoes Smiley's opinion that the novel is moralizing, noting that:

> In consequence, *Hard Times* is a morality drama, stark, formalized, allegorical, dominated by the mood of piercing through to the underlying *meaning* of the industrial scene rather than describing it in minute detail.... In the Gradgrind world there are to be no imagination, no fancy, no emotion, only fact and the utilitarian calculus [II: 803–804; 807].

Despite the tendency of the novel to brevity and a reduction of a number of characters to seemingly formulaic roles, the novel succeeds in its mission to discredit the three-headed monster of facts, ineffective government, and laissez-faire capitalism run rampant.

Dickens's attack of facts to the exclusion of imagination or "fancy" began in the eighteen-thirties, when he prepared to write *Nicholas Nickleby*. In February 1838, Dickens traveled to Yorkshire with his illustrator, Hablot K. Browne (Phiz), to visit a number of schools in Yorkshire which had gained notoriety for the poor treatment of students. His visit led to the inclusion of Dotheboys Hall, run by its sadistic schoolmaster, Wackford Squeers, in the novel. It is believed that Dickens's portrayal of Squeers was based on the life of William Shaw, who ran the Bowes Academy in Yorkshire; yet Dickens's attack against the administration of these schools is meant to be more universal in nature and not merely an indictment of a particular school. Dickens wrote a letter to his wife Catherine on February 1, 1838, regarding the trip to Yorkshire; it is short on details about the schools, with the notable exception of the mistress of a Yorkshire school who was rather eccentric and long on descriptions of the lodging and weather. Michael Slater provides a number of details about the trip to Yorkshire in *Charles Dickens*, and writes:

> On 2 February Dickens and Browne saw the one-eyed William Shaw, proprietor of Bowes Academy, one of the biggest schools in the area, and Dickens made a note to himself to research newspaper reports of prosecutions brought against this man fifteen years earlier after two boys had gone blind at his school. Later, he wrote about this "scoundrel" to the literary philanthropist Anna Marie Hall and about his stumbling on a gravestone in the local churchyard erected in memory "of a boy, eighteen long years old, who had died—suddenly, the inscription said; I suppose his heart broke ... at that wretched place [Shaw's School]" [116].

The Yorkshire schools were Dickens's first experience with a failing school system but it was not the last time he took an interest in schools. In 1843, he traveled to a "Ragged School" in Field Lane in an attempt to help Angela

Dotheboys Hall, illustration by H.K. Browne (Phiz) of the school where Nicholas Nickleby taught. It is believed that Dotheboys Hall is modeled after the Bowes Academy in Yorkshire and its headmaster, William Shaw (British Library, London).

Burdett Coutts establish a series of schools where poor children could receive an education.[3] His letter to Ms. Coutts, dated September 16, 1843, describes the condition he witnessed at the school:

I have very seldom seen, in all the strange and dreadful things I have seen in London and elsewhere, anything so shocking as the dire neglect of soul and body exhibited in these children. And although I know; and am as sure as it is possible for one to be of anything which has not happened; that in the prodigious misery and ignorance of the swarming masses of mankind in England, the seeds of its certain ruin are sown, I never saw the Truth so staring out in hopeless characters, as it does from the walls of this place.... The school is miserably poor, you may believe, and is almost entirely supported by the teachers themselves. If they could get a better room (the house they are in, is like an ugly dream); above all, if they could provide some convenience for washing; it would be an immense advantage. The moral courage of the teachers is beyond all praise. They are surrounded by every possible adversity, and every disheartening circumstance that can be imagined [*SL* 122–123].

The combination of the atrocities he witnessed at the Yorkshire schools, along with the poor conditions he saw at the Ragged Schools, led Dickens to attempt to ameliorate the conditions of students in these schools, and to act as an outspoken advocate of schooling as a means of improving conditions for the working classes. In a speech he delivered on December 30, 1853, at Birmingham for the benefit of the Birmingham and Midland Institute, just prior to the start of publication of *Hard Times*, Dickens expressed his views on the benefits of education for the working classes:

I have no fear here of being misunderstood—of being supposed to mean too much in this. If there ever was a time when any one class could of itself do much for its own good, and for the welfare of society—which I greatly doubt—that time is unquestionably past. It is in the fusion of different classes, without confusion; in the bringing together of employers and employed; in the creating of a better common understanding among those whose interests are identical, who depend upon each other, who are vitally essential to each other, and who never can be in unnatural antagonism without deplorable results, that one of the chief principles of a Mechanics' Institution should consist. In this world a great deal of the bitterness among us arises from an imperfect understanding of one another. Erect in Birmingham a great Educational Institution, properly educational; educational of the feelings as well as of the reason; to which all orders of Birmingham men contribute; in which all orders of Birmingham men meet; wherein all orders of Birmingham men are faithfully represented—and you will erect a Temple of Concord here which will be a model edifice to the whole of England [*SP* 48].

In this speech, in addition to speaking about the benefits of education, Dickens returned to one of the themes that he wrote about throughout his life: the separation of people into polar categories of "us" and "them." He believed that as people became better educated, these arbitrary distinctions between "us" and "them" would cease.

Dickens feared that an education which relied on facts alone, a reliance bred in the doctrine of Utilitarianism, would lead to a loss of imagination or "fancy" and would culminate in a citizenry that viewed everything in binary fashion; right versus wrong; black versus white; rich versus poor. Dickens believed that the theory of Utilitarianism, which propounded that society should be concerned with the greatest good for the greatest number of people, was too vague. Depending on whose definition of good was used, Utilitarianism could justify any number of practices

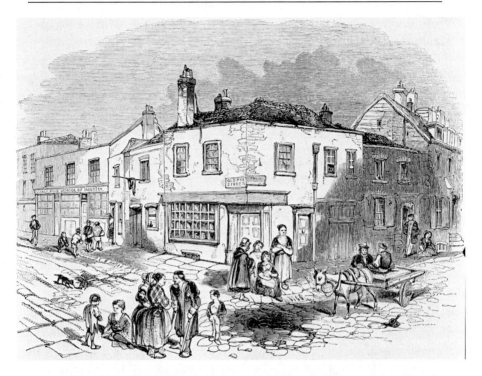

Ragged School, Old Pye Street; wood engraving by Frederick Napoleon Shepard, 1849. Dickens visited several ragged schools and helped administer a school located in Field Lane and supported by the philanthropist, Angela Burdett Coutts (London Metropolitan Archives).

which, in fact, might be harmful to society.[4] Karen Odden makes this point succinctly:

> I suggest that in *Hard Times* this word "something" repeatedly gestures towards Dickens's profound need to "express" his own apprehension about a Victorian habit of mind that made him almost unspeakably anxious: black-and-white thinking. I borrow this phrase from Dickens's working notes for the novel, in which he lists a series of possible titles, one of which is "Black and White." It is underlined twice. Like *Martin Chuzzlewitt*, which addresses the problem of Selfishness, and *Dombey and Son* (1846–1848), which addresses the flaw of Pride, *Hard Times* too has a single serious object of critique. For Dickens, black-and-white thinking effectively forestalls nuanced logic, intuition, sympathy, listening, forbearance, and compromise. As groups become further separated, conflicts grow and power struggles inhibit and even replace alliances. In chapter 6 of the third book, we see the end result of simplistic, extreme, binary logic: death. For Dickens, it is an insidious, dangerous, and widespread mode of thought that must be untaught [xxiv].

From the very beginning of the novel, Dickens strikes home with the opposition of fact to fancy when he introduces the reader to Mr. Gradgrind, master of the school in Coketown, who is:

> A man of facts and calculations. A man who proceeds upon the principle that two and two are four, and nothing over, and who will not be talked into allowing anything over. Thomas Gradgrind, Sir—peremptorily Thomas—Thomas Gradgrind. With a rule and a pair of scales, and the multiplication table always in his pocket, Sir, ready to weigh and measure any parcel of human nature, and tell you exactly what it comes to. It is a mere question of figures, a case of simple arithmetic [*HT* 10].

When Mr. Gradgrind invites a government official to address the students the officer asks whether the students would paper a room with representations of horses, of which half the room believes that such a representation would be acceptable, while the other half expresses the opinion that a representation would be incorrect. He responds to them as follows: "'Of course, No,' said the gentleman, with an indignant look at the wrong half. 'Why, then, you are not to see anywhere, what you don't see in fact; you are not to have anywhere, what you don't have in fact. What is called Taste, is only another name for Fact'" (*HT* 13). When Sissy Jupe questions the government official's opinion about wallpaper that featured horses, she is admonished that, "'Ay, ay, ay! But you mustn't fancy,' cried the gentleman, quite elated by coming so happily to his point. 'That's it! You are never to fancy'" (*HT* 14). As if this rejoinder were not enough to settle the argument once and for all, the official announces that: "'We hope to have, before long, a board of fact, composed of commissioners of fact, who will force the people to be a people of fact, and of nothing but fact'" (*HT* 14).

When Mr. Gradgrind finds his children at Mr. Sleary's circus, an amusement devoted to equestrian activities, he is stunned and asks his children why they are at such a place:

> "In the name of wonder, idleness, and folly!" said Mr. Gradgrind, leading each away by a hand; "what do you do here?"
> "Wanted to see what it was like," returned Louisa, shortly.
> "What it was like?"
> "Yes, father."
> There was an air of jaded sullenness in them both, and particularly in the girl: yet, struggling through the dissatisfaction of her face, there was a light with nothing to rest upon, a fire with nothing to burn, a starved imagination keeping life in itself somehow, which brightened its expression. Not with the brightness natural to cheerful youth, but with uncertain, eager, doubtful flashes, which had something painful in them, analogous to the changes on a blind face groping its way [*HT* 19].

In this passage, Dickens makes it plain that there is something missing in the life of the Gradgrind children; a something that Mr. Gradgrind does not see or comprehend, with his constrained view that education and life itself should be limited to facts. Mr. Gradgrind, talking to his associate, Josiah Bounderby, about finding his children at Sleary's circus asks

"whether any instructor or servant can have suggested anything? Whether Louisa or Thomas can have been reading anything? Whether, in spite of all precautions, any idle story-book can have got into the house? Because, in minds that have been practically formed by the rule and line, from the cradle upwards, this is so curious, so incomprehensible" [*HT* 24–25].

The incongruousness of the situation is much appreciated by Mr. Bounderby, who is also a man of facts and figures, as well as being a responsible proprietor of one of the largest factories in Coketown. The person of Bounderby, and his position as one of the owners of the manufactory in Coketown, leads the narrator to speculate rhetorically that there is a connection between the Gradgrind children and the workers in the Coketown factories:

Is it possible, I wonder, that there was any analogy between the case of the Coketown population and the case of the little Gradgrinds? Surely, none of us in our sober senses and acquainted with figures, are to be told at this time of day, that one of the foremost elements in the existence of the Coketown working-people had been for scores of years deliberately set at nought? That there was any Fancy in them demanding to be brought into healthy existence instead of struggling on in convulsions? That exactly in the ratio as they worked long and monotonously, the craving grew within them for some physical relief—some relaxation, encouraging good humour and good spirits, and giving them a vent—some recognized holiday, though it were but for an honest dance to a stirring band of music—some occasional light pie in which even M'Choakumchild had no finger—which craving must and would be satisfied aright, or must and would inevitably go wrong, until the laws of the Creation were repealed? [*HT* 29–30]

In this direct address to his readers, Dickens is explicitly linking the concepts of a misguided educational system and of unbridled capitalism together. If both focused solely on facts and efficiency, to the exclusion of everything else including "fancy," it would lead to disaster. On several occasions Dickens commented on the necessity of providing amusements, or "fancy" as he termed it, for the working class. In *Sketches by Boz*, he wrote about the sights at Vauxhall Gardens and at Astley's Circus; sights which provided affordable amusements for the working classes. In *A Christmas Carol*, he railed against the Poor Laws which resulted in the formation of workhouses in order to discourage those who were destitute from becoming "idle," as the supporters of these laws maintained. In addition, Dickens leveled an attack against a growing tide of Sabbatarianism which sought to prohibit entertainment on Sundays and which was alluded to in *A Christmas Carol* when Scrooge blamed the Spirit of Christmas

Present of wishing to deny amusements to the poor.[5] The linking of a misguided educational system and unbridled capitalism is made more explicit when Misters Gradgrind and Bounderby journey with Sissy Jupe, girl number twenty in Mr. Gradgrind's school, to Sleary's Circus to speak to Sissy's father. While at the circus the proprietor of the establishment, Mr. Sleary, addresses the two gentlemen and explains to them that:

> "People must be amuthed, Thquire, thomehow," continued Sleary, rendered more pursy than ever, by so much talking; "they can't be alwayth a working, nor yet they can't be alwayth a learning. Make the betht of uth; not the wurtht. I've got my living out of the horthe-riding all my life, I know; but I conthider that I lay down the philothophy of the thubject when I thay to you, Thquire, make the betht of uth: not the wurtht!" [*HT* 45–46]

Yet, despite Mr. Sleary's somewhat distorted speech, his advice is worthwhile; unfortunately, neither Mr. Gradgrind nor Mr. Bounderby heed his advice.

Gradgrind's personality was established early in the novel. Dickens then proceeds to inform the reader about the personality of Josiah Bounderby, that bastion of capitalist efficiency, in the following quotation:

> ... [Bounderby was] a rich man: banker, merchant, manufacturer, and what not. A big, loud man, with a stare, and a metallic laugh. A man made out of a coarse material, which seemed to have been stretched to make so much of him. A man with a great puffed head and forehead, swelled veins in his temples, and such a strained skin to his face that it seemed to hold his eyes open, and lift his eyebrows up. A man with a pervading appearance on him of being inflated like a balloon, and ready to start. A man who could never sufficiently vaunt himself a self-made man. A man who was always proclaiming, through that brassy speaking-trumpet of a voice of his, his old ignorance and his old poverty. A man who was the Bully of humility [*HT* 20].

Mr. Bounderby, like all the other manufacturers in Coketown, believed in facts, and the facts pointed to the conclusion that the workers in Coketown were idlers, and not to be trusted. They were lazy, inefficient, and had to be prodded to work optimally. They were not even accorded proper names, but were referred to as "hands," as if they served one function only: to act as mere extensions of the machines on which they worked. According to Mr. Bounderby, "There's not a Hand in this town, Sir, man, woman or child, but has one ultimate object in life. That object is, to be fed on turtle soup and venison with a gold spoon!" (*HT* 126). According to Mr. Bounderby, the "hands" wished to live a luxurious life and must be forced to apply themselves to tending their machines. The implication is that the factory owners, and not the "hands," are the only ones who should be allowed to live in luxury. The reliance on facts allowed the factory owners to calculate to the smallest degree the amount of output that the "hands" could produce but like the schools where imagination was not taught and was left to languish, the factory owners could not understand the inner workings of their employees, as the narrator of the book makes clear in the following passage:

> So many hundred Hands in this Mill; so many hundred horse Steam Power. It is known, to the force of a single pound weight, what the engine will do; but, not all the calculators of the national Debt can tell me the capacity for good or evil, for love or hatred, for patriotism or discontent, for the decomposition of virtue into vice, or the reverse, at any single moment in the soul of one of these its quiet servants, with the composed faces and the regulated actions. There is no mystery in it; there is an unfathomable mystery in the meanest of them, for ever.—Supposing we were to reserve our arithmetic for material objects, and to govern these awful unknown quantities by other means! [*HT* 71]

Of course, if one of the "hands" objected that they were pushed too hard or paid too little, that the air in the factories was pestilent, or that there was little hope for the future, the manufacturers had a pat answer for them: work hard, and you too can make a fortune, just as I did:

> This, again, was among the fictions of Coketown. Any capitalist there, who had made sixty thousand pounds out of sixpence, always professed to wonder why the sixty thousand nearest Hands didn't each make sixty thousand pounds out of sixpence, and more or less reproached them every one for not accomplishing the little feat. What I did you can do. Why don't you go and do it? [*HT* 118]

The one salient point lost in such an argument is why would anyone continue to work in such conditions if he/she could miraculously transform sixpence into sixty thousand pounds?

Hobsbaum, commenting on the character of Bounderby, claims that he is not merely a capitalist, a man of facts, a self-made man but a sadist, not content unless he can inflict pain on others. This assertion is in line with his steadfast claim that he was abandoned by his mother and given to his grandmother to be raised. She was a wicked old woman addicted to strong drink, and who sold his shoes in order to procure alcohol. This treatment fuels his need to inflict on others what he himself experienced:

> An assertion of will for Bounderby evidently has no satisfaction unless it involves the deprivation or misery of someone else. Put another way; Bounderby cannot see that anyone is in his power unless they are undergoing conditions which no one in their right mind would possibly seek. No doubt Bounderby can justify polluting the atmosphere and misusing the Hands; Utilitarianism is a highly subjectivist creed and can be used to justify almost anything [181].

By having Gradgrind elected to Parliament for the district of Coketown, Dickens is able to unite the three themes of the work in the persons of Bounderby and Gradgrind. Both characters believe in facts and disdain imagination. Bounderby is seen as the ultimate capitalist who ruthlessly works his "hands" to extract the last bits of efficiency he can from them. Gradgrind is a representative of a governing body that caters to its own needs and offers no respite for the people it is intended to serve. In a scathing indictment of Parliament, and the people who serve there, the narrator indicates that the election of Mr. Gradgrind to Parliament did not alter any aspect of that gentleman's character,

> Except one, which was apart from his necessary progress through the mill. Time hustled him into a little noisy and rather dirty machinery, in a by-corner, and made him Member of Parliament for Coketown: one of the respected members of the multiplication table, one of the deaf honourable gentlemen, dumb honourable gentlemen, blind honourable gentlemen, lame honourable gentlemen, dead honourable gentlemen, to every other consideration. Else wherefore live we in a Christian land, eighteen hundred and odd years after our Master? [HT 92–93]

In this passage, Dickens once again disparages a Parliament that he characterizes as ineffective. It is a theme that gestated during his time as a Parliamentary reporter and was born into the light of day in *Bleak House*, and was to emerge full-blown as the center of incompetence and nepotism that somehow gained control of all governmental functions, the Circumlocution Office, in *Little Dorrit*. Continuing his denunciation of the august body that was responsible for drafting legislation for England, Dickens makes an analogy between Gradgrind's office and an observatory, commenting:

> As if an astronomical observatory should be made without any windows, and the astronomer within should arrange the starry universe solely by pen, ink, and paper, so Mr. Gradgrind, in his Observatory (and there are many like it), had no need to cast an eye upon the teeming myriads of human beings around him, but could settle all their destinies on a slate, and wipe out all their tears with one dirty little bit of sponge [HT 95].

In the universe that was dominated by wealthy industrialists, it was expected that the legislators would be amenable to the interests of the manufacturers and neglect the interest of the "hands." If, for some reason, the Members of Parliament did not agree with those interests the industrialists would simply appeal to a higher authority:

> Whenever a Coketowner felt he was ill-used—that is to say, whenever he was not left entirely alone, and it was proposed to hold him accountable for the consequences of any of his acts—he was sure to come out with the awful menace, that he would "sooner pitch his property into the Atlantic." This had terrified the Home Secretary within an inch of his life, on several occasions [HT 111–112].

Thus, a parasitic relationship was established between the host, Parliament, and the parasite, the Coketown manufacturers. Dickens, no doubt, thought of this relationship as being an allegory for the actual relationship that existed between Parliament and the industrialists in Victorian England.

The denouement of the novel begins with the marriage of Louisa Gradgrind to Mr. Bounderby. At first, Louisa continues to believe in the strictures of her father and her husband but after visiting one of the workers at her husband's factory, she realizes that the system in which she was brought up does not apply to the lives of the workers. She recognizes that the workers are not:

> Something to be worked so much and paid so much, and there ended; something to be infallibly settled by laws of supply and demand; something that blundered against those laws, and floundered into difficulty; something that was a little pinched when wheat was dear, and over-ate itself when wheat was cheap; something that increased at such a rate of percentage, and yielded such another percentage of crime, and such another percentage of pauperism; something wholesale, of which vast fortunes were made; something that occasionally rose like a sea, and did some harm and waste (chiefly to itself), and fell again; this she knew the Coketown Hands to be. But, she had scarcely thought more of separating them into units, than of separating the sea itself into its component drops [*HT* 155].

This passage is an attack against the theory developed by Thomas Malthus, who proposed that there were arithmetical principles governing population growth, wealth formation, and employment; propositions which Dickens renounces in the novel. Louisa, although possessed of new-found knowledge, realizes that what she lacks in her life is not factual principles but imagination and love. She searches for these two qualities in her life and observes that her father and husband cannot provide them. In vain, she tries to find these qualities in another Parliamentary man, James Harthouse. Harthouse hints at his character when he tells Louisa that he, like other refined men in London, does not believe in the efficacy of Parliament to fix the wrongs plaguing society nor does he believe in imagination and has no sympathy for the "hands." He claims that MPs are men, "'Whom none of us believe, my dear Mrs. Bounderby, and who do not believe themselves. The only difference between us and the professors of virtue or benevolence, or philanthropy—never mind the name—is, that we know it is all meaningless, and say so; while they know it equally and will never say so'" (*HT* 162–163).

Despite the hints that Harthouse throws her way, she ignores them and eventually learns his true nature: he is selfish and self-satisfied, and as a result, she rejects him as a possible source of love. She returns to her father's house and leaves that of Mr. Bounderby, who renounces her. Mr.

Gradgrind, chastened by the death of his wife and Mr. Bounderby's treatment of his daughter, has a change of heart. He understands that there is more to life than facts and figures; that imagination and fancy have a part to play, as Mr. Sleary warned him years earlier.

When Mr. Gradgrind approaches Bounderby in an attempt at a reconciliation between husband and wife, he is met with a stern rebuke by the industrialist:

> "You have had your say; I am going to say mine. I am a Coketown man. I am Josiah Bounderby of Coketown. I know the bricks of this town, and I know the works of the town, and I know the chimneys of this town, and I know the smoke of this town, and I know the Hands of this town. I know 'em all pretty well. They're real. When a man tells me anything about imaginative qualities, I always tell that man, whoever he is, that I know what he means. He means turtle soup and venison, with a gold spoon, and that he wants to be set up with a coach and six. That's what your daughter wants. Since you are of opinion that she ought to have what she wants, I recommend you to provide it for her. Because, Tom Gradgrind, she will never have it from me" [*HT* 234].

There is no reconciliation between the two and Bounderby goes on his way, bullying people and exhorting them to pull themselves up by their bootstraps and make something of themselves, as he had done. Bounderby's claims to self-reliance, hard work, and lack of formal education, prove false when his mother, Mrs. Pegler, a mother he claimed had abandoned him, appeared at his house with Mr. Gradgrind present:

> "Josiah in the gutter!" exclaimed Mrs. Pegler. "No such a thing, Sir. Never! For shame on you! My dear boy knows, and will give *you* to know, that though he come of humble parents, he come of parents that loved him as dear as the best could, and never thought it hardship on themselves to pinch a bit that he might write and cipher beautiful, and I've his books at home to show it!" ... And I'll give you to know, Sir—for this my dear boy won't—that though his mother kept but a little village shop, he never forgot her, but pensioned me on thirty pounds a year—more than I want, for I put by out of it—only making the condition that I was to keep down in my own part, and make no boasts about him, and not trouble him. And I never have, except with looking at him once a year, when he has never knowed it" [*HT* 252].

One by one, the claims made by Bounderby, and by extension, the rich industrialists in Coketown and by the members in Parliament, come crashing down. The strict educational system practiced by Mr. Gradgrind and endorsed by Bounderby, produces stunted adults who, while filled with facts, lack imagination and love. The "hands," who are held in contempt by Bounderby and his cohorts, are seen to be better people than are their employers. The notion of the self-made man, who without assistance or education of any kind, raises himself from the gutter to become rich, is given the lie by a simple woman who was granted thirty pounds a year to keep her son's past a secret. In the end, Josiah Bounderby is exposed as a fraud and by extension the whole notion of Utilitarianism, founded as it is on the basis of unbridled laissez-faire capitalism, is also exposed as a bankrupt fraud.

There is little in the way of a happy ending in this novel; lives are destroyed and beliefs once cherished are riven asunder. Towards the end of the novel, Mr. Sleary tells Mr. Gradgrind a tale about a dog that belonged to Sissy Jupe's father. The story is a sort of morality tale that sums up the themes of the novel. Sissy's father, who abandoned Sissy as a child, had a dog that went away with the father. Years later, after the death of Mr. Jupe, the dog came back to the circus and died when he recognized his old circus friends. Mr. Sleary, in his simple, lisping way, as he relates his tale of the dog, speaks for the circus performers, and all the working people who have been degraded by the likes of Bounderby:

> "It theemth to prethent two thingth to a perthon, don't it, Thquire?" said Mr. Sleary, musing as he looked down into the depths of his brandy and water: "one, that there ith a love in the world, not all Thelf-interetht after all, but thomething very different; t'other, that it hath a way of ith own of calculating or not calculating, whith thomehow or another ith at leatht ath hard to give a name to, ath the wayth of the dogth ith!" [*HT* 280]

For Dickens, facts and figures, without imagination and love, make for a life that is incomplete. Power and wealth that is based on oppressing those less fortunate while at the same time neglecting friends and family, leads to a sterile, heartless, life. A legislature that is not responsive to the needs of its people fails in the purpose for which it was created. *Hard Times* may be allegorical, it may be moralizing, but it expresses Dickens's belief that life is meant to be lived: it is not a theory which proposes the greatest good for the greatest number of people. Furthermore, people are not easily categorized into neat black and white polarities. What was true for Dickens's time, is true for our time as well: if life is reduced to a series of polarities; if education is to be based strictly on facts with no room for imagination; if government is not responsible to those governed; if power and wealth are concentrated in the hands of the few; then there will be *Hard Times for These Times,* as well.

Chapter Six

Prison

The execution differed little from other similar exhibitions. On Monday the barriers were put up, and on Monday night a fringe of eager sightseers assembled, mostly sitting beneath the beams, but ready on a moment's notice to rise and cling to the front places they had so long waited for. There were the usual cat-calls, comic choruses, dances, and even mock hymns, till towards 2 o'clock, when the gaiety inspired by alcohol faded away as the public houses closed, and popular excitement was not revived till the blackened deal frame which forms the base of the scaffold was drawn out in the dawn, and placed in front of the door from which Barrett was to issue. Its arrival was accompanied with a great cheer, which at once woke up those who had been huddled in doorsteps and under barricades, and who joined in the general acclamation. The arrival of the scaffold did much to increase the interest, and through the dawn people began to flock in, the greater portion of the newcomers being young women and little children. Never were they more numerous than on this occasion, and blue velvet hats and huge white feathers lined the great beams which kept the mass from crushing each other in their eagerness to see a man put to death. The crowd was most unusually orderly, but it was not a crowd in which one would like to trust. It is said that one sees on the road to the Derby such animals as are never seen elsewhere; so on an execution morning one see faces that are never seen save round the gallows or near a great fire. Some laughed, some fought, some preached, some gave tracts, and some sang hymns; but what may be called the general good-humoured disorder of the crowd remained the same, and there was laughter at the preacher or silence when an open robbery was going on. None could look on the scene, with all its exceptional quietness, without a thankful feeling that this was to be the last public execution in England. Towards 7 o'clock the mass of people was immense. A very wide open space was kept round the gallows by the police, but beyond this the concourse was dense, stretching up beyond St. Sepulchre's Church, and far back almost, into Smithfield— a great surging mass of people which, in spite of the barriers, kept swaying to and from like waving corn. Now and then there was a great laughter as a girl fainted, and was passed out hand over hand above the heads of the mob, and then there came a scuffle and a fight, and then a hymn, and then a sermon, and then a comic song, and so on from hour to hour, the crowd thickening as the day brightened, and the sun shone out with such a glare as to extinguish the very feeble light which showed itself faintly through the glass roof above where the culprit lay. It was a wild, rough crowd, not so numerous nor nearly so violent as that which thronged to see Muller or the pirates die. In one way they showed their feeling by loudly hooting a magnificently-

130

attired woman, who, accompanied by two gentlemen, swept down the avenue kept open by the police, and occupied a window afterwards right in front of the gallows. This temporary exhibition of feeling was, however, soon allayed by coppers being thrown from the window for the roughs to scramble for. It is not right, perhaps, that a murderer's death should be surrounded by all the pious and tender accessories which accompany the departure of a good man to a better world, but most assuredly the sight of public executions to those who have to witness them is as disgusting as it must be demoralizing even to all the hordes of thieves and prostitutes it draws together. Yesterday the assembly was of its kind an orderly one, yet it was such as we feel grateful to think will under the new law never be drawn together again in England [Lloyd].

The preceding account of the last public execution in England, of one Michael Barrett, a member of the Irish Republican Brotherhood who was executed for exploding a bomb outside the Clerkenwell prison which killed twelve people and injured one hundred and twenty additional people, appeared in the *Times* on May 27, 1868. The description is fairly typical of the events surrounding a public execution, as well as the people who attended such executions. In the period from 1800 through 1899, there were 4,396 people executed in England, Scotland and Ireland; prior to 1868, all were executed publicly (Clark).

To the modern reader, it is difficult to imagine the attraction of a public execution. It is equally difficult to understand why such a spectacle was encouraged by the courts and why it was sanctioned by the monarchy. Michel Foucault, in his book *Discipline and Punish*, provides an answer to this dilemma:

We must regard the public execution, as it was still ritualized in the eighteenth century, as a political operation. It was logically inscribed in a system of punishment, in which the sovereign, directly or indirectly, demanded, decided and carried out punishments, in so far as it was he who, through the law, had been injured by the crime [53].

As Foucault explains, through the eighteenth century, crime was considered to be an affront to the person of the monarch, and as such, the punishment to be meted out must be displayed publicly; it must be made clear that an attempt to suborn the privileges of the monarch would be met with a very public manifestation of the monarch's displeasure. Although this monarchical process was replaced in the nineteenth century by a juridical process, the practice of public executions lasted through mid-century, partly because of the slow progress any new form of custom takes to replace an established form of custom, partly because such spectacles provided a very real release of pent-up emotion.

In order to prevent the release of emotions from spreading into something more dangerous, public executions in France prior to the Revolution were accompanied by "A whole military machine [that] surrounded the scaffold.... This was intended, of course, to prevent any escape or show of force; it was also to prevent any outburst of sympathy or anger on the part of the people" (Foucault 50).

According to Foucault, the people, that is, the general populace, were an essential element in the spectacle of the execution: "In the ceremonies of the public execution, the main character was the people, whose real and immediate presence was required for the performance. An execution that was known to be taking place, but which did so in secret, would scarcely have had any meaning" (57–58). The execution then, was a performance, a performance which recognized the power of the king initially, and later, the power of the state, to judge and punish malefactors.

As the century progressed, the idea that criminality was an offense against the crown began to shift to the idea that criminality was an offense against the state. This change in attitude was accompanied by the changes in society that have been alluded to previously: the rise of industrialism, the movement from rural to urban living, the generation of moveable wealth accompanied by a shift in crime from crimes against persons to crimes against property, as Foucault notes:

> In fact, the shift from a criminality of blood to a criminality of fraud forms part of a whole complex mechanism, embracing the development of production, the increase of wealth, a higher juridical and moral value placed on property relations, stricter methods of surveillance, a tighter partitioning of the population, more efficient techniques of locating and obtaining information: the shift in illegal practices is correlative with an extension and a refinement of punitive practices [77].

Under the old notion of criminality, where crime was an offense against the monarch, public execution was required to indicate the displeasure of the monarch and to enforce a disproportionate punishment on the offender: "This enables us to understand some of the characteristics of the liturgy of torture and execution—above all, the importance of a ritual that was to deploy its pomp in public. Nothing was to be hidden of this triumph of the law" (Foucault 49). Under the new notion of criminality, which made use of juridical procedure, charges against the criminal were made known beforehand, and a trial was conducted to determine guilt or innocence through the process of interrogation. Moreover, no longer was crime to be punished in an arbitrary manner by the will of the monarch, but punishment was to be meted out to be commensurate with the nature of the crime, and that punishment was meted out by the judiciary. Furthermore, the gallows were replaced by the prison as the primary method of punishment.

To the reformers of the nineteenth century, the abolition of capital punishment, and the replacement of the gallows with the prison, was not enough. Incarceration, by itself, did not produce an effective outcome. If, at the end of a criminal's sentence he/she was not reformed, what was the point of incarceration? If society was to be truly served, merely locking up a criminal served no real purpose; in order to truly serve society, a criminal must be reformed, changed, improved. Foucault comments on this very notion of reform as having a tripartite purpose, as follows:

> Imprisonment, with the purpose of transforming the soul and conduct, made its entry into the system of civil laws. The preamble of the bill, written by Blackstone and Howard, describes individual imprisonment in terms of its triple function as an example to be feared, instrument of conversion and condition for an apprenticeship: subjected to "isolated detention, regular work and the influence of religious instruction," certain criminals might not only inspire terror in those who would be tempted to imitate them, "but also to correct themselves and to acquire the habit of work" (Preamble of the bill of 1779) [123].

This change in crime and punishment was gradually accepted as being more humane, more conducive to reforming the criminal so that he/she could become a valued member of society after release from prison, and being more equitable in matching the form of punishment to the nature of the crime. For Dickens, this was theory; practice was another matter altogether.

Dickens would likely agree with the facts of punishment and reform laid out in Foucault's book, growing up as he did, with a first-hand experience of incarceration, which was the result of his father's imprisonment. He also developed an empathy born of his experiences; as a result, while Dickens might have agreed with the theory of prison reform, he was staunchly opposed to both the death penalty and the condition of the prisons and their wards. He used this information in his letters and non-fictional writings, as well as his fictional work, particularly the vision of the world as a prison which he depicted in his novel, *Little Dorrit.*

Dickens's first narrative of events related to prison occurred in *Sketches by Boz*, a collection of pieces originally written for various magazines and newspapers. The *Sketches* make use of a fictional narrator, *Boz*, a name which was a corruption of the name "Moses," a character in Oliver Goldsmith's novel, *The Vicar of Wakefield.*[1] The combined sections were published in two parts by John Macrone in 1836 and 1837. Dickens would continue to revise *Sketches by Boz* throughout his life, and issued revised copies of the book in 1839, 1850, and 1868. Two of the *Sketches* are relevant to the discussion of prisons, "Criminal Courts," and "A Visit to Newgate."

The first paragraph of "Criminal Courts" suggests that the author is writing autobiographically, although his readers did not know that Dickens had first-hand experience of prison life as a result of his family living in the Marshalsea Prison. Dickens, writing as Boz, begins:

> We shall never forget the mixed feelings of awe and respect with which we used to gaze on the exterior of Newgate in our schoolboy days. How dreadful its rough heavy walls, and low massive doors, appeared to us—the latter looking as if they were made for the express purpose of letting people in, and never letting them out again. Then the fetters over the debtor's door, which we used to think were a *bona fide* set of irons, just hung up there, for convenience sake, ready to be taken down at a moment's notice, and riveted on the limbs of some refractory felon! We were never tired of wondering how the hackney-coachmen on the opposite stand could cut jokes in the presence of such horrors, and drink pots of half-and-half so near the last drop [*SB* 229].

This first paragraph suggests that the narrator is recalling a scene from memory and is an example of reporting, an occupation which Dickens had developed as a journalist for *The Evening Chronicle*, and later for *The Morning Chronicle*. Later in the piece, Dickens describes the spectators and participants in the courthouse:

> Look upon the whole group in the body of the Court—some wholly engrossed in the morning papers, other carelessly conversing in low whispers, and others, again, quietly dozing away an hour—and you can scarcely believe that the result of the trial is a matter of life or death to one wretched being present.
> Turn your eyes to the dock; watch the prisoner attentively for a few moments, and the fact is before you, in all its painful reality. Mark how restlessly he has been engaged for the last ten minutes, in forming all sorts of fantastic figures with the herbs which are strewed upon the ledge before him; observe the ashy paleness of his face when a particular witness appears, and how he changes his position and wipes his clammy forehead, and feverish hands, when the case for the prosecution is closed, as if it were a relief to him to feel that the jury knew the worst [*SB* 232].

This passage retains the feeling of reporting, but there are additional elements present. The first such element is the detail conveyed by the workings of the court; here Dickens displays the knowledge he gained of court procedure in his years of legal and Parliamentary reporting. Secondly, Dickens captures the feeling of the courtroom; its bustle, the attitude of the spectators, the details of the witness stand. The final element that is noteworthy is Dickens's observation of the character of the defendant, and an attempt at understanding his feelings as he sits in the dock as a witness appears to testify, and while he awaits the final verdict of the jury.

In "A Visit to Newgate," there are glimpses of Dickens the mature writer, who has seen too much of prisons and punishment, and is disturbed by what he witnesses. In a passage at the beginning of the sketch, Dickens

Old Newgate Prison, view from the N.W.; photographer unknown. Dickens frequently refers to prisons in his works. In "Criminal Courts," which appears in *Sketches by Boz*, he reflects on his impressions of the Newgate Prison as a young man. His impressions were likely influenced by his family's residence in the Marshalsea Prison during his childhood (University of Michigan Library Digital Collections).

reflects upon the prisoners waiting for their sentences to be consummated and imbues the sketch with a feeling of empathy for the accused:

> How much more awful is it to reflect on this near vicinity to the dying—to men in full health and vigour, in the flower of youth or the prime of life, with all their faculties and perceptions as acute and perfect as your own; but dying, nevertheless—dying as surely—with the hand of death imprinted upon them as indelibly—as if mortal disease had wasted their frames to shadows, and loathsome corruption had already begun! [*SB* 234–235]

In another passage, Dickens writes of a woman prisoner who is met by her daughter, a child whose life has been blighted by poverty and neglect. Dickens returns to the connection between poverty, disease and criminality in his writings, a connection which he believed was all too common in Victorian England. The connection between poverty and criminality is made apparent in this piece about a woman and daughter who live in poverty and have been forced to live in a debtor's prison. Once again, the fragment seems autobiographical, the young Dickens recognizing elements from his own experience in the life of the young girl:

The girl belonged to a class—unhappily but too extensive—the very existence of which should make men's hearts bleed. Barely past her childhood, it required but a glance to discover that she was one of those children born and bred in poverty and vice, who have never known what childhood is; who have never been taught to love and court a parent's smile, or to dread a parent's frown. The thousand nameless endearments of childhood, its gaiety and its innocence, are alike unknown to them. They have entered at once upon the stern realities and miseries of life, and to their better nature it is almost hopeless to appeal in aftertimes, by any of the references which will awaken, if it be only for a moment, some good feeling in ordinary bosoms, however corrupt they may have become. Talk to *them* of parental solicitude, the happy days of childhood, and the merry games of infancy! Tell them of hunger and the streets, beggary and stripes, the gin-shop, the station-house, and the pawnbrokers, and they will understand you [SB 238–239)[2]

Recorded in this passage are traces of the young boy who pawned his father's books, worked in a blacking factory while other boys his age played games, who was estranged from his mother because of her desire to keep him working as a "laboring hind," but who, to his own amazement as he related to Forster, did not pursue the life of a criminal.

Pickwick Papers is his first venture into a sustained piece of fiction. Despite its relatively early appearance, *Pickwick Papers* was published in 1837, and it is, in many ways, a remarkably mature production for such a young author (Dickens was twenty-four years old when the book was published), as well as being an instant success, at least after Sam Weller appeared on the scene in chapter 10. Sam Weller has been described as one of Dickens's most successful comic creations, owing to the contrast of his worldliness (as opposed to the naiveté of Mr. Pickwick) with his cockney accent and homespun truths. Prior to Sam's appearance on the scene, sales of *Pickwick* lagged; they skyrocketed after Sam's appearance and maintained their torrid pace of publication until the book was finished.[3]

It is in *Pickwick Papers* that the reader is presented with the first extended look at prison life in Dickens's work. In this novel, Mr. Samuel Pickwick is accused of breach of a marriage contract by Mrs. Bardell, his landlady. The marriage proposal was never proffered by Mr. Pickwick, and the entire incident which led to the marriage proposal is a series of misunderstandings. Mr. Pickwick refuses to honor the marriage contract, is found guilty of violating the contract by a court of law, and refuses to make restitution for the breach. As a result of his refusal, he is sent to the Fleet Prison, a debtor's prison in London. Dickens provides a view of the prison in chapter 41:

"Oh," replied Mr. Pickwick, looking down a dark and filthy staircase, which appeared to lead to a range of damp and gloomy stone vaults beneath the ground, "and those,

I suppose, are the little cellars where the prisoners keep their small quantities of coals. Unpleasant places to have to go down to; but very convenient, I dare say."

"Yes, I shouldn't wonder if they was convenient," replied the gentleman, "seeing that a few people live there pretty snug. That's the Fair, that is."

"My friend," said Mr. Pickwick, "you don't really mean to say that human beings live down in those wretched dungeons?"

"Don't I?" replied Mr. Roker with indignant astonishment. "Why shouldn't I?"

"Live! Live down there!" exclaimed Mr. Pickwick [*PP* 623].

Perhaps this is the voice of the boy who, at age twelve, first encountered the Marshalsea Prison, speaking through Mr. Pickwick. Perhaps it is the boy who expresses his horror at the conditions of a prison where people dwell in squalid conditions.

The prison, as depicted in *Pickwick Papers,* is barely fit for human habitation; yet despite the conditions, despite the overcrowding, life goes on. The prison becomes a microcosm of Victorian society, complete with all manner of occupations and people, as this passage from *Pickwick Papers* makes clear:

In all the galleries themselves, and more especially on the staircases, there lingered a great number of people who came there, some because their rooms were empty and lonesome, others because their rooms were full and hot; the greater part because they were restless and uncomfortable, and not possessed of the secret of exactly knowing what to do with themselves. There were many classes of people here, from the labouring man in his fustian jacket to the broken-down spendthrift in his shawl dressing-gown, most appropriately out at elbows, but there was the same air about them all—a listless jail-bird careless swagger, a vagabondish who's-afraid sort of bearing, which is wholly indescribable in words, but which any man can understand in one moment, if he wish, by setting foot in the nearest debtor's prison and looking at the very first group of people he sees there, with the same interest as Mr. Pickwick did [*PP* 623].

Although written during the time when prison reform was beginning in England and when sentencing was beginning to be standardized, the effects on the prisoners themselves differed markedly in places like the Fleet Prison. Since the Fleet was a debtor's prison, the population was mixed; there were inveterate neer-do-wells, first time offenders, and unlucky tradesmen who were brought together in the prison population. Mr. Pickwick and Sam Weller discuss the various effects prison life has on the inhabitants of the Fleet prison:

"Ah, that's just the wery thing, sir," rejoined Sam "*they* don't mind it; it's a regular holiday to them—all porter and skittles. It's the t'other vuns as gets done over vith this sort o' thing; them downhearted fellers as can't svig away at the beer nor play at skittles neither; them as vould pay if they could, and gets low by being boxed up. I'll tell you wot it is, sir: them as is always a'idlin' in public-houses it don't damage at all, and them as is alvays a-workin' wen they can it damages too much. 'It's unekal,' as my father used to say wen his grog worn't made half-and half. It's unekal, and that's the fault on it" [*PP* 627].

The inequality of the system was perhaps most troubling to Dickens. He had a keen aversion to the "system," whether it be the Parliamentary system, the school system, the sanitary system, or the penitentiary system. This aversion was based on the fact that none of these "systems" seemed to work as they were designed. Parliament did not work for the benefit of the people, and was populated by such incompetents that Dickens resorted to calling them by several derogatory names in *Bleak House*: Boodle, Coodle, Doodle, Foodle, Goodle, Joodle, Loodle, Moodle, and Noodle, to name but a few; the schools were mismanaged and corporal punishment was perhaps the only lesson some students remembered; the sanitary system produced cholera, dysentery and pestilence, and was anything but sanitary; the prisons did not produce reform, but instead recreated the life outside the prison walls, a microcosm of the streets of London.

Squalor, decay, over-crowding, death; these were the scenes of life in Fleet Prison. In one of the more moving passages in *Pickwick Papers*, Sam Weller and Mr. Pickwick encounter the body of one of the prison "lifers," a man who had been incarcerated for a period of twenty years, and died gasping for fresh air which was untainted by the pestilent fumes of the Fleet Prison:

> ... and all was noise and tumult—save in a little miserable shed a few yards off, where lay, all quiet and ghastly, the body of the Chancery prisoner who had died the night before, awaiting the mockery of an inquest. The body! It is the lawyer's term for the restless whirling mass of cares and anxieties, affections, hopes, and griefs that make up the living man. The law *had* his body; and there it lay, clothed in grave clothes, an awful witness to its tender mercy [*PP* 697].

"The law *had* his body," is an apt description of the notion of punishment that Dickens reviled. The punishment of the body, after all, was the message that was delivered at public executions. The majesty of the monarch, and later, of the state, the right of the government to take vengeance on the body of the criminal was the lesson to be learned at the public executions and in the prisons. It was a combination of the abhorrent nature of the punishment, and the behavior of the crowds at these executions, that led Dickens to write a letter to the Editor of the *Times* newspaper on November 13, 1849, documenting the scene of a public execution, and urging that such spectacles be abandoned:

> I was a witness of the execution at Horsemonger-lane this morning. I went there with the intention of observing the crowd gathered to behold it, and I had excellent

opportunities of doing so, at intervals all through the night, and continuously from daybreak until after the spectacle was over....

I believe that a sight so inconceivably awful as the wickedness and levity of the immense crowd collected at that execution this morning could be imagined by no man, and could be presented in no heathen land under the sun. The horrors of the gibbet and of the crime which brought the wretched murderers to it, faded in my mind before the atrocious bearing, looks, and language, of the assembled spectators. When I came upon the scene at midnight, the *shrillness* of the cries and howls that were raised from time to time, denoting that they came from a concourse of boys and girls already assembled in the best places, made my blood run cold. As the night went on, screeching, and laughing, and yelling in strong chorus of parodies on Negro melodies, with substitutions of "Mrs. Manning" [one of the persons executed, along with her husband for the crime of murder] for "Susannah," and the like, were added to these. When the day dawned, thieves, low prostitutes, ruffians and vagabonds of every kind, flocked on to the ground, with every variety of offensive and foul behaviour....

I have seen, habitually, some of the worst sources of general contamination and corruption in this country, and I think there are not many phases of London life that could surprise me. I am solemnly convinced that nothing that ingenuity could devise to be done in this city, in the same compass of time, could work such ruin as one public execution, and I stand astounded and appalled by the wickedness it exhibits. I do not believe that any community can prosper where such a scene of horror and demoralization as was enacted this morning outside Horsemonger-lane Gaol is presented at the very doors of good citizens, and is passed by, unknown or forgotten. And when, in our prayers and thanksgivings for the season, we are humbly expressing before God our desire to remove the moral evils of the land, I would ask your readers to consider whether it is not a time to think of this one, and to root it out [*SL* 205–206].

The reader is struck by the similarity of the descriptions of a public execution noted in the *Times* article cited at the beginning of the chapter, and Dickens's editorial written in 1849. It was to take almost twenty years before Dickens's wish for an end to public executions was granted.

Shortly after *Pickwick Papers* was written, two systems of incarceration were being developed in the United States, and their success or failure was closely monitored in England. The first system was known as the Auburn model, founded at the penitentiary in Auburn, New York, which

... prescribed the individual cell during the night, work and meals in common, but under the rule of absolute silence, the convicts being allowed to speak only to the warders, with their permission and in a low voice. It was a clear reference to the monastic model; a reference too, to the discipline of the workshop. The prison must be a microcosm of a perfect society in which individuals are isolated in their moral existence, but in which they come together in a strict hierarchical framework, with no lateral relation, communication being possible only in a vertical direction. The advantage of the Auburnian system, according to its advocates, was that it formed a duplication of society itself [Foucault 238].

An interesting Account of the life, Trial, Execution and Dying Behaviour of Joseph Hutton And other Men who Suffered at Newgate, this Morning; Broadside, author unknown. Dickens wrote several articles to the *Times* newspaper expressing his revulsion of public executions which were carried out in London. It would take until 1868 for public hangings to cease in London (British Library, London).

The second model, known as the Philadelphia system, prescribed total isolation, which attempted not only

> ... the application of a common law, but of the relation of the individual to his own conscience and to what may enlighten him from within. Alone in his cell, the convict is handed over to himself; in the silence of his passions and of the world that surrounds him, he descends into his conscience, he questions it and feels awakening within him the moral feeling that never entirely perishes in the heart of man (*Journal des economistes*, II, 1842) [Foucault 238].

It was hoped that these two models would transform the penal system into a more humane method of incarceration in the United States, just as the old system of criminality was transformed from one based upon the will of the monarch into a system which relied on the judiciary.[4] During his first trip to North America in 1842, Dickens was able to visit the Eastern Penitentiary in Philadelphia, a prison founded on the methods of the Philadelphia system. Dickens imagined himself in the place of one of the prisoners and records his thoughts on the effects solitary confinement would have on that prisoner in his travel log, *American Notes*. He begins by intimating that when the man is newly confined to his cell he:

... is stunned. His confinement is a hideous vision; and his old life a reality. He throws himself upon his bed, and lies there abandoned to despair. By degrees the insupportable solitude and barrenness of the place rouses him from this stupor, and when the trap in his grated door is opened, he humbly begs and prays for work. "Give me some work to do, or I shall go raving mad!" [*AN* 106]

As the years wear on, the prisoner adapts himself to his work, but despairs when he thinks of the remaining years he must spend in the prison. Eventually, he begins to become disoriented, and wonders whether he is the only inhabitant of the prison, or whether there are other prisoners nearby:

There is no sound, but other prisoners may be near for all that. He remembers to have heard once, when he little thought of coming here himself, that the cells were so constructed that the prisoners could not hear each other, though the officers could hear them. Where is the nearest man—upon the right, or on the left? or is there one in both directions? Where is he sitting now—with his face to the light? or is he walking to and fro? How is he dressed? Has he been here long? Is he much worn away? Is he very white and spectre-like? Does *he* think of his neighbor too? [*AN* 106]

Finally, after long years of confinement, the man loses hold of reality and sinks into a condition of madness and terror:

... slowly he begins to feel that the white walls of the cell have something dreadful in them: that their colour is horrible: that their smooth surface chills his blood: that there is one hateful corner which torments him.... By slow but sure degrees, the terrors of that hateful corner swell until they beset him at all times; invade his rest, make his dreams hideous, and his nights dreadful. At first, he took a strange dislike to it; feeling as though it gave birth in his brain to something of corresponding shape, which ought not to be there, and racked his head with pains. Then he began to fear it, then to dream of it, and of men whispering its name and pointing to it. Then he could not bear to look at it, nor yet to turn his back upon it. Now, it is every night the lurking-place of a ghost: a shadow:—a silent something, horrible to see, but whether bird, or beast, or muffled human shape, he cannot tell [*AN* 107].

In these passages, Dickens has tolled out the stages of incredulity, despair, boredom, feelings of uselessness, impotence and loss, which finally descend into fear, sleeplessness, terror and then, to madness; this is the reality of the system of isolation which is the outcome of the grand design of the Philadelphia system. The madness that Dickens imagines for this prisoner is similar to the reveries and dreams which he employs in several of the novels, and the description of the prisoner's isolation possesses the surreal quality of many dreams. Clearly, Dickens understood the psychology of a person who undergoes isolation, and then descends into madness, and portrayed it vividly in the preceding passage. Dickens would return to the idea of solitary confinement, and the effects such confinement had on a prisoner in *A Tale of Two Cities*.

In the U.K., a system somewhat analogous to the Philadelphia system was developed by Jeremy Bentham. A prison designed under this system has a circular structure, with cells arranged around the circumference of the circle. Each prisoner is isolated from other prisoners, and is observed at all times from a central tower located in the middle of the structure (Foucault 195–228). Unable to communicate with others, constantly subjected to observation, the prisoners in these institutions gradually grow mad, as Dickens describes in his travel log in *American Notes*.

With the passage of time, the two systems developed in the United States fell out of favor, and the Panopticon, the system devised by Jeremy Bentham, while surviving to the present day in some areas, has also fallen out of favor.[5] It is not surprising that Dickens rejected any type of system which led to isolation, despair, and madness, and which treated prisoners so poorly. To a man such as Dickens, a system which led to real reformation of character, instead of the theoretical benefits of character reformation espoused by solitary confinement, communal discipline, or continual observation, was required. Accordingly, Dickens suggested the adoption of a modified version of the "mark system," developed by Alexander Maconochie in 1840 for use in Urania Cottage. The cottage was founded in 1846 as an institution developed for the rehabilitation of prostitutes under the auspices of Angela Burdett Coutts. In a letter to Ms. Coutts, dated May 26, 1846, Dickens describes the workings of the "mark system,"

> A woman or girl coming to the Asylum, it is explained to her that she has come there for *useful* repentance and reform, and because her past way of life has been dreadful in its nature and consequences, and full of affliction, misery, and despair to *herself*. Never mind Society while she is at that pass. Society has used her ill and turned away from her, and she cannot be expected to take much heed of its rights or wrongs. It is destructive to *herself*, and there is no hope in it, or in her, as long as she pursues it. It is explained to her that she is degraded and fallen, but not lost, having this shelter, and that the means of Return to Happiness are now about to be put into her own hands, and trusted to her own keeping. That with this view, she is, instead of being placed in this probationary class for a month, or two months, or three months, or any specified *time* whatever, required to earn there, a certain number of Marks (they are mere scratches in a book) so that she may make her probation a very short one, or a very long one, according to her own conduct....
>
> What they would be taught in the house, would be grounded in religion, most unquestionably. It must be the basis of the whole system. But it is very essential in dealing with this class of persons to have a system of training established, which, while it is steady and form, is cheerful and hopeful. Order, punctuality, cleanliness, the whole routine of household duties—as washing, mending, cooking—the establishment itself would supply the means of teaching practically, to every one [*SL* 163–164].

After successful rehabilitation the ward in Urania House would emigrate to Australia, New Zealand, South Africa, and Canada to begin a new life.[6]

Duplicate view of HBS No. PA-1729-126—Eastern State Penitentiary, photographed by Jack Boucher. Dickens visited the Eastern State Penitentiary in 1842, and wrote an account of the state of mind of a prisoner located there in *American Notes* (Library of Congress).

In some cases, the women returned to their former life as prostitutes or engaged in other forms of criminal behavior. The Cottage was closed in 1861 or 1862. Dickens's involvement in the Cottage ended in 1858, after Dickens separated from his wife Catherine; the closing of the Cottage was due, in part, to the strain in Dickens's friendship with Angela Burdett Coutts as a result of his marital difficulties. Miss Coutts was disturbed by Dickens's separation from his wife; Dickens and Miss Coutts continued a correspondence, but their relationship was never the same.

Yet, despite the closure of Urania Cottage, the institution provided an alternative life for some of the women whose lives were squandered before their attendance at the cottage. But perhaps the real benefit of the cottage was not the domestic duties that Dickens emphasized to these women, but the system of reform that the cottage tried to utilize in dealing with these women; it was instilled in the very charter of Urania Cottage. The system would reward good behavior while not punishing behavior that was deemed to be counter-productive. How different from the barbarous practices of the prior century, when merely failing to kneel to passing monks resulted in being tortured and put to death!

Shortly after the Dickens's involvement with Urania Cottage, he returned to a fictional account of prison in *A Tale of Two Cities*, which was published in 1859. The novel is concerned with the events leading up to the French Revolution, as well as the rioting which accompanied this period in French history. Dickens relied upon Thomas Carlyle's *The French Revolution: A History* to obtain a sense of the workings of the French aristocracy and the plight of the peasantry in the period leading up to the Revolution. In a passage early in the novel, Dickens writes about the system of punishments meted out by the crown, a passage which mirrors the non-fictional accounts of monarchical abuse highlighted in Foucault's work:

> Under the guidance of her Christian pastors, she [France] entertained herself, besides, with such humane achievements as sentencing a youth to have his hands cut off, his tongue torn out with pincers, and his body burned alive, because he had not kneeled down in the rain to do honour to a dirty procession of monks which passed within his view, at a distance of some fifty or sixty yards [*TTC* 2].

A passage later in the novel emphasizes that France was not alone in exacting strict measures of punishment for the most trivial offenses, and that England also engaged in such barbaric practices:

> But indeed, at that time, ... the forger was put to death; the utterer of a bad note was put to Death; the unlawful opener of a letter was put to Death; the purloiner of forty shillings and sixpence was put to Death; the holder of a horse at Tellson's door, who made off with it, was put to Death; the coiner of a bad shilling was put to Death; the

sounders of three-fourths of the notes in the whole gamut of Crime, were put to Death [*TTC* 50].

Dickens continues his condemnation of the criminal practices in use in England in the 1780s in *A Tale of Two Cities*:

> They hanged at Tyburn, in those days, so the street outside Newgate had not obtained one infamous notoriety that has since attached to it. But, the gaol was a vile place, in which most kinds of debauchery and villainy were practiced, and where dire diseases were bred, that came into court with the prisoners, and sometimes rushed straight from the dock at my Lord Chief Justice himself, and pulled him off the bench. It had more than once happened, that the Judge in the black cap pronounced his own doom as certainly as the prisoner's, and even died before him. For the rest, the Old Bailey was famous as a kind of deadly inn-yard, from which the pale travellers set out continually, in carts and coaches, on a violent passage into the other world: traversing some two miles and a half of public street and road, and shaming few good citizens, if any. So powerful in use, and so desirable to be good use in the beginning. It was famous, too, for the pillory, a wise old institution, that inflicted a punishment of which no one could foresee the extent; also, for the whipping-post, another dear old institution, very humanising and softening to behold in action; also, for extensive transactions in blood-money, another fragment of ancestral wisdom, systematically leading to the most frightful mercenary crimes that could be committed under Heaven. Altogether, the Old Bailey, at that date, was a choice illustration of the precept, that "Whatever is is right"; an aphorism that would be as final as it is lazy, did not include the troublesome consequence, that nothing that ever was, was wrong [*TTC* 56].

In these passages, the reader can understand Dickens's contempt for a society that would inflict such punishment on its members, while at the same time hypocritically asserting that the punishment was meted out for the good of the transgressors. Dickens's reply to the adage that "might makes right," could be summed up by indicating: no, your majesties; no your honors; no to every man who believes that some good can come from such cruel practices.

Against this background of cruel punishment for small or insignificant offenses, Dickens paints a portrait of the effects of incarceration on Dr. Manette. When the reader first encounters the doctor, he has been imprisoned for a period of eighteen years. He is hidden in a garret attached to the wine shop owned by Monsieur Ernest Defarge; the garret is dark, and Dr. Manette is seated on a bench, making shoes. Dickens opens the scene with a dialogue between Monsieur Defarge and the doctor:

> "You are still hard at work, I see?"
> After a long silence, the head was lifted for another moment, and the voice replied, "Yes—I am working." This time, a pair of haggard eyes had looked at the questioner, before the face had dropped again [*TTC* 38].

Dickens continues in his description of the doctor, who has regressed into the character of a shoe cobbler as a result of his years of imprisonment.

In this scene, Dickens recalls the opening of the novel, where Mr. Lorry speculates about the fate of the doctor, jailed for eighteen years. Yet, the reality of the doctor's condition, reduced to a pitiable shoe cobbler lodged in a garret above a wine shop, is much worse than the fate imagined by Mr. Lorry. In his description of the doctor, Dickens focuses on his voice, which was:

> ... pitiable and dreadful.... It was like the last feeble echo of a sound made long and long ago. So entirely had it lost the life and resonance of the human voice, that it affected the senses like a once beautiful colour faded away into a poor weak stain. So sunken and suppressed it was, that it was like a voice underground. So expressive it was, of a hopeless and lost creature, that a famished traveller, wearied out by lonely wandering in a wilderness, would have remembered home and friends in such a tone before lying down to die [*TTC* 38].

Here is the man in jail in the Philadelphia prison in *American Notes*, reimagined as Dr. Manette. The effects of solitary confinement have done their work; he is no longer an educated, respected physician, but a shoe maker, afraid of human contact, unable to bear the faintest light of day, a man reduced to snatches of conversation and compared to a dead man. His voice, once active and animated, is now reduced to a voice that can only be heard in a whisper, the whisper of a man who was buried alive for eighteen years. Indeed, as the note delivered to Mr. Lorry in the second chapter intimates, Dr. Manette is "recalled to life." But what kind of life is it?

In the novel, it is only through the continual solicitude of the doctor's daughter, Lucie Manette, and the good graces of his banker and friend, Mr. Lorry, that the doctor regains some sense of normalcy after a period of five years. Yet, after learning that his daughter Lucie wishes to marry Charles Darnay, and after the revelation of Mr. Darnay's true identity as Charles St. Evremonde, son to the Marquis who imprisoned him, the doctor relapses into the character of the shoe maker:

> Nothing would induce him to speak more. He looked up, for an instant at a time, when he was requested to do so; but, no persuasion would extract a word from him. He worked, and worked, and worked, in silence, and words fell on him as they would have fallen on an echoless wall, or on the air. The only ray of hope that Mr. Lorry could discover, was, that he sometimes furtively looked up without being asked. In that, there seemed a faint expression of curiosity or perplexity—as though he were trying to reconcile some doubts in his mind [*TTC* 186].

The doctor eventually recovers, only to have a relapse at the trial of Charles Darnay, now revealed as Charles St. Evremonde. The doctor's notes from prison are read before a tribunal assembled by the peasants, who have seized control of the courts of law as the revolution swept through the city of

Paris. The notes explain the details behind the doctor's imprisonment for treating a young woman who was raped by the Marquis St. Evremonde, and the killing of the woman's husband and brother by the Marquis St. Evremonde and his brother. The notes also reveal the eventual death of the young woman who was raped, as well as the fact that the doctor was imprisoned simply because he treated the young wife and her brother, and because the Marquis' secret was revealed to him. He was given no trial, no sentence, but was taken to the Bastille where he spent eighteen years in detention.

In *A Tale of Two Cities*, Dickens develops a psychological portrait of a man who has been unjustly imprisoned, and who is completely innocent of any crime; he is jailed to hide the criminal deeds of two noblemen who are above the law and cannot be held accountable for their actions. Over the course of eighteen years of incarceration, he is reduced to a state of fear and forgets his prior life, ultimately descending into a state of madness. The portrait of Dr. Manette is informed by Dickens's first-hand observations of solitary confinement at the Philadelphia prison, nearly twenty years before he wrote *A Tale of Two Cities*.

Dickens would continue to write about prisons in his next novel, *Great Expectations*, written during the period from 1860 to 1861. In the novel, a convict, Abel Magwitch, escapes from one of the prison hulks in the estuary of the River Thames. The hulks were derelict merchant ships, no longer fit for duty, which were used to house criminals. Upon his escape from the hulks, Magwitch terrorizes a local boy, Pip, into bringing him food and drink. Magwitch is later captured by the constable and a group of soldiers. When captured, Magwitch does not implicate Pip for providing food and drink for him, but claims that he stole the food from the blacksmith shop where Pip works with his brother-in-law, Joe Gargery. So begins the tale of Pip's fortunes, his meeting with Miss Havisham and Estella, his renouncing of Joe Gargery, and the subsequent revelation that his fortune was left to him not by Miss Havisham, as he supposed, but by the escaped convict, Abel Magwitch.

The theme of imprisonment permeates the novel: Pip is imprisoned by his notions of what constitutes a gentleman, and his belief that money is equated with gentility. His love for Estella, despite her warnings that she cannot reciprocate his love, does not allow him to find happiness with another woman. Miss Havisham is imprisoned in her decaying house as a result of being jilted in marriage. Rather than continue with her life, she suspends time so that it is fixed at the date of her canceled marriage, and becomes a prisoner of that date and time. Estella is raised to be Miss

The Criminal Prisons of London and scenes of prison life. With numerous illustrations from photographs, **by Henry Mayhew and John Binny. Hulks were decommissioned ships used to house prisoners in the eighteenth and nineteenth centuries. This scene depicts a prison hulk similar to the one from which Magwitch escaped in** *Great Expectations* **(British Library, London).**

Havisham's punishment to mankind; she is taught to be cold and heartless, to wreak vengeance on those who have harmed her patroness. Estella is trapped by Miss Havisham's need for revenge; she is forced into a marriage with a brute in order to fulfill Miss Havisham's wishes.

In the course of the novel, Pip lives a dissolute life in London, living off the funds he believes are provided to him by Miss Havisham. While in London, Pip stumbles upon an acquaintance, Mr. Wemmick, who works on behalf of Pip's attorney, Mr. Jagger. Wemmick, on a case involving a man accused of robbery, is on his way to Newgate, and invites Pip to join him. Pip records his impressions of Newgate:

> We were at Newgate in a few minutes, and we passed through the lodge where some fetters were hanging up on the bare walls among the prison rules, into the interior of the jail. At that time, jails were much neglected, and the period of exaggerated reaction consequent on all public wrong-doing—and which is always its heaviest and longest punishment—was still far off. So, felons were not lodged and fed better than soldiers (to say nothing of paupers), and seldom set fire to their prisons with the excusable object of improving the flavour of their soup. It was visiting time when Wemmick took me in; and a potman was going his rounds with beer; and the prisoners, behind bars in yards, were buying beer, and talking to friends; and a frouzy, ugly, disorderly, depressing scene it was [*GE* 260].

At first glance, the passage seems indeterminate. On the one hand, it seems to imply that prison conditions were not as bad as they seemed and that felons "seldom set fire to their prisons with the excusable object of improving the flavour of their soup." On the other hand, Pip's description of the conditions of the prison at the close of the paragraph would seem to indicate otherwise. The passage which relates to the prisoner's soup refers to an incident which occurred in February 1861, in which the convicts at Chatham prison rioted as a result of the inadequacy of their food. The riot was covered in the local newspapers, and speculation developed that prison reform had gone too far (*GE* 499, footnote 1). It is obvious that Dickens was being ironic in his comments about the conditions of prisons and prisoners in the mid eighteen-hundreds, when the events of the novel were to have occurred; hopefully, his readers understood the irony.

That Dickens intended the passage to be ironic is demonstrated by Pip's observation concerning his visit to Newgate, a visit that seemed to link his past with his current situation, and his advancement as an aspiring gentleman:

> I consumed the whole time in thinking how strange it was that I should be encompassed by all this taint of prison and crime; that, in my childhood out on our lonely marshes on a winter evening I should have first encountered it; that, it should have reappeared on two occasions, starting out like a stain that was faded but not gone; that, it should in this new way pervade my fortune and advancement [*GE* 264].

Of course, Pip could not know at the time how this visit with Mr. Wemmick foreshadowed his later trip to the prison, when he would care for Magwitch.

Returning to the original capture of Magwitch at the beginning of the novel, the court, in a rare display of mercy, spared Magwitch's life but imposed the penalty of transportation to Australia, with the further provision that if he returned, he would be executed. While in Australia, Magwitch made a fortune which allowed him to provide funds to Pip. For Magwitch, giving money to Pip was a way to show his gratitude to the young boy. Eventually, the desire to see the results of his handiwork, making a gentleman of Pip, was too great, and Magwitch returned to England, only to be recaptured and sent to Newgate in order to be executed. Pip describes how he tended to Magwitch after his capture:

> He lay in his prison very ill, during the whole interval between his committal for trial, and the coming round of the Sessions. He had broken two ribs, they had wounded one of his lungs, and he breathed with great pain and difficulty, which increased daily. It was a consequence of his hurt, that he spoke so low as to be scarcely audible; therefore, he spoke very little. But, he was ever ready to listen to me, and it became the first duty of my life to say to him, and read to him, what I knew he ought to hear.

> Being far too ill to remain in the common prison, he was removed, after the first day or so, into the infirmary. This gave me opportunities of being with him that I could not otherwise have had. And but for his illness he would have been put in irons, for he was regarded as a determined prison-breaker, and I know not what else [GE 455].

In the interval between Magwitch's capture and his death, Pip learns that Estella is Magwitch's daughter. Magwitch believed that his daughter had perished, and on his deathbed, Pip reveals that Estella is alive, and that he is in love with her. Magwitch finally dies, with a chastened Pip by his side. After the death of Magwitch, Pip goes to the Far East as a partner in an import firm, and returns to England ten years later, a wiser man.

By the end of the novel, Magwitch is recognized by Pip as his benefactor. As the novel concludes, Pip has learned that being a gentleman is more than just possessing money; the title of gentleman is won by actions, and a good heart. Joe Gargery and Abel Magwitch have earned that title, Joe by his steady, faithful support of Pip; Abel Magwitch by his earlier refusal to compromise Pip near the prison hulks, and his later return to see how his young friend has prospered in life. In many ways, Abel Magwitch fulfilled the hope Dickens had of the reformed convict; a man whose life was changed as a result of a good act, and who endeavored to repay that act with kindness.

That Dickens was affected by his knowledge of prison life, and that he wrote about prisons and prisoners almost obsessively, cannot be denied. Philip Hobsbaum writes about Dickens's seeming obsession with prisons and his writing about prisons in his novels:

> One cannot exaggerate the part prison and the sense of imprisonment plays in Dickens, from the debtors' prison in *Pickwick Papers* to Harmony Jail in *Our Mutual Friend*; and indeed one novel, *Little Dorrit*, is entirely given up to the idea. That it was deeply ingrained in Dickens, no doubt as a result of his father's improvidence in his unhappy childhood, is clear enough. It is the dynamic in many of the *Sketches* [25].

Like many things in Dickens's life, his writing about, and knowledge of, prisons produced deeply ambivalent feelings in him. On the one hand, he was the ardent supporter of prison reform, a champion for better rights for prisoners, and for the prostitutes whom he and Angela Burdett Coutts sought to help. On the other hand, he was the little boy who felt abandoned by his parents, who walked the streets of London alone at night, without friends, without succor, with only his dreams of becoming a learned man. From this ambivalence came great literature, but it left the man wounded, hurt, and unable to become intimate with those closest to him.

Although Dickens wrote about prisons in *Sketches by Boz*, *The Pick-*

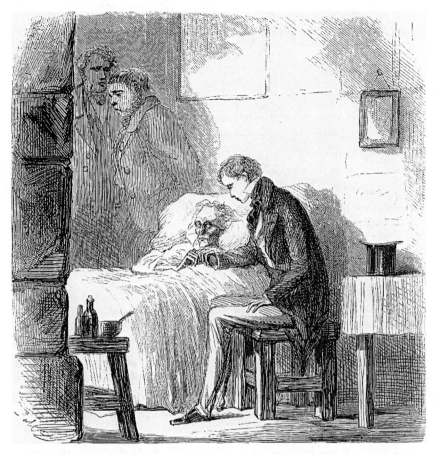

Illustration by John McLenan depicting Pip with Magwitch on his deathbed in *Great Expectations.* At the conclusion of the novel, Pip recognizes Magwitch as his benefactor, and learns the true meaning of becoming a gentleman (British Library, London).

wick Papers, American Notes, A Tale of Two Cities and *Great Expectations,* he saved his most telling blow against the futility of the prison system for the novel *Little Dorrit.* Prisons, ineffective governmental agencies, social conventions that no longer function properly, organized religions which no longer satisfy the needs of their congregations, evil characters who prey upon good people; these are all manifestations of a dysfunctional society, a society imprisoned by its own attitudes, that Dickens portrays in the novel, *Little Dorrit.* Philip Hobsbaum comments on this society and its lack of responsibility, which permeates through all aspects of Victorian life, until the entire world is seen as a prison:

> It appears as an indictment of irresponsibility, seen in the machinery of government; a series of portraits showing irresponsible or repressive parents; a study of dehumanization in the case of repressed children; the portrayal at once of society in a prison and Society *as* a prison; and indications both at large and in minute particular of an economy hopelessly out of control [189].

This is not the prison that Foucault recorded in the France of the seventeenth and eighteenth centuries; this was more like the nightmare of the Panopticon, where every member of society was in some way touched by the evil effects of prison life; a society where its very essence was infected by the pestilence that oozed from a man like Merdle.

Fittingly, the novel opens in a prison located in Marseilles, with one of the archetypal villains, in the person of Monsieur Rigaud, railing against the society which has placed him, a "citizen of the world," in prison (Dickens, *LD* 5). The scene next shifts to the quarantine area in Marseilles, where a group of European travelers have been placed, awaiting their release in order to return to England. The next scene shifts to England, where an invalid, Mrs. Clenham, sits in her wheeled chair, confined to a single room in a ramshackle house, where she sits in self-imprisoned exile. Next, the reader is shown the Marshalsea Debtor's Prison, where the Dorrit family live "locked up in narrow yards surrounded by high walls with spikes at the top" (*LD* 34). For those fortunate enough to escape the Marshalsea, the prospect of Bleeding Heart Yard is not much better, and for those who cannot afford a roof over their heads, they are condemned to the workhouse, a far more horrific place than the debtor's prison, "much worse fed and lodged and treated altogether than … malefactors" (*LD* 72).

The world of *Little Dorrit* is a prison world, where even the governmental agencies, which should assist the population, are instead the locus of cronyism, ineffectiveness and nepotism; and where the functionaries are trapped in the world they constructed, and from which there is no escape. The motto of that institution, the Circumlocution Office, was "How Not To Do It," and its tentacles spread through every phase of government: "In short, all the business of the country went through the Circumlocution Office, except the business that never came out of it; and *its* name was Legion" (*LD* 53). That the Circumlocution Office was another form of imprisonment is made clear by Dickens on page 275: "The shady waiting-rooms of the Circumlocution Office, where he [Arthur Clenham] passed a good deal of time in company with various troublesome Convicts who were under sentence to be broken alive on that wheel…" (*LD*). Hobsbaum writes that the Circumlocution Office is a symbol for all dysfunctional governments everywhere, a feeling that Dickens certainly would have agreed with:

Northeast view of the original Marshalsea prison, taken from *The Gentleman's Magazine*, September 1803. The Dickens family, minus young Charles, was sent to the Marshalsea as a result of John Dickens's improvidence in 1824. The novel *Little Dorrit* was set in the Marshalsea, circa 1826, at approximately the same time as the imprisonment of the Dickens family. Dickens employed the metaphor of imprisonment affecting every aspect of English life from the Marshalsea Prison to the Circumlocution Office, to society in general.

> The Circumlocution Office is a government department that symbolizes all government departments, indeed, Government itself. It is a network of jobbery and nepotism, mostly a result of intermarriage between the Barnacle and Stiltstalking families, and the assignment of posts to the scions thereof; ... but [it] suggests any form of government without personal feel: Dickens's great theme, in fact, of System in lieu of human contact [191].

The Circumlocution Office was populated with a species of animal life known as the Barnacles, whose job it was to make sure that the principle of "How Not to Do It" was strictly adhered-to: "The Barnacles were a very high family, and a very large family. They were dispersed all over the public offices, and held all sorts of public places" (*LD* 54). The primary job of this species was to propagate itself and stick to anything that might hold promise of remuneration or advancement:

> ... There was to be a convocation of Barnacles on the occasion ... sticking to that post was a Barnacle.... Thus the Barnacles were all over the world, in every direction— despatch-boxing the compass ... on which there was nothing (except mischief) to be done and anything to be pocketed, it was perfectly feasible to assemble a good many Barnacles [*LD* 203].

True to their charter, the Barnacles effectively ignored the needs of the poor or needy in their quest for self-aggrandizement; their neglect of the condition of the poor folks assembled in Bleeding Heart Yard serves to illustrate this point: "That high old family, the Barnacles, had long been too busy with their great principle to look into the matter [the decrepit conditions in Bleeding Heart Yard]; and indeed the matter had nothing to do with their watchfulness in outgeneralling all other high old families except the Stiltstalkings" (*LD* 70).

Life outside of prison was composed of a series of parlor games, known as "Society," which is portrayed by Dickens with a combination of disgust, satire, and loathing as he develops the characters who populate this squalid universe. Chief among the outward social luminaries are the Merdles. As noted previously, Mrs. Merdle, described by Dickens as "the bosom," is an affected, transparent woman who claims to detest the social conventions of her time and professes a desire to return to a simpler lifestyle, as her conversation with Little Dorrit and her sister, Fanny, makes clear: "A more primitive state of society would be delicious to me.... If a few thousand persons moving in Society, could only go and be Indians, I would put my name down directly; but as, moving in Society, we can't be Indians, unfortunately—Good morning!" (*LD* 123). Yet, she is not above flaunting her wealth and looking down upon the lower social classes as characterized in the persons of Fanny and Amy Dorrit. Mrs. Merdle makes it perfectly clear that her position in society is superior to that of Fanny and Amy, and that it would be impossible for her to recognize either of them socially (*LD* 123).

The husband of "the bosom," Mr. Merdle, was professed by all to be "the man of his time. The name of Merdle is the name of the age" (*LD* 246). Perhaps Dickens is intimating in this passage that excrement was, indeed, an apt term for a society which, he believed, placed wealth before truth, honor, and hard work (perhaps the name itself is a play on the French word for excrement, "merde").[7] Mr. and Mrs. Merdle threw parties that were attended by all the "right" people, and society for its part, sanctioned the Merdles: "Society was aware of Mr. and Mrs. Merdle. Society had said 'let us license them; let us know them'" (*LD* 125). Yet, despite their false and avaricious natures, it seemed that the Merdles acted solely for the benefit of the glittering society which they populated. Mr. Merdle, who fancied himself as a patron of society, is mockingly referred to as disinterested and unmindful of gain, even as he solicits contributions to his sham enterprise among the guests at his house.

Like Midas, everything Merdle touched was turned to gold, and investment turned to admiration, which quickly proceeded to adulation: "All the people knew (or thought they knew) that he had made himself

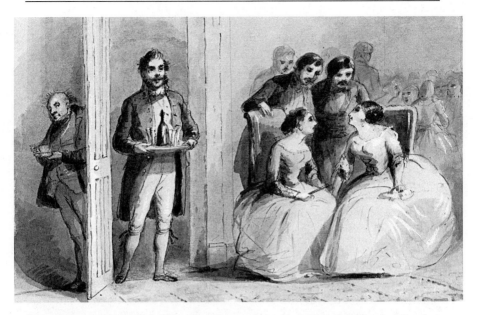

Scene from *Little Dorrit*. "Mr. Merdle stands in awe of his chief butler, & takes his tea behind the door, when that magnificent functionary appears"; wash on paper by Alfred Jacob Miller. Mr. Merdle, who is hiding from view in this scene, was declared to be the man of his age. He is exposed as a fraud and slits his wrists in a public bath house. His suicide leads to the ruin of many investors in his bank, including Arthur Clenham (Walters Art Museum).

immensely rich; and, for that reason alone, prostrated themselves before him, more degradedly and less excusably than the darkest savage creeps out of his hole in the ground to propitiate, in some log or reptile, the Deity of his benighted soul" (*LD* 282). This Merdle, ascending the social ladder like a comet, became affiliated with that other highly connected, one might say, tight family, the Barnacles, and was proposed for a peerage; such is the power of money, as portrayed by Dickens.

Not to be outdone by the rich and famous, Fanny Dorrit, formerly of the Marshalsea, was herself adept in the posturings of Society. Considering herself to be superior in every way to her colleagues, or "collegians," in the Marshalsea, Fanny expressed her attitude toward Society to her sister Amy: "If I am ever a little provoking, I am sure you'll consider what a thing it is to occupy my position and feel a consciousness of being superior to it" (*LD* 120). Once released from the stifling confines of the Marshalsea where her societal luster was dimmed, Fanny thrust herself into Society with a will: "As to Miss Fanny, she had become the victim of an insatiate mania for what she called 'going into society'" (*LD* 244).

It might seem odd that a person raised in the confines of a notorious debtor's prison should develop an attitude of superiority towards other members of society. Fanny's sense of entitlement was a learned response, a response perfected by her father, William Dorrit. That illustrious gentleman, known as the "Father of the Marshalsea," had over long years become convinced that his largely honorific title, a title earned due to his longevity in the prison, conveyed a sense of importance and respect which he cultivated. Mr. Dorrit, in observing the perquisites he believed were owed to him in the Marshalsea, had come to expect to be given small "tributes" as a mark of respect that he believed were owed to him as the benefactor of the prison and its inhabitants. Failure to provide a sufficient monetary emolument met with Mr. Dorrit's displeasure, and past favors earned no merit with him on this sensitive topic, as Arthur Clenham learned: "Mr. Clenham did not increase with favour with the Father of the Marshalsea in the ratio of his increasing visits. His obtuseness on the great Testimonial question was not calculated to awaken admiration in the paternal breast, but had rather a tendency to give offence in that sensitive quarter" (*LD* 129).

So great was Mr. Dorrit's sense of entitlement that he referred to his behavior as a manifestation of "spirit": "At the same time, I preserve in doing this, if I may—ha—if I may use the expression—Spirit, Becoming Spirit" (*LD* 189). His tendency to take offense at perceived slights to his person became more pronounced after an inheritance freed him from the constraints of the debtor's prison and launched him into society. Travelling with his family in Italy, Mr. Dorrit arranged to rent a villa, where he and his family would spend time in order to become more "polished," that is, more fit for polite society. Upon his arrival at the villa, Mr. Dorrit was upset to learn that his accommodations were not ready, and complained to the agent of the villa: "You have treated this family with disrespect; you have been insolent to this family" (*LD* 233).

It was at this villa that Mr. Dorrit became acquainted with Mrs. Merdle, an acquaintance that would result in the marriage of Edmund Sparkler, Mrs. Merdle's son by a prior marriage, to Fanny Dorrit. The marriage resulted in an alliance that combined the Merdles, Dorrits and Barnacles, so that prison life and social life became nearly indistinguishable, as Little Dorrit mused to herself one day:

> It appeared on the whole, to Little Dorrit herself, that this same society in which they lived, greatly resembled a superior sort of Marshalsea. Numbers of people seemed to come abroad, pretty much as people had come into the prison; through debt, through idleness, relationship, curiosity, and general unfitness for getting on at home. They

were brought into these foreign towns in the custody of couriers and local followers, just as the debtors had been brought into the prison. They prowled about the churches and picture-galleries, much in the old, dreary, prison-yard manner. They were usually going away again to-morrow or next week, and rarely knew their own minds, and seldom did what they said they would do, or went where they said they would go; in all this again, very like the prison debtors. They paid high for poor accommodations, and disparaged a place while they pretended to like it: which was exactly the Marshalsea custom [*LD* 259–260].

A number of critics have pointed out an autobiographical element in Dickens's portrayal of Mr. Dorrit, who bears a striking resemblance to John Dickens, himself a "collegian" of the Marshalsea, as well as to Mr. Micawber of *David Copperfield* fame. The comparison does not end with the prison, however. Mr. Dorrit, Mr. Micawber, and John Dickens also shared an inability to manage money; as a result, all three spend time in debtor's prison. John Dickens, like Mr. Dorrit and Wilkins Micawber, had an affinity for language, a certain oratorical flourish, which Dickens captures so well in the novel.

After their release from prison the Dorrit family embarked on a European tour, and Mr. Dorrit hired a governess, Mrs. General, to provide training in the social graces to Amy and Fanny. Neither daughter embraced the training provided by Mrs. General, but Fanny at least, being supercilious by nature, recognized her new-found position in society; Little Dorrit did not, leading to the following impassioned speech by Mr. Dorrit:

"I said I was hurt. So I am. So I—ha—am determined to be, whatever is advanced to the contrary. I am hurt that my daughter, seated in the—hum—lap of fortune, should mope and retire and proclaim herself unequal to her destiny. I am hurt that she should—ha—systematically reproduce what the rest of us blot out; and seem—hum— I had almost said positively anxious—to announce to wealthy and distinguished society that she was born and bred in—ha hum—a place that I myself decline to name. But there is no inconsistency—ha—not the least, in my feeling hurt, and yet complaining principally for your sake, Amy. I do; I say again, I do. It is for your sake that I wish you, under the auspices of Mrs. General, to form a—hum—a surface. It is for your sake that I wish you to have a—ha—truly refined mind, and (in the striking words of Mrs. General) to be ignorant of everything that is not perfectly proper, placid, and pleasant" [*LD* 243].

Despite the halting expression, the "ha's and hum's," Dickens portrays a man who has practiced the art of rhetoric, formed through years of seeking small "tributes" from visitors to the Marshalsea, and can use these rhetorical tricks to his advantage. Yet despite the volubility, despite the professions of his superiority to those around him, neither he nor his brother Fredrick nor Amy nor Tip can escape the prison, which is physically represented by the Marshalsea, and symbolically represented as the entire Victorian world.

On his return to England to invest some money with Mr. Merdle, Mr. Dorrit is visited at his hotel by John Chivery, the son of the gatekeeper at the Marshalsea. Young John, as he is known in the novel, brings Mr. Dorrit a gift of cigars, a practice which he instituted in prison as a sign of respect to the "Father of the Marshalsea." Mr. Dorrit's response is both a show of his imagined social superiority and his inability to escape the Marshalsea, despite his attempts to forget his life in prison:

> "How do you presume to come here? How dare you insult me?"
> "Insult you sir?" cried Young John. "Oh!"
> "Yes, sir," returned Mr. Dorrit. "Insult me. Your coming here is an affront, an imper-tinence, an audacity. You are not wanted here. Who sent you here? What—ha—the Devil do you do here?"
> "I thought, sir," said Young John, with as pale and shocked a face as ever had been turned to Mr. Dorrit's in his life—even in his College life. "I thought, sir, you mightn't object to have the goodness to accept a bundle—"
> "Damn your bundle, sir!" cried Mr. Dorrit, in irrepressible rage. "I—hum—don't smoke."
> ... "Young John, I am very sorry to have been hasty with you, but—ha—some remem-brances are not happy remembrances, and—hum—you shouldn't have come" [*LD* 322].

The connection between the Marshalsea and polite society, the notion that there is no escape from the prison-world of Victorian society is made clear when Mr. Dorrit attends a party thrown by the Merdles, and addresses the crowd, composed of the "best" people in society as follows:

> "Ladies and gentlemen, the duty—ha—devolves upon me of—hum—welcoming you to the Marshalsea! Welcome to the Marshalsea! The space is—ha—limited—limited— the parade might be wider; but you will find it apparently grow larger after a time— a time, ladies and gentlemen—and the air is, all things considered, very good. It blows over the—ha—Surrey hills. Blows over the Surrey hills. This is the Snuggery. Hum. Supported by a small subscription of the—ha—Collegiate body. In return for which— hot water—general kitchen—and little domestic advantages. Those who are habituated to the—ha—Marshalsea, are pleased to call me its Father. I am accustomed to be com-plimented by strangers as the—ha—Father of the Marshalsea. Certainly, if years of residence may establish a claim to so—ha—honourable a title, I may accept the— hum—conferred distinction. My child, ladies and gentlemen. My daughter. Born here!" [*LD* 330]

Here is the same volubility, the same oratorical flourish he employs throughout the novel, but it is marred by the effects of a stroke which has left Mr. Dorrit unaware of his surroundings. Perhaps, it is fitting that he can no longer distinguish between the Marshalsea and the outside world; this is undoubtedly what Dickens intended. Mr. Dorrit's lack of awareness, although pitiable, helps to reinforce the point that there is no real distinc-tion between life lived in the Marshalsea Prison and life outside the prison, even in the highest levels of society.

No mention of the disdain in which Dickens holds social conventions would be complete without acknowledging one of his great comic creations, Mrs. General, keeper of the proprieties by way of "prunes, prisms, poultry, and potatoes." That estimable personage was retained to impart a "surface" on Amy and Fanny Dorrit by means of applying a "varnish" to their exterior. Mrs. General was one of those personages whose ideas of propriety were bounded by their limited intellectual achievements: "She had a little circular set of mental grooves or rails on which she started little trains of other people's opinions, which never overtook one another, and never got anywhere" (*LD* 229). She, like the Barnacles, was never concerned with the realities of life which might interfere with her limited scope of understanding. Her advice to Amy Dorrit could have come from Lord Decimus Tite Barnacle himself:

> Nothing disagreeable should ever be looked at. Apart from such a habit standing in the way of that graceful equanimity of surface which is so expressive of good breeding, it hardly seems compatible with refinement of mind. A truly refined mind will seem to be ignorant of the existence of anything that is not perfectly proper, placid, and pleasant [*LD* 242].

That Mrs. General's ideas of imparting a "surface" were somewhat hollow, is reflected in Amy Dorrit's ruminations: "Prunes and Prism, in a thousand combinations, having been wearily in the ascendant all day—everything having been surface and varnish and show without substance—Little Dorrit looked as if she had hoped that Mrs. General was safely tucked up in bed for some hours" (*LD* 256). It is fitting that Mrs. General slinks away after Mr. Dorrit's stroke; having discovered that the family origins lie in the Marshalsea, Mrs. General can no longer present herself in polite society with the Dorrit family, and must find another family upon whom she may impart her proprieties.

Unable to find solace from the dysfunction of the world-view of the novel, it might be natural to expect that the characters would turn to organized religion for comfort. However, the only religion to be found in the novel is that of the warped, Old Testament vindictiveness exhibited by Mrs. Clenham. Mrs. Clenham's idea of religion was formed around the principles of retribution, wrath and hatred:

> She then put on the spectacles and read certain passages aloud from a book—sternly, fiercely, wrathfully—praying that her enemies (she made them by her tone and manner expressly hers) might be put to the edge of the sword, consumed by fire, smitten by plagues and leprosy, that their bones might be ground to dust, and that they might be utterly exterminated [*LD* 18].

Her implacable nature, combined with her self-righteousness, reduced her life to one of retribution and self-imprisonment. She professes a form of religion where the only courses of action are self-denial and punishment. The following speech, uttered to Mr. Blandois, illustrates her belief system:

> If I forgot that this scene, the Earth, is expressly meant to be a scene of gloom, and hardship, and dark trial, for the creatures who are made out of its dust, I might have some tenderness for its vanities. But I have no such tenderness. If I did not know that we are, every one, the subject (most justly the subject) of a wrath that must be satisfied, and against which mere actions are nothing, I might repine at the difference between me, imprisoned here, and the people who pass that gateway yonder [*LD* 182].

Mrs. Clenham's bitterness and vindictiveness have led her to set up an idol, rather than worship God. The idol is made in her own image, for she, like many of the characters in the novel, has mistaken the order of creation: "Yet, gone those more than forty years, and come this Nemesis now looking her in the face, she still abided by her old impiety—still reversed the order of Creation, and breathed her own breath into a clay image of her Creator" (*LD* 394). For the Barnacles, the Merdles, Mrs. Clenham, Mrs. General, Fanny and William Dorrit, and others like them, religion offers no refuge from the society they have created, and the prisons which they have constructed for themselves.

Dickens adds one final touch of depravity to the picture of society painted in *Little Dorrit* in the form of the evil people who prey upon the unfortunate characters inhabiting the poorer portions of the city. As Little Dorrit passes through Covent Garden, Dickens apostrophizes those members of society who have neglected the poor, leading to:

> ... desolate ideas of Covent Garden, ... where the miserable children in rags among whom she had just now passed, like young rats, slunk and hid, fed on offal, huddled together for warmth, and were hunted about (look to the rats young and old, all ye Barnacles, for before God they are eating away our foundations, and will bring the roofs on our heads!) ... [*LD* 84].

Two characters stand apart from the other evil personages in the novel, two characters who display sociopathic tendencies which mark them as the final piece to the puzzle of social decay in *Little Dorrit*. The first, a woman, displays her antisocial tendencies early in the novel, when she informs Mr. Meagles while quarantined in Marseilles: "'If I had been shut up in any place to pine and suffer, I should always hate that place and wish to burn it down, or raze it to the ground. I know no more'" (*LD* 12). Miss Wade is meant to be a counterpoint to Little Dorrit, who, despite being locked away in Marshalsea some twenty years, has grown to venerate the prison as a result of the associations of family she developed there. Miss

Wade, she of the "unhappy temper," invents insults where none are intended, and cherishes the slights she feels, as she relates to Arthur Clenham: "Let him [Blandois] look round him (she said) and judge for himself what general intelligence was likely to reach the ears of a woman who had been shut up there while it was rife, devouring her own heart" (*LD* 334).

Miss Wade's character, which devours her own heart, is formed as a result of her early upbringing as an orphan, one of the many orphans who occupy not only this novel, but many of Dickens's works. Her conversation with Mr. Meagles concerning Tattycoram, sheds some light on her early childhood: "What your broken plaything is as to birth, I am. She has no name, I have no name. Her wrong is my wrong. I have nothing more to say to you" (*LD* 169). The kindness exhibited by her guardians is interpreted as condescension by Miss Wade, and she turns all good acts performed on her behalf into a personal affront, resulting in her rejection of love and her anti-social behavior. Later, she explains herself to Arthur Clenham, and provides an insight into her character in the process: "'For this reason [her rejection of Mr. Gowan's love] I have for some time inclined to tell you what my life has been—not to propitiate your opinion, for I set no value on it; but that you may comprehend, when you think of your dear friend and his dear wife, what I mean by hating'" (*LD* 336).

Miss Wade's hatred extended even to her closest friends, as she related in the account of her life to Arthur Clenham. During her stay at her "grandmother's" house, which was in reality a lodging house for orphans, she developed a fondness for one of the children living in the house. Over time, Miss Wade convinced herself that her childhood friend was plotting against her for the affections of the other residents in the household, and related to Mr. Clenham that: "...I would hold her in my arms till morning: loving her as much as ever, and often feeling as if, rather than suffer so, I could so hold her in my arms and plunge to the bottom of a river—where I would still hold her after we were both dead" (*LD* 338).

Miss Wade is a portrait of a sociopath, but the formation of her character is in some ways the fault of a social system that does not know how to care for orphans, that does not know how to exhibit compassion or human kindness. Miss Wade's character is an indictment of the systems which Dickens dislikes, and to which he returns time and again, in an attempt to effect real social change.[8] As a result, Miss Wade, in an attempt to ameliorate the hurt she has experienced, traps herself in a prison of her own making, a prison where only hatred and bitterness can grow. Instead of the kindness and mercy that Little Dorrit exhibits, Miss Wade can only sow hatred and self-loathing.

That Miss Wade should form an alliance with another evil person, one identified several times with the devil, is not surprising. A known murderer, blackmailer, and scoundrel, Blandois is Dickens's idea of evil incarnate. From his introduction to the reader in the prison in Marseilles to his involvement in uncovering the mystery of Mrs. Clenham's secret, Blandois is unfailingly presented as all that is evil in society, despite his somewhat genteel appearance. Mr. Gowan, the dilettante painter and isolated scion of the Barnacle family tree, sees though Blandois' exterior to the essence of the man within: "'There he stands, you see' ... 'a murderer after the fact. Show that white hand of yours, Blandois. Put it outside the cloak. Keep it still....' 'He was formerly in some scuffle with another murderer, or with a victim, you observe...'" (*LD* 250).

Blandois commits his crimes as a form of retribution for his treatment at the hands of society, a treatment he resolves to avenge early in the novel: "'Such are the humiliations that society has inflicted upon me, possessing the qualities I have mentioned, and which you know me to possess. But society shall pay for it'" (*LD* 67). Blandois, like Mrs. Clenham and Miss Wade, keeps a scrupulous ledger of the insults he receives and calculates the cost of those insults with the precision of a merchant: "'I sell anything that commands a price. How do your lawyers live, your politicians, your intriguers, your men of the Exchange? How do you live? How do you come here? Have you sold no friend? Lady of mine! I rather think yes!'" (*LD* 381).

His actions are calculated to do the most harm to the society which he despises, a fitting circumstance where the prisoner takes retribution on the various forms of prison that populate the novel: "Society sells itself and sells me: and I sell society" (*LD* 381). When he falls, as all proud persons must in the novel, he takes down the house of Clenham (literally) along with its partners, Mr. Flintwinch and Mrs. Clenham. In the end, the Merdles are destroyed, the Barnacles embarrassed, the inheritance of Mr. Dorrit is squandered, Blandois killed, Mrs. Clenham the victim of a stroke which makes her an invalid (this time her imprisonment is imposed externally as opposed to internally), bankers ruined, the general populace involved in the fall of Merdle's empire. The entire social structure comes crashing down like the house of Clenham, itself built upon deceit and treachery. Hobsbaum notes the effects of jail on the members of society and comments on the lack of responsibility of those who are charged with governing the institutions that are supposed to benefit the population. He likens these people charged with governance to poor parents, specifically, poor fathers:

> The area of destruction wrought by the jailers in *Little Dorrit* is seen to be far-reaching. That these jailers are represented as bad fathers—true even of the masculine Mrs. Clenham—is not accidental. For behind them all is the abdication of responsibility on the part of Society, alike represented by the Circumlocution Office, by the Marshalsea, and by the circumscribed world of Mrs. General, Mrs. Merdle, and the Magnates [210].

Dickens draws a parallel between bad government and bad parenting. The failure of a parent to adequately provide for his/her children, in Dickens's worldview, leads to the same lack of care in the functioning of government; one form of neglect begets the other.

Is there a saving grace in the novel, an antidote to the contagion that sweeps through the town and destroys everything in its wake, like the Merdle-disease that wracked the inhabitants of Bleeding Heart Yard? Unfortunately, no such antidote exists on a universal scale. Dickens, disillusioned, is unable to develop a program which would cure the ills he paints in the dysfunctional view of the world of *Little Dorrit*. Instead, he offers provisional hope that the good characters in the novel can somehow eke out a living amid the squalor and hopelessness that pervades London. It is only this provisional, personal form of salvation that Dickens can offer. The blight of the city, the indifference of governmental institutions, the hypocrisy of social conventions, the useless hope that panders to the populace by means of organized religion, the almost blind pursuit of wealth, the evil of characters like Blandois and Miss Wade cannot be white-washed away. At best, the good characters can only hope to lead a life such as Arthur and Amy Clenham, who:

> Went down into a modest life of usefulness and happiness. Went down to give a mother's care, in the fullness of time, to Fanny's neglected children no less than to their own, and to leave that lady going into Society for ever and a day. Went down to give a tender nurse and friend to Tip for some few years, who was never vexed by the great exactions he made of her in return for the riches he might have given her if he had ever had them, and who lovingly closed his eyes upon the Marshalsea and all its blighted fruits. They went quietly down into the roaring streets, inseparable and blessed; and as they passed along in sunshine and shade, the noisy and the eager, and the arrogant and the froward and the vain, fretted and chafed, and made their usual uproar [*LD* 420].

Is there no more? Is there no salvation, no cure to the dysfunction that permeates the novel? Can Dickens develop no antidote to the disease of life in London? In this, his most mature novel, he admits that such an universal cure is beyond him. Perhaps, like Arthur and Amy, the best that can be hoped for is to walk quietly in the sunshine and the shade while the world roars along, indifferent to the lives of individual men and women.

Afterword

This book has attempted to understand Dickens's fictional and non-fictional writing and his philanthropic endeavors by examining a number of themes in his works. The selection of the themes covered in this book is based on my desire to better understand Dickens's life and work. Other themes could have been selected, and in fact, some may argue with the selection of themes made in this book. Hopefully, the themes selected, and the analysis provided, will help readers to appreciate Dickens's literary and philanthropic efforts.

In following the life of an author, especially one with the literary output of Dickens, a careful reading will reveal the author's mastery of his craft. Dickens's proficiency as an author grew over time and so did his desire to effect changes in Victorian society. The number of causes that Dickens championed has a common theme: his desire to help those in need. Whether the cause was for the establishment of better working conditions for common laborers; for the provision of education for the poor; for improved sanitary condition in London; a second chance for women engaged in prostitution; the establishment of funds to provide for authors and actors who died leaving families behind; for the creation of a universal system of copyright; Dickens pursued these endeavors with the single-minded determination that enabled him to rise from poverty to the best loved writer of his generation.

Yet, despite his desire to effect change during his lifetime, some changes are too difficult to accomplish. The "system," that impersonal set of nameless bureaucrats who populate governmental agencies, acts like inertia, wearing down the efforts of all persons who attempt to make profound changes. Over time, Dickens's invectives against the "system" did not stop, but his belief that change could come through hard work and determination, waned. By the end of his career, he recognized that change only happens incrementally, and absent some grand plan, perhaps change can only be effected provisionally and on a personal level.

Like many people, Dickens was a study in contrasts. He wrote tirelessly about the need for nuclear families to provide stability and a safe environment for children, but he failed to provide such an environment for his own children. His belief in the sanctity of marriage was real, but he was unable to maintain his own marriage. He preached about the evils inherent in money for its own sake, but worked tirelessly to earn money; an endeavor which cost him his health and life. Yet, these are human faults, and weighed against the great good he accomplished his faults can be pardoned.

Some one hundred and sixty odd years ago, Charles Dickens wrote the opening to *David Copperfield.* It began: "Whether I shall turn out to be the hero of my own life, or whether that station will be held by anybody else, these pages must show" (*DC* 1). Somewhat surprisingly, Charles Dickens later admitted to John Forster that he did not realize that the initials of the hero of his novel, D.C, were the reverse of his own initials, C.D. Perhaps, in reversing the initials of his fictional character with his own initials, Dickens was unconsciously thinking that he, too, was the hero of his own life.

Some one hundred and ten years after the publication of *David Copperfield*, an American writer, in her first novel, attempted to define courage, and in the process, offered a definition of a hero: "I wanted you to see something about her—I wanted you to see what real courage is, instead of getting the idea that courage is a man with a gun in his hand. It's when you know you're licked before you begin but you begin anyway and you see it through no matter what." These words were spoken by Atticus Finch to his son Jem in Harper Lee's novel *To Kill a Mockingbird* (128).

Sometime after the publication of *David Copperfield*, Dickens must have known that, despite his best efforts, Victorian society was not about to change. The poor would be with him always; sanitary conditions would improve slowly, if at all; the courts would continue to plod along, and squander men's resources and lay waste their lives; Parliament would continue to promote the interests of its members and neglect the interests of its constituents; men would continue to be men: venal, selfish, wicked, foolish, self-serving. Yet, after the publication of *David Copperfield*, he wrote six additional novels, each one hammering away at one of the ills which Dickens saw in the society in which he lived.

He began these novels knowing that he was "licked before he began," but he continued anyway. In the process, he never lost his faith in individual people; never lost his faith that imagination and "fancy" were worth fighting for; never lost his sense of humor that carried him through when things looked bleakest; never lost hope that better days might be had for those people who worked hard and attempted to help their fellow men.

The words written some one hundred sixty odd years ago have been judged by posterity; for the millions of readers who have hoped that Oliver Twist would be given more gruel; who have wondered with people standing on the docks of New York Harbor "Is Little Nell dead?"; who have hoped that Charles Darnay would be spared a death, and who read the famous last words of Sydney Carton: "It is a far, far, better thing that I do, than I have ever done; it is a far, far better rest that I go to than I have ever known"; Charles Dickens has earned the right to be called the hero of his own life.

Appendix: Suggested Reading

For those wishing to become more familiar with Dickens's life, I suggest Jane Smiley's *Charles Dickens: A Life*, as a good starting point. Similarly, Peter Ackroyd's book, *Dickens: Public Life and Private Passion* that was released in conjunction with a BBC television series on Dickens is both informative and entertaining. For those readers who are interested in a deeper knowledge of Dickens' life, John Forster's two-volume edition *The Life of Charles Dickens* is an invaluable guide written by the man who was closest to Dickens during his lifetime and was personally selected by Dickens to write his official biography. There are several abridged versions of Forster's books that are available and I recommend the recently published *The Life of Charles Dickens: The Illustrated Edition* as being less daunting while retaining Forster's insights into Dickens's life. Edgar Johnson's work *Charles Dickens: His Tragedy and Triumph* (in either the abridged or the unabridged version) is an exploration of Dickens's life, psychology, and works. Johnson provides an empathetic reading of Dickens's life and makes a case that despite his impoverished childhood, Dickens was able to overcome his early misfortunes and develop into one of the greatest English authors. Finally, Michael Slater's recent biography, *Charles Dickens*, is the work of the man considered the foremost Dickens scholar of his generation.

There are a number of web sites which provide information about Charles Dickens. *David Perdue's Charles Dickens Page* is highly informative and can be found at: http://charlesdickenspage.com/. The Charles Dickens Museum is a repository of information on the life of the "Inimitable." The website is located at: http://dickensmuseum.com/. As an added bonus to those interested in Dickens's life, the Museum hosts a reading of *The Christmas Carol* by Michael Slater each year. *The Victorian Web* provides information about Charles Dickens and presents an overview of Victorian life; it can be located at: http://victorianweb.org/.

Finally, for those interested in joining a group of readers and scholars dedicated to all things Dickensian, The Dickens Society provides a welcoming environment to read, learn and write about Charles Dickens. The Society publishes the *Dickens Quarterly* and holds an annual meeting where papers are presented and discussed. The website is located at: http://dickenssociety.org/.

Chapter Notes

Introduction

1. Michael Slater comments on Dickens's dashed hopes of becoming a gentleman after the family moved from Chatham to London, as well as his subsequent work in Warren's Blacking Factory in the first chapter of his biography *Charles Dickens*.

2. A sponging house was a private residence where debtors were taken by a bailiff prior to being consigned to debtor's prison. Confinement at a sponging house lasted for a period of a few days, and was an attempt to provide debtors with some time to raise funds to pay their debt prior to being sent to prison.

3. Dickens changed publishers on several occasions because he felt that the publishers were somehow short-changing him. He left his first publisher, John Macrone, and switched to Chapman and Hall, then to Bradbury and Evans as a result of conflicts over publishing fees.

His separation from Catherine was the result of marital incompatibility. Dickens proposed to publish a public letter addressing his separation from his wife, and asked the advice of John Forster about such a course of action. Forster advised him not to publish the letter, but Dickens did not heed his advice. Dickens produced a written letter to an associate, Arthur Smith, who was Dickens's organizer for a series of reading tours and encouraged him to show the letter to anyone who was friendly to him. The letter made its way into London papers and caused a scandal.

It has become known as the "Violated Letter," and its treatment of Catherine shows a vindictive side of Dickens's character that is difficult to understand in a man so firmly a champion of domestic life and happiness. See the *Selected Letters*, pages 337–338, for the full text of the "Violated Letter," as well as several other letters which Dickens wrote about his failed marriage.

4. Dickens, in a letter to Maria Winter (née Beadnell), dated February 15, 1851, indicated that as a result of her rejection of him, he could not show his affections, "even to my children, except when they are very young." (Dickens *SL*).

5. While in Italy, Dickens composed a letter to Catherine Dickens, dated November 8, 1844, who remained at the couple's home in Devonshire Terrace. In the letter he urged Catherine to "Keep things in their places. I can't bear to picture them otherwise," (Dickens *SL*). In a similar vein, there is a passage in *David Copperfield*, where David invites a few of his friends to celebrate the start of his life in London. At the celebration, the mutton that was intended as the main course for the meal was ruined, causing Wilkins Micawber, one of the invited guests at the party to exclaim: "My dear friend Copperfield ... accidents will occur in the best-regulated families..." (*DC* 413). A similar assertion is made by Mr. Jingle in *The Pickwick Papers*: "I see—never mind—accidents will happen—best-regulated families—never say die..." (*PP* 31).

Chapter One

1. Frederick William Roe, in his "Introduction" to the anthology *Victorian Prose*, notes the destabilization brought about by the migration of people from rural to urban areas during the Victorian era: "The vast material expansion, we may be sure, meant concomitant changes and problems affecting the whole structure of society. No previous social order in all history had seen such rapid and revolutionary mutation as the Victorians saw unfolding before their astonished eyes. A little before this age began, the ways of human life were not radically different from what they had been for centuries...."

2. The New Poor Law was passed in 1834 and mandated that all able-bodied persons should work, and not accept charity. In the event that an able-bodied person could not find employment, he/she would be consigned to a workhouse and supplied with food and lodging in exchange for his/her labor. In addition to the persons who were unable to find employment, the workhouses also housed illegitimate children, lunatics and criminals. Each administrative parish (the smallest unit of local government in England) was required to set up its own workhouse which was administered by the local authorities. As a result of the local nature of the parish administration, the quality of life afforded to the people housed by the various workhouses differed dramatically. A Poor Law Commission was established in an attempt to regulate the administration of the workhouses, and the Commission was charged with formulating regulations for the administration of the various parishes, although compliance with the regulations was not scrupulously enforced. For a brief description of the Poor Laws, see the *New Encyclopaedia Britannica*, volume 9. A more complete description of the New Poor Law can be found at the *Victorian Web*, http://www.victorianweb.org/history/poorlaw/plaatext.html, as well as *The National Archive* at: http://www.nationalarchives.gov.uk/education/resources/1834-poor-law/. A PDF of the full text of the New Poor Law of 1834 can be found at: http://www.educationengland.org.uk/documents/acts/1834-poor-law-amendment-act.html.

3. A number of quotations from Chadwick's *Report* follow. Commenting on the housing arrangements of the laboring population in Liverpool, a Dr. Duncan notes the lack of sewers which lead to poor drainage and unsanitary conditions: "There can be no doubt that the emanations from this pestilential surface, in connection with other causes, are a frequent source of fever among the inhabitants of these undrained localities" (18).

Commenting on the lack of potable water, Chadwick notes: "No previous investigations had led me to conceive the great extent to which the labouring classes are subjected to privations, not only of water for the *purpose* of ablution, house cleansing, and sewerage, but of wholesome water for drinking, and culinary purposes" (35).

The lack of sufficient land drainage and its contribution to disease is noted by Chadwick: "In considering the circumstances external to the residence which affect the sanitary conditions of the population, the importance of a general land drainage is developed by the inquiries as to the cause of the prevalent diseases, to be of a magnitude of which no conception had been formed at the commencement of the investigation: its importance is manifested by the severe consequences of its neglect in every part of the country..." (44).

Chadwick next quotes from the Commission of the Metropolitan Police regarding the spread of disease from several occupations including bone-pickers, a subject which Dickens explores in *Our Mutual Friend*: "We cannot wonder at the rapidity with which contagion often spreads. Both in and out of doors, it seems facilitated on every way; within doors every article of furniture and wearing apparel is disfigured with filth; every spot seems encrusted with its layers, and the foulest odors abound everywhere. Out of doors, at least in warm seasons, our churchyards, slaughter-houses, and the masses of filth and offal with which our streets and lanes are disgraced contribute no less to the propagation of contagion" (52).

Turning to the deaths of orphans and the number of widows prevalent in the tailoring industry, Chadwick writes: "The frequency of cases of early death, and orphanage, and widowhood amongst one class of labourers, the journeymen tailors, led me to make some inquiries as to the causes affecting them; and I submit the following evidence ... bad ventilation and overcrowding..." (53).

Chadwick's denunciation of the poor working conditions of the tailors is followed up by a description of the conditions in the mines, specifically the sleeping quarters of the miners: "...yet from 39 to 40 persons slept there [in a space of about eight by fifteen feet].... The beds had not been slept in for Friday, Saturday and Sunday nights preceding, yet was the smell most noxious.... What this place must be in the summer nights is, happily for those who have never felt it, utterly inconceivable.... In such a dense accumulation of bodies, one man who might be ill was a disturbance to all the rest.... Men coming from the mine at 12 o'clock at night, and frying their bacon at the fire below, sent up an odour which added to the already too suffocating smell of the sleeping-room above" (60).

A Dr. Walker, surgeon at the Greenock Infirmary, comments on the overcrowded conditions in private houses: "The rooms are in most instances small, and frequently far too much crowded. It is not unusual to see ten or twelve human beings occupying a room not as many feet square. The lower classes in these districts are grossly filthy in their persons and dwellings; and even many of our operatives who receive paid wages are extremely inattentive to cleanliness, both in person and in dwelling" (66).

4. Carlyle was a personal friend of Dickens. Dickens dedicated the novel *Hard Times for These Times* to Carlyle and used Carlyle's *The French Revolution: A History* as research for the novel *A Tale of Two Cities*. In a letter dated July 13, 1854, Dickens asked Carlyle's permission to dedicate *Hard Times* to him adding: "I know it contains nothing in which you do not think with me, for no man knows your books better than I" (*SL* 278–279).

5. The novel *Barnaby Rudge* was written in 1841 before Dickens's letter to Forster and prior to his departure for Italy in 1844. During this time period, Dickens was beginning to become dissatisfied with English society and worried that failure to enact social reforms would lead to a series of uprisings similar to the Gordon Riots. In 1859, having read Carlyle's *The French Revolution* and completed his novel *A Tale of Two Cities*, Dickens's views on the need for social reform become more bleak. He feared that something more akin to the French Revolution might occur in England. A letter written to John Forster on February 4, 1855 illustrates Dickens's increasing frustration with the lack of social reform: "I am hourly strengthened in my old belief, that our political aristocracy and our tuft-hunting are the death of England. In all this business I don't see a gleam of hope" (*SL* 282).

6. The success of the *Sketches* led the proprietors of the newly established firm of Chapman and Hall to propose that Dickens write the narrative pieces that were meant to accompany the illustrations provided by Robert Seymour for a series entitled the "Nimrod Club." The "Club" was originally conceived as a series of adventures of a group of country sportsman. Dickens convinced the publishers that this plan would not work and it was replaced by the adventures of the men comprising the Pickwick Club. See chapter 4 of Michael Slater's book *Charles Dickens* for further details of the writing of the *Sketches* and *Pickwick*. Edgar Johnson comments on the writing of the *Sketches* and *Pickwick* in chapters 6 and 7 of his book *Charles Dickens: His Tragedy and Triumph* (abridged edition).

7. An alternative reading may be argued that the use of the pronoun "we" is an attempt at inclusion on the part of Dickens. Benedict Anderson makes the argument that a common language is one of the requirements leading to the development of an imagined community which eventually leads to the formation of the nation-state. He goes on to argue that language is not exclusive, but inclusive. Viewed from this vantage point, Dickens's use of the pronoun "we" can be seen as an

attempt to make the characters depicted in the *Sketches* inclusive, a part of a larger group. While this argument has some appeal, I do not believe that Dickens intended the *Sketches* to portray a community, imagined or otherwise, of fully integrated people functioning in a large group setting. See Benjamin Anderson's *Imagined Communities* for a complete description of the formation of communities based on official languages.

In other works, Dickens uses the word "we" to establish a connection among his characters and with his readers. In fact, Dickens used the prefaces of his novels to directly address his readers as the opening of *David Copperfield* suggests: "So true are these avowals at the present day, that I can now only take the reader into one confidence more. Of all my books, I like this the best" (*DC*).

8. Dickens met Maria Beadnell in 1829 when he was seventeen. He developed an infatuation for her which continued for several years. At first Mr. and Mrs. Beadnell tolerated Dickens's presence at various parties and family gatherings, but by 1831 Mr. Beadnell learned that John Dickens had been sent to the Marshalsea Prison and the Beadnell's relations with Dickens became more reserved. Finally, in an attempt to discourage Maria's affections for Dickens, she was sent to Paris to complete her education. Upon her return to London in 1832, Maria broke off her relationship with Dickens. Please see chapter 5 of Edgar Johnson's *Charles Dickens: His Tragedy and Triumph* (abridged edition) for a more complete discussion of Dickens's courtship of Maria Beadnell.

Chapter Two

1. In addition to the characters of Alfred Jingle and Sally Brass, there are a number of additional characters whose names seem suggestive of their personality, including: Serjeant Buzfuz and Mr. Fogg in *The Pickwick Papers*; Mr. Bumble in *Oliver Twist;* the Cheerybles, Smike, Pluck and Pyke in *Nicholas Nickleby;* Sampson Brass in *Old Curiosity Shop;* Mr. Mould, Chevy Slyme, Jefferson Brick, and Doctor John Jobling in *Martin Chuzzle-*

witt; Doctor Blimber, Captain Cuttle, Mrs. Mac-Stinger and Lucretia Tox in *Dombey and Son;* Mr. Creakle, Steerforth, Mr. Edward Murdstone and his sister Jane Murdstone in *David Copperfield;* Miss Flite, Lawrence Boythorn, Harold Skimpole, Guppy, Mr. Jarndyce, Tony Jobling, The Smallweeds, Sir Leicester and Lady Dedlock, Mr. Vholes, and Mrs. Jellyby in *Bleak House;* Mr. Bounderby, Mr. Gradgrind, M'Choakumchild in *Hard Times;* the Barnacles, Mrs. General, Edmund Sparkler, the Merdles, and Flora Finching in *Little Dorrit;* Bradley Headstone, the Podsnaps, and the Veneerings in *Our Mutual Friend.*

2. In this quotation, it appears that Micawber is repeating himself. The first use of the word nineteen refers to pounds; the second use of the word nineteen refers to shillings.

3. The number of orphaned and fatherless children in Dickens's fiction is staggering. There are orphans in *Oliver Twist* (Oliver, Fagin's pickpockets, Nancy, Bill Sikes); *Nicholas Nickleby* (Smike, a number of the boys at Dotheboys Hall); *Martin Chuzzlewitt* (Martin, Mary Graham, Tom Pinch and his sister Ruth); *Old Curiosity Shop* (Little Nell, her brother, Fred Trent, The Marchioness, Dick Swiveller, Miss Edwards and her sister, the little scholar); *David Copperfield* (David, Emily, Traddles, Rosa Dartle, Ham, the Orfling, Dora after her father's death); *Bleak House* (Esther Summerson {at least before the discovery of Lady Dedlock's earlier life}, Jo, Richard Carstone, Ada Clare); *Little Dorrit* (Miss Wade and Maggy); *Our Mutual Friend* (John Harmon/Julius Handford/ John Rokesmith, Eugene Wrayburn, Lizzie Hexam after the death of her father); *Great Expectations* (Pip, Estella, Mrs. Joe Gargery, Biddy). In addition to the proliferation of orphans, there are motherless or fatherless children in each of the aforementioned novels, as well as in *Barnaby Rudge* (Barnaby, Edward Chester) *Dombey and Son* (Paul Jr., and Florence Dombey, Walter Gay, Mrs. Edith Dombey) *Hard Times* (Sissy Jupe, Josiah Bounderby), *A Tale of Two Cities* (Lucie Manette, Charles Darnay). In fact, each of Dickens's novels deals, in some way, with dysfunctional familial relationships.

4. The identification between the parental figure and the government is noted in Hobsbaum's book *A Reader's Guide to Charles Dickens*, when he writes: "Submerged deeper beneath the surface is a consuming rancor against the weakness of his father. The dynamics, not just of *David Copperfield*, but of many other Dickens novels, is a condemnation of father images; and, beyond that, of social institutions, for their failure to act on behalf of those who most stood in need.... Private charity, the interference of the strong on behalf of the weak—this was Dickens's panacea for the ills he saw all around him.... Behind all this is the feeling that fathers ought to be a protection against the world and that mothers ought to be a solace for its injustices" (114).

5. In 1847, Dickens, working with Angela Burdett Coutts, established Urania Cottage as a home to rehabilitate prostitutes. He composed a letter to the potential candidates for the home that is known as the "Letter to Fallen Women." In it, Dickens emphasizes that the women lodged in the home had made mistakes but that through hard work they can be rehabilitated. Dickens stresses that the habits formed at the home would enable the women to lead useful, productive lives as wives and mothers.

His philanthropic efforts included the production of plays and periodic writings for the benefit of fellow writers and actors whose death caused hardship to their families. After staging a number of these philanthropic efforts as one-off events, Dickens and Edward Bulworth Lytton decided to form a permanent society to help their fellow authors and actors. Accordingly, the two men founded the Guild of Literature and Art in 1850 to provide stability for those families in need of financial assistance.

The legacy of the Lytton family continues to the present day. Knebworth house, home to Edward Bulwer Lytton, is a museum and the Knebworth Trust provides educational opportunities relating to the Renaissance and Victorian time periods. Knebworth hosts an annual concert and has featured some of the most famous rock bands in the world.

6. Dickens makes use of a technique which presents two characters who are alike in manner, speaking or temperament. He intends that these characters should in some way complement one another. Dickens's technique of multiplying characters in such a way has been termed "doubling" by a number of critics. For a discussion of Dickens's technique of doubling characters, please see "Dickens: Doubles:: Twain: Twins," by Susan K. Gillman and Robert L. Patten.

7. The similarity between John Dickens and the characters of Wilkins Micawber and William Dorrit has been noted by many critics. In his life of Dickens, Forster notes that John Dickens was the basis for the character of Micawber noting that he "humoured and remembered the foibles of his original, found its counterpart in that of his readers for the creation itself, as its part was played out in the story" (Forster II: 127).

8. The relationship between the female characters like Esther Summerson, Little Nell and Agnes Wickfield, among others, has been noted by a number of critics. Edgar Johnson comments on Dickens's use of his sister-in-law Mary, as a template for these characters: "Indeed, out of his imagination she never died. Throughout almost his entire literary career his novels continue to reveal glimpses of now one and now another aspect of her shining image. Mary's gaiety and tenderness animate loving, laughing Ruth Pinch in *Martin Chuzzlewitt*. His vision of her nobler qualities recurs again and again, in Florence Dombey's devotion to her brother and father, in David Copperfield's serene and perhaps too perfect Agnes, in the sacrificial spirit of Little Dorrit. The very sentimentality that we sometimes find in their delineation is only a further index to the transcendent goodness with which he endowed Mary in his heart" (Johnson I. 128).

9. The Bildungsroman is a novel which portrays the growth of its protagonist from a young man or woman into a mature, fully developed human being. The story follows a progression where the protagonist undergoes some sort of tragedy. The tragedy causes the main character to embark on a series of adventures in an attempt

to discover him/her self. During the adventures, the main character overcomes a series of obstacles and, in so doing, comes to a realization of his true nature. An alternate name for the Bildungsroman is a "coming of age" novel.

10. Michael Slater discusses the care Dickens used in developing names for his novels and characters in *Charles Dickens*. As an example, Slater notes that Dickens considered as many as 16 different titles for the novel that was to become *David Copperfield*. Similarly, Slater notes that Dickens considered various names for the novel's protagonist, including "Flowerbury," "Copperboy" and that he took similar pains to name Copperfield's aunt including "Trotfield" and "Trotbury" (Slater 386–388).

11. There is no evidence that Dickens read the works of Plato and Aristotle, yet that does not in itself indicate that Dickens was unaware of the debate regarding naming and the notion that a name somehow conveys a sense of the inner nature of a person. Forster provides a listing of the books Dickens read as a child which included *Peregrine Pickle, Humphrey Clinker, Tom Jones, the Vicar of Wakefield, Don Quixote, Gil Blas, Robinson Crusoe, the Arabian Nights* and the tales of the *Genii* (9). Later, he mentions that Dickens was familiar with the *Tattler*, the *Spectator*, the *Idler*, the *Citizen of the World* and a *Collection of Farces* (13). Forster then lists some additional books that were lent to Dickens, including the *Scottish Chiefs, Dance of Death* and *Broad Grins* (18). R.F Dibble notes that Dickens was familiar with many of the prominent literary figures of the day and adds several additional books that Dickens was familiar with, including: George Eliot's *Scenes of a Clerical Life*, Mrs. Gaskell's novel *Mary Barton*, Tennyson's *Idylls*, Ruskin's *Lamps of Architecture*, Charles Knight's *Biography of Shakespeare*, Forster's *Life of Goldsmith*, Landor's *Imaginary Conversations* and Boswell's *Life of Johnson* (336–339). Brian Murray notes Dickens's admiration of the writings of Thomas Carlyle, Thomas Arnold, Robert Browning, Washington Irving, William Cullen Bryant, and Bret Harte (135–136). Dickens was also aware

of the writings of Edwin Chadwick on the sanitary conditions prevalent in England in the 1840s and familiar with Henry Mayhew's three volume work *on London Labour and the London Poor* published in the 1860s.

12. In the early parts of the novel, he is called by various names, including: "Master Davy, Master and My pet" by Peggoty; "Davy and Dear Davy" by his mother; "Sir and Mas'r Davy" by Mr. Peggoty, Ham and Mrs. Gummidge; "David and Brooks of Sheffield" by Mr. Murdstone; "Boy" by Miss Murdstone; "Master David" by Dr. Chillip; "The young Suffolker and the little gent" by the boys and men at Murdstone and Grinby's; "Copperfield" by Mr. and Mrs. Micawber; "Trotwood, Master Trotwood, pretty fellow, poor fellow, and Trot" by Aunt Betsey; and "Little Copperfield, Young Davy, and Daisy" by Steerforth.

13. I am indebted to Joseph Bottum, and his paper, "The Gentleman's True Name: *David Copperfield* and the Philosophy of Naming," for his insight into the character of the Micawbers, and their reluctance to assume a responsibility toward David as a small child, and not a grown-up companion, in the early parts of the novel. In addition, Mr. Bottum's paper notes the class distinctions between the Peggoty family and David on the one hand, as well as between the Steerforth family and David, on the other.

14. The list of orphans includes David, Emily, Dora, Ham, Steerforth, Traddles, Clara Copperfield, Rosa Dartle, Agnes Wickfield, Uriah Heep, Anne Strong, and the Orfling. To the list of broken families can be added a listing of the widowed, which includes Clara Copperfield, Mr. Murdstone, Peggoty, Mrs. Steerforth, Aunt Betsey, Mrs. Heep, and Mr. Omer.

15. Dickens's marriage to Catherine continued until 1858. Prior to abandoning his wife, Dickens wrote to Forster explaining that his temperament and career played a part in his estrangement from Catherine: "But the years have not made it easier to bear for either of us; and, for her sake as well as mine, the wish will force itself upon me that something might be done. I know too well it is impossible. There is the fact,

and that is all one can say. Nor are you to suppose that I disguise from myself what might be urged on the other side. I claim no immunity from blame. There is plenty of fault on my side, I dare say, in the way of a thousand uncertainties, caprices, and difficulties of disposition; but only one thing will alter all that, and that is, the end which alters everything" (*SL* 325). This was the closest Dickens would come to admitting his part in the estrangement from Catherine; later, he would paint Catherine as primarily responsible for their marital difficulties.

Chapter Three

1. Dickens makes use of the theme of angels in *The Old Curiosity Shop*, although it is not readily apparent. In addition to the quoted passages, there are two illustrations which appear in the Oxford Illustrated edition of the novel which shed further light on Dickens's use of angels in the book. Early in the novel (between pages 16 and 17), there is an illustration of Nell sleeping in her room. On the right-hand side of the bed is a crucifix and near it, two figures who appear to be hooded figures or spirits. On the last page of the book, page 555, there is a picture of Nell being wafted to heaven in the company of three angels, while a fourth angel plays a harp.

2. For a discussion of how mythology attempts to make sense of the chaos of daily life, see *Myth and Meaning: Cracking the Code of Culture* by Claude-Levi-Strauss. Joseph Campbell makes a similar point in *Myths to Live By*, noting that: "For not only has it been the way of multitudes to interpret their own symbols literally, but such literally read symbolic forms have always been—and still are, in fact—the supports of their civilizations, the supports of their moral orders, their cohesion, their vitality, and creative powers. With the loss of them there follows uncertainty, and with uncertainty, disequilibrium, since life, as both Nietzsche and Ibsen knew, requires life-supporting illusions; and where these have been dispelled, there is nothing secure to hold on to, no moral law, nothing firm."

Chapter Four

1. Here is Matthew's original passage: "Therefore I say unto you, Take no thought for your life, what ye shall eat, or what ye shall drink; nor yet for your body, what ye shall put on. Is not the life more than meat, and the body than raiment? /Behold the fowls of the air: for they sow not, neither do they reap, nor gather into barns; yet your heavenly Father feedeth them. Are ye not much better than they?" (6:25–26)

Chapter Five

1. Dickens began using the serial method of publication with the release of the *Pickwick Papers*. Each installment was issued on a monthly basis and featured thirty-two pages of text and one or two illustrations. The installments were bound in green covers with an illustration on each cover; advertisements were generally included in each installment. The monthly installment cost one shilling, which contributed to the popularity of the format. The final installment of each of the novels was published in a double issue, which included sixty-four pages of text and at least four illustrations. Hard bound copies of the novels were issued after the full novel was published in serial format. Dickens's two magazine offerings, published weekly, *Household Words* and *All the Year Round*, also made use of the serial form of publication.

2. Dickens was the "conductor" of *Household Words* (he declined to use the word editor), as well as being part owner of the magazine along with the publishers Bradbury and Evans. *Household Words* was published from 1850 to 1859, and was disbanded when he argued with his publishers regarding his separation from Catherine Dickens. The title of the magazine is derived from Henry V, Act IV, scene iii, when the King gives his St. Crispin Day speech, telling his followers that their deeds will be "Familiar in the mouth as household words" (Shakespeare I: 556). The magazine included articles on current events, news, inventions, editorials, and works of fiction. Dickens personally edited

each submission, often re-writing entire sections of an article or literary piece, and in a letter to William H. Wills, sub-editor of the magazine, urged him to scrupulously edit each piece with the adjuration: "Brighten it, brighten it, brighten it!" (*SL* 259–260). After publication of *Household Words* ceased, Dickens began a new weekly magazine, *All the Year Round*, which was published until 1893, several years after Dickens's death in 1870.

3. The Ragged Schools were a series of private institutions that were established as charitable organizations and were funded by private individuals. The aim of these schools was to provide a rudimentary knowledge of reading, handwriting and arithmetic to children whose families were too poor to send them to private institutions. Formalized, state run schooling was not adopted in England until 1870, when the Elementary Education Act was made law.

4. The notion that Utilitarianism can mean different things to different people is raised by Philip Hobsbaum in his discussion of the novel *Hard Times*: "It [the image of Coketown] is, however, powerfully backed by the figure of Thomas Gradgrind, who links it up with Utilitarianism. This philosophy is based upon Bentham's dictate concerning social legislation: that government should aim towards the greatest happiness of the greatest number of people. It is quite plain, on closer scrutiny, that this argument is open-ended; depending entirely upon who is defining 'greatest' and 'happiness' and from what position in life they are considering the proposition" (175).

5. Sabbatarianism was a movement that originated in the Puritan belief that the Bible required Christians to refrain from all activities on the Sabbath, including work and recreational activities. Dickens opposed this movement, believing that workers, who commonly worked six days a week, for twelve hours a day, had only one day—Sunday—to enjoy leisure activities.

Chapter Six

1. Dickens related to Forster that his younger brother, Augustus, was unable to pronounce the name Moses, and rendered the name Boses, which then became Boz (Forster I: 64).

2. Monroe Engle notes the connection between poverty, disease and crime in his paper "The Politics of Dickens' Novels": "He habitually linked poverty with filth and disease, and the connections between poverty, sanitation, and disease provide perhaps the most exploited subject in both *Household Words* and *All the Year Round*. Crime too he sees as a product of poverty and its companion, ignorance" (957).

3. Chapman and Hall published *The Pickwick Papers* in a series of monthly installments meant to act as textual accompaniment to a series of sporting sketches produced by the famous illustrator, Robert Seymour. The booklets were published on cheap paper set between green covers; the first installment sold 500 copies. Dickens decided that precedence should be given to the text and that the illustrations should be tailored to the story, not the other way around. Seymour, a proud man, committed suicide and Hablot Knight Browne "Phiz," was selected as the new illustrator, and was only too happy to follow Dickens's lead. The combination of the sketches by "Phiz" and the appearance of Sam Weller in chapter 10 caused sales of *The Pickwick Papers* to skyrocket and it publication rose to 40,000 copies per month. See Edgar Johnson's *Charles Dickens: His Tragedy and Triumph* (abridged version), chapter nine for a description of the success of *Pickwick Papers* and the increase in sales of the serial installments after the introduction of Sam Weller.

4. Neither system could be said to be preferable to the other; in fact, they appealed to different groups of people. The Auburn Model appealed to those people who believed that the prison should mimic the outside world, with a set of rewards and punishments that were designed to be enforced by the authorities. The prisoners complied because they were made to comply; to the extent that they could be reformed, they were reformed based on obedience and compliance.

The Philadelphia System appealed to those people who believed that the convict could be rehabilitated by reflecting on his crimes and applying the lessons learned in contemplation to his own particular situation. In this, it was similar to an ecclesiastical order which emphasized communal gatherings, in silence, followed by reflection and penitence. See Foucault's *Discipline and Punish*, part 4, chapter 1, for a description of the two types of prison systems that were adopted in the United States.

5. The Panopticon was a prison designed by Jeremy Bentham, and is formed from the Latin (pan, all-encompassing) and opticon (capable of being seen). The prison was designed as a circular structure, with a guard house at the center of the circle. The intent of the prison design was to enable each prisoner to be seen by the jailor at all times; as a result, the prisoner was deprived of privacy. A number of prisons, including Santo Stefano in Italy, the Rathway Prison in New Jersey and the Stateville Penitentiary in Illinois, have been built using the concept of the Panopticon, but none of them were built to Bentham's precise specifications. Critics of these types of prisons contend that they violate the prisoners' rights to privacy and that they lead to psychic disturbances. See Foucault's *Discipline & Punish*, part 3, chapter 3 concerning the Panopticon. Also, see *New Encyclopaedia Britannica*, volume 9 for a short description of the Panopticon designed by Jeremy Bentham.

6. Jenny Hartley, editor of the *Selected Letters of Charles Dickens*, has produced a book which traces the lives of the women who were wards in Urania House. The book is entitled *Charles Dickens and the House of Fallen Women*. In chapter 14, part 4, Hartley notes that of the 30 women who emigrated from England, 3 went to Canada, 1 to New Zealand, 6 to South Africa, leaving 20 women who emigrated to Australia. In chapter 15, part 4, Hartley writes that Jane Westaway originally emigrated to Australia where she married an American miner originally from Illinois, Thomas Stanfield. Records of Jane Westaway and Thomas Stanfield after their marriage cannot be traced and Hartley speculates that they may have returned to America.

Hartley notes that Urania Cottage closed in 1861 or 1862 and that Dickens's involvement in the Cottage ended in 1858 (Epilogue).

7. A number of critics have commented on the name Merdle and its association with the French word merde. Trey Philpotts in *The Companion to Little Dorrit* makes the following observation about Mr. Merdle's name on page 244: "In French merde means excrement, and merdaille a heap of dung. 'Merdle' also suggests 'mired,' 'marred,' 'murdered,' and 'muddle.'" On page 115, he mentions an interesting connection between Mr. Dorrit, who invests in Merdle's bank, and a dung beetle: "'Dor' or 'dorr' also means a dung beetle, particularly appropriate given William and Fanny Dorrit's interest in the Merdles (merde is French for excrement.)"

8. In the January 14, 1851 edition of *Household Words*, Dickens wrote a piece entitled "The Last Words of the Old Year," in which the departing year, 1850, addresses the readers of the magazine. The piece is a catalog of a number of the social problems which concerned Dickens, and was printed prior to his beginning work on *Bleak House*. In the piece, the old year lists the things which he accomplished in his 365 days of existence, including: blighting the farmers, destroying the land, his responsibility for the lack of reform on the part of the Commissioners of Sewers and the Board of Health, the lack of educational reform and the poverty which led children to small crimes of theft to relieve their hunger. The year places special emphasis on the construction of the Crystal Palace, designed to show the world the might of England, while at the same time, the country neglected the issues which affected its own population (Dickens, *HW* 337–339).

Works Cited

Ackroyd, Peter. *The Life and Times of Charles Dickens*. Irvington, New York: Hydra Publishing, 2002. Print.

Adrian, Arthur. *Dickens and the Parent-Child Relationship*. Athens, Ohio: Ohio University Press, 1984. Print.

Ainsworth, Mary D. Salter and Leonard H. Ainsworth. *Measuring Security in Personal Adjustment*. Toronto: University of Toronto Press, 1958. Print.

Anderson, Benedict. *Imagined Communities*. London: Verso, 2006. Print.

Bottum, Joseph. "The Gentleman's True Name: *David Copperfield* and the Philosophy of Naming." *Nineteenth-Century Fiction* 49.4 (1995): 435–55. Print.

Burke, Alan R. "The Strategy and Theme of Urban Observation in *Bleak House*." *Studies in English Literature, 1500–1900* 9.4 (1969): 659–76. Print.

Campbell, Joseph. *Myths to Live By*. New York: Penguin Compass, 1972. Print.

Carlyle, Thomas. "Signs of the Times." *Victorian Prose*. Ed. Roe, Frederick William. New York: The Ronald Press Company, 1947. 5–18. Print.

Carmichael, Virginia. "In Search of Beein': Nominon Du Pere in *David Copperfield*." *ELH* 54.3 (1987): 653–67. Print.

Chadwick, Edwin. *Report on the Sanitary Condition of the Labouring Population and on the Means of Its Improvement*. London 1842. Print.

Clark, Richard. "The History of Judicial Hanging in Great Britain 1735–1964." The Capital Punishment U.K. Website 1995. Web. 1/2/2016 2016.

Davies, Hayley. "Children, Family and Kinship." *Sociology* 45.4 (2011): 554–69. Print.

Dibble, R.F. "Dickens: His Reading." *Modern Language Notes* 35.6 (1920): 334–39. Print.

Dickens, Charles. *The Adventures of Oliver Twist*. The Oxford Illustrated Dickens: Oxford University Press, 1989. Print.

_____. *American Notes and Pictures from Italy*. The Oxford Illustrated Dickens. Oxford: Oxford University Press, 1989. Print.

_____. *Barnaby Rudge*. London: J. M. Dent & Sons Ltd., 1972. Print.

_____. *Bleak House*. The Modern Library Classics. Modern Library Paperback Edition ed. New York: The Modern Library, 2002. Print.

_____. *Christmas Books. A Christmas Carol*. The Oxford Illustrated Dickens. Oxford: Oxford University Press, 1989. Print.

_____. *David Copperfield*. New York: Washington Square Press, 1971. Print.

_____. "Dickens Journals Online." *Household Words*. 1850. Web.

_____. *Dombey and Son*. The Oxford Illustrated Dickens. Oxford: Oxford University Press, 1989. Print.

_____. *Great Expectations*. Harmondsworth: Penguin Classics, 1996. Print.

_____. *Hard Times*. Barnes and Noble Classics. Ed. Stade, George. New York: Barnes and Noble Classics, 2004. Print.

_____. "The Last Words of the Old Year." *Household Words* [London] March 22, 1851. http://www.archive.org/details/householdwords02dickmiss.

_____. *Little Dorrit. Great Books of the*

Western World. Ed. Adler, Mortimer J. Vol. 47. 60 vols. Chicago: Encyclopaedia Britannica, 2007. Print.

_____. *Martin Chuzzlewitt.* The Oxford Illustrated Dickens. Oxford: Oxford University Press, 1989. Print.

_____. *Nicholas Nickleby.* Barnes and Noble Classics. Ed. Stade, George. New York: Barnes and Noble Classics, 2005. Print.

_____. *The Old Curiosity Shop.* Harmondworth: The Penguin English Library, 1972. Print.

_____. *Our Mutual Friend.* The Oxford Illustrated Dickens`. Oxford: Oxford University Press, 1989. Print.

_____. *Pickwick Papers.* New York: Signet Classics, 1964. Print.

_____. *The Selected Letters of Charles Dickens.* Oxford: Oxford University Press, 2012. Print.

_____. *Sketches by Boz.* Penguin Classics. London: Penguin Books, 1995. Print.

_____. *Speeches: Literary and Social.* Sandy, Utah: Quiet Vision Publishing, 2003. Print.

_____. *A Tale of Two Cities.* The Oxford Illustrated Dickens. Oxford: Oxford University Press, 1989. Print.

Douglas-Fairhurst, Robert. *Becoming Dickens.* Cambridge: The Belknap Press of Harvard University Press, 2011. Print.

Eliot, George. "The Natural History of German Life." *Westminster Review* (1856): 71–72. Print.

Engel, Monroe. "The Politics of Dicken's Novels." *PMLA: Publications of the Modern Language Association of America* 71.5 (1956): 945–74. Print.

Finch, Janet. "Names: Kinship, Individuality and Personal Names." *Sociology* 42.4 (2008): 709–25. Print.

Forster, John. *The Life of Charles Dickens.* Vol. I. II vols. London: Chapman & Hall, LD., 1899. Print.

_____. *The Life of Charles Dickens.* Vol. II. II vols. London: Chapman & Hall, 1899. Print.

Foucault, Michel. *Discipline and Punish: The Birth of the Prison.* New York: Vintage Books, 1977. Print.

Freud, Sigmund. *The Major Works of Sigmund Freud.* Great Books of the Western World. Ed. Hoiberg, Dale H. Vol. 54.

60 vols. Chicago: Encyclopaedia Britannica, 1990. Print.

Gillard, Derek. "Education in England the History of Our Schools." 2010–2016. Web. 5/11/2016. http://www.education england.org.uk/documents/acts/1834-poor-law-amendment-act.html.

Gillman, Susan K. and Robert L. Patten. "Dickens: Doubles:: Twain: Twins." *Nineteenth-Century Fiction* 39.4 (1985): 441–58. Print.

Greenhut, Morris. "Henry Lewes as a Critic of the Novel." *Studies in Philology* 45.3 (1948): 491–511. Print.

Grillo, Virgil. *Charles Dickens' "Sketches by Boz": End in the Beginning.* Boulder, Colorado: Colorado Associated University Press, 1974. Print.

Hartley, Jenny. *Charles Dickens and the House of Fallen Women.* 2012. Web.

Hobsbaum, Philip. *A Readers' Guide to Charles Dickens.* New York: Farrar, Straus and Giroux, 1972. Print.

James, Louis. "Cruikshank and Early Victorian Caricature." *History Workshop* 6 (1978): 107–20. Print.

James, William. *William James, The Great Books of the Western World.* Ed. Adler, Mortimer J. Vol. 53. 60 vols. Chicago: Encyclopaedia Britannica, 2007. Print.

Johnson, Edgar. *Charles Dickens: His Tragedy and Triumph.* Vol. I. II vols. New York: Simon & Schuster, 1952. Print.

_____. *Charles Dickens: His Tragedy and Triumph.* Vol. II. II vols. New York: Simon & Schuster, 1952. Print.

_____. *Charles Dickens: His Tragedy and Triumph Revised and Abridged.* New York: Viking Press, 1952. Print.

The King James Version of the Bible, Cambridge Paragraph Bible 1873 Version. Ed. Scrivener, F.H.A. Grand Rapids: Zondervan, 2002. Print.

Lee, Harper. *To Kill a Mockingbird.* New York: Harper Perennial Classics, 1960. Print.

Levi-Strauss, Claude. *Myth and Meaning: Cracking the Code of Culture.* New York: Schocken Books, 1979. Print.

Levine, Richard A. "The Two Nations, and Individual Possibility." *Studies in the Novel* 1.2 (1969): 157–80. Print.

Lloyd, Matthew. "The Times Report of the Last Public Hanging in England." The

Music Hall and Theatre History Website 2001. Web. 1/2/2016 2016.

Locke, John. *John Locke, Berkeley, Hume: Great Books of the Western World*. Ed. Adler, Mortimer J. Vol. 33. 60 vols. Chicago: The Encyclopaedia Britannica, 2007. Print.

Miller, J. Hillis and David Borowitz. "Charles Dickens and George Cruikshank: Papers Read at a Clark Library Seminar on May 9, 1970." *Clark Library Seminar*. 1971. Print.

Murray, Brian. *The Bedside, Bathtub & Armchair Companion to Dickens*. London: Continuum International Publishing Group, 2009. Print.

"The National Archives." Web. 5/11/2016. http://www.nationalarchives.gov.uk/education/resources/1834-poor-law/.

The New Encyclopaedia Britannica. Fifteenth ed. Chicago: Encyclopaedia Britannica, 1992. Vol. 8. 29 vols. Print.

Odden, Karen. "Introduction." *Hard Times*. New York: Barnes and Noble Classics, 2004. xv–xxxv. Print.

Patten, Robert. "From *Sketches* to *Nickleby*." *The Cambridge Companion to Charles Dickens*. Ed. Jordan, John O. Cambridge: Cambridge University Press, 2001. 16–33. Print.

Philpotts, Trey. *The Companion to Little Dorrit*. Mountfield: Helm Information, 2003. Print.

Plato. *The Dialogues of Plato. The Great Books of the Western World*. Ed. Adler, Mortimer J. Vol. 6. 60 vols. Chicago: Encyclopaedia Britannica, 2007. Print.

Potter, Jonathan. "Constructing Social and Personal Identities in Dickens' *David Copperfield*." The Victorian Web. Web. 5/27/2013.

Roe, Frederick William. "Introduction." *Victorian Prose*. Ed. Roe, Frederick William. New York: The Ronald Press Company, 1947. xi–xxxiii. Print.

Sacks, Oliver. *An Anthropologist on Mars*. New York: Vintage Books, 1995. Print.

_____. *The Man Who Mistook His Wife for a Hat and Other Clinical Tales*. New York: Simon & Schuster, 1985. Print.

Said, Edward. "Reflections on Exile." *Reflections on Exile and Other Essays*. Cambridge: Harvard University Press, 2002. 137–49. Print.

Shakespeare, William. *William Shakespeare: The Plays and Sonnets, Volume I. The Great Books of the Western World*. Ed. Adler, Mortimer J. Vol. 25. 60 vols. Chicago: The Encyclopaedia Britannica. Print.

Slater, Michael. *Charles Dickens*. New Haven: Yale University Press, 2009. Print.

Smiley, Jane. *Charles Dickens a Life*. New York: Penguin Group, 2002. Print.

Tomalin, Claire. *Charles Dickens: A Life*. New York: The Penguin Group, 2011. Print.

"The Victorian Web." 1987–2015. Web. 5/11/2016 2016. http://www.victorian-web.org/history/poorlaw/plaatext.html.

Walder, Dennis. "Introduction." *Sketches by Boz*. London: Penguin Books 1995. ix–xxxiv. Print.

Watkins, Gwen. *Dickens in Search of Himself*. Houndmills: Macmillan Press, 1987. Print.

Wilson, Angus. *The World of Charles Dickens*. New York: The Viking Press, 1970. Print.

Wilson, Ben. *The Making of Victorian Values*. New York: The Penguin Press, 2007. Print.

Additional Sources

Ainsworth, Mary D. Salter. "Attachment, Exploration, and Separation: Illustrated by the Behavior of One-Year-Olds in a Strange Situation." *Child Development* 41.1 (1970): 49–67. Print.

_____. "Attachments Beyond Infancy." *American Psychologist* 44.4 (1989): 709–16. Print.

_____. "Dependency, and Attachment: A Theoretical Review of the Infant-Mother Relationship." *Child Development* 40.4 (1969): 969–1025. Print.

Ayres, Brenda. *Dissenting Women in Dickens's Novels*. Westport. Connecticut: Greenwood Press, 1998. Print.

Bar-Yosef, Eltan. "'It's the Old Story': David and Uriah in II Samuel and *David Copperfield*." *The Modern Language Review* 101.4 (2006): 957–65. Print.

Baumgarten, Murray. "Fictions of the City." *The Cambridge Companion to Charles Dickens*. Ed. Jordan, John O. Cambridge: Cambridge University Press, 2001. 106–19. Print.

Berry, Laura C. *The Child, the State, and the Victorian Novel*. Charlottesville: University Press of Virginia, 1999. Print.

Blain, Virginia. "Double Vision and the Double Standard in *Bleak House*: A Feminist Perspective." *New Casebooks: Bleak House*. Ed. Tambling, Jeremy. New York: St. Martin's Press, 1998. 65–86. Print.

Boege, Fred W. "Point of View in Dickens." *PMLA: Publications of the Modern Language Association of America* 65.2 (1950): 90–105. Print.

Brantlinger, Patrick. "Dickens and the Factories." *Nineteenth-Century Fiction* 26.3 (1971): 270–85. Print.

Breslow, Julian W. "The Narrator in *Sketches by Boz*." *ELH* 44.1 (1977): 127–49. Print

Broderick, James H, and John E. Grant. "The Identity of Esther Summerson." *Modern Philology* 55.4 (1958): 252–58. Print.

Butt, John. ""Bleak House" in the Context of 1851." *Nineteenth-Century Fiction* 10.1 (1955): 1–21. Print.

Chase, Karen. "Bleak House: Plot, Character, and the Tragic Sense." *Eros & Psyche: The Representation of Personality in Charlotte Bronte, Charles Dickens, and George Eliot*. New York: Methuen, 1952. 92–111. Print.

Costigan, Edward. "Drama and Everyday Life in *Sketches by* Boz." *The Review of English Studies* 27.108 (1976): 403–21. Print.

Davies, Philip. *Lost London: 1870–1945*. Hertfordshire: Transatlantic Press, 2009. Print.

Deen, Leonard. "Style and Unity in "*Bleak House*."" *Criticism* 1967: 206–18. Print.

Delespinasse, Doris Stringham. "The Significance of Dual Point of View in *Bleak House*." *Nineteenth-Century Fiction* 23.3 (1968): 253–64. Print.

Dennis, Carl. "Dickens' Moral Vision." *Studies in Literature and Language* 11.3 (1969): 1237–46. Print.

Dickens, Charles. *The Life of Our Lord: Written for His Children During the Years 1846 to 1849*. New York: Simon & Schuster, 1999. Print.

_____. *Selected Letters of Charles Dickens.* Ed. Paroissien, David. Boston: Twayne Publishers, 1985. Print.

Dickens Hawksley, Lucinda. *Dickens' Bicentenary 1812 –2012: Charles Dickens.* San Rafael, California: Insight Editions, 2011. Print.

Donovan, Robert A. "Structure and Idea in *Bleak House.*" *ELH* 29.2 (1962): 175–201. Print.

Dunlop, C.R.B. "Samuel Warren: A Victorian Law and Literature Practitioner." *Cardozo Studies in Law and Literature* 12.2 (2000): 265–91. Print.

Dyson, A.E. Rev. of Bleak House. *Bleak House: A Casebook.* The Spectator. Bristol: Macmillan, 1969. 55–59. Print.

Fawkner, Harald William. *Animation and Reification in Dickens's Vision of the Life-Denying Society.* Uppsala, New York: University of Uppsala, 1977. Print.

Fradin, Joseph I. "Will and Society in *Bleak House.*" *PMLA: Publications of the Modern Language Association of America* 81.1 (1966): 95–109. Print.

Frank, Lawrence. "'Through a Glass Darkly': Esther Summerson and *Bleak House.*" *Critical Essays on Charles Dickens's Bleak House.* Ed. Bowen, Zack. Critical Essays on British Literature. Boston: G.K. Hall & Co., 1989. Print.

Gest, John Marshall. "The Law and Lawyers of Charles Dickens." *The American Law Register* 53.7 (1907): 401–26. Print.

Gilbert, Elliot L., ed. *Critical Essays on Charles Dickens's Bleak House.* Boston: G.K. Hall & Co., 1989. Print.

Gill, Stephen C. "Allusion in *Bleak House*: A Narrative Device." *Nineteenth-Century Fiction* 22.2 (1967): 145–54. Print.

Goldberg, Michael. "From Bentham to Carlyle: Dicken's Political Development." *Journal of the History of Ideas* 33.1 (1972): 61–76. Print.

Graver, Suzanne. "Writing in a Womanly Way and the Double Vision of *Bleak House.*" *Dickens Quarterly* (1987): 3–15. Print.

Holbrook, David. *Charles Dickens and the Image of Woman.* New York: New York University Press, 1993. Print.

Holdsworth, William S. *Charles Dickens as a Legal Historian.* New Haven: Yale University Press, 1929. Print.

Hornbeck, Bert G. *Noah's Architecture: A Study of Dickens' Mythology.* Athens, Ohio: Ohio University Press, 1972. Print.

Houston, Gail Turley. *Consuming Fictions: Gender, Class and Hunger in Dickens's Novels.* Carbondale, IL: Southern Illinois University Press, 1994. Print.

Korg, Jacob, ed. *Twentieth Century Interpretations of Bleak House.* Englewood Cliffs: Prentice-Hall, 1968. Print.

Larson, Janet L. *Dickens and the Broken Scripture.* Athens: University of Georgia Press, 1985. Print.

Laurence, Dan H, and Martin Quinn, eds. *Shaw on Dickens.* New York: Frederick Ungar Publishing Co., 1985. Print.

Leavis, FR & QD. "Bleak House: A Chancery World." *Dickens the Novelist.* New Brunswick: Rutgers University Press, 1979. 118–83. Print.

LeBaron, Michelle. *Bridging Cultural Conflicts: A New Approach for a Changing World.* San Francisco: Jossey-Bass, 2003. Print.

Luyster, Deborah B. "English Law Courts and the Novel." *Law and Literature* 14.3 (2002): 595–605. Print.

McLaughlin, Kevin. "Losing One's Place: Displacement and Domesticity in Dickens's *Bleak House.*" *MLN* 108.5 (1993): 875–90. Print.

McMaster, Juliet. "Visual Design in *Pickwick Papers.*" *Studies In English Literature, 1500–1900* 23.4 (1983): 595–614. Print.

Michie, Helena. "'Who Is This in Pain?': Scarring, Disfigurement, and Female Identity in "Bleak House" and "Our Mutual Friend.'" *Novel: A Forum in Fiction* 22.2 (1989): 199–212. Print.

Miller, J. Hillis. "Moments of Decision in *Bleak House.*" *The Cambridge Companion to Charles Dickens.* Ed. Jordan, John O. Cambridge: Cambridge University Press, 2001. 49–63. Print.

Millhauser, Milton. "*David Copperfield*: Some Shifts of Plan." *Nineteenth-Century Literature* 27.3 (1972): 339–45. Print.

Moseley, Merritt. "The Ontology of Esther's Narrative in "Bleak House.'" *South Atlantic Review* 50.2 (1985): 35–46. Print.

Moskovitz, Richard M.D. *Lost in the Mirror: An inside Look at Borderline Per-*

sonality Disorder. Lanham, Md: Taylor Trade Publishing, 2001. Print.

Orwell, George. "Charles Dickens." *A Collection of Essays.* Orlando: Harcourt Brace, 1981. 48–103. Print.

Ousby, Ian. "The Broken Glass: Visions and Comprehension in *Bleak House.*" *Nineteenth-Century Fiction* 29.4 (1975): 381–92. Print.

Peltason, Timothy. "Esther's Will." *ELH* 59.3 (1992): 671–91. Print.

Ponzio, Peter. *Attached to Life Again: Esther Summerson's Struggle for Identity and Acceptance in Bleak House.* Saarbrucken: VDM Verlag, 2008. Print.

_____. "Dickens and the Visual: Realism and Mimesis in *Sketches by Boz.*" *Global Journal of Human-Social Science: A Arts & Humanities-Psychology* 14.1 (2014): 52–57. Print.

Potts, Alex. "Picturing the Modern Metropolis: Images of London in the Nineteenth Century." *History Workshop* 26 (1988): 28–56. Print.

Ramachandran, V.S. *A Brief Tour of Human Consciousness.* New York: Pi Press, 2004. Print.

Roth, Kimberlee, and Freda B Friedman, PhD. *Surviving a Borderline Parent: How to Heal Your Childhood Wounds & Build Trust, Boundaries and Self-Esteem.* Oakland, CA: New Harbinger Publications, Inc., 2003. Print.

Sadoff, Diane F. "The Dead Father: *Barnaby Rudge, David Copperfield,* and *Great Expectations.*" *EBSCO* (2002): 36–57. Print.

Sadrin, Anny. *Parentage and Inheritance in the Novels of Charles Dickens.* Cambridge: Cambridge University Press, 1994. Print.

Sanders, Andrew. *Authors in Context: Charles Dickens.* Oxford World Classics. Ed. Ingham, Patricia. Oxford: Oxford University Press, 2003. Print.

Seed, David. "Touring the Metropolis: The Shifting Subjects of Dickens's London Sketches." *The Yearbook of English Studies* 34 (2004): 155–70. Print.

Serlen, Ellen. "The Two Worlds of *Bleak House.*" *ELH* 43.4 (1976): 551–66. Print.

Shatto, Susan. *The Companion to Bleak House.* London: Unwin Hyman, 1988. Print.

Stoehr, Taylor. "*Bleak House*: The Novel as Dream." *Bleak House: A Casebook.* Ed. Dyson, A.E. Bristol: Macmillan, 1965. 235–43. Print.

Storey, Graham. *Landmarks of Literature: Dickens Bleak House.* Cambridge: Cambridge University Press, 1987. Print.

Tambling, Jeremy, ed. *New Casebooks: Bleak House.* New York: St. Martin's Press, 1998. Print.

Tillotson, Kathleen, and John Butt. *Dickens at Work.* London: Methuen & Co., 1957. Print.

Van Boheemen-Saaf, Christine. "The Universe Makes an Indifferent Parent." *New Casebooks: Bleak House.* Ed. Tambling, Jeremy. New York: St. Martin's Press, 1998. 254. Print.

Waters, Catherine. *Dickens and the Politics of the Family.* Cambridge: Cambridge University Press, 1997. Print.

_____. "Gender, Family and Domestic Ideology." *The Cambridge Companion to Charles Dickens.* Ed. Jordan, John O. Cambridge: Cambridge University Press, 2001. 120–35. Print.

Welsh, Alexander. *Dickens Redressed: The Art of Bleak House and Hard Times.* New Haven: Yale University Press, 2000. Print.

Wilt, Judith. "Confusion and Consciousness in Dickens's Esther." *Nineteenth-Century Fiction* 32.3 (1977): 285–309. Print.

Winters, Warrington. "Dickens and the Psychology of Dreams." *PMLA: Publications of the Modern Language Association of America* 63.3 (1948): 984–1006. Print.

Zwerdling, Alex. "Esther Summerson Rehabilitated." *PMLA: Publications of the Modern Language Association of America* 88.3 (1973): 429–39. Print.

Index